I0541758

Thoughts
on my
Thoughts
IV

Thoughts
on my
Thoughts
IV

The <u>TALES</u> That Wagged This Veterinarian

Walter R. Hoge, DVM

Printed in the United States of America

ISBN 979-8-89114-117-9 (hc)
ISBN 979-8-89114-115-5 (sc)
ISBN 979-8-89114-116-2 (e)

Library of Congress Control Number: 2024917580

2024.11.05

MainSpring Books
5901 W. Century Blvd
Suite 750
Los Angeles, CA, US, 90045

www.mainspringbooks.com

Table of Contents

ABOUT THE COVER

Michelangelo was one of the greatest artists of the Italian Renaissance, and his legacy lives on today. His greatest masterpiece was probably the interior of the Sistine Chapel, which he adorned with a stunning array of Biblical frescoes, an astonishing feat of artistic endeavor that took him over six years to complete, from 1508-1512. One of the most talked about frescoes within the Sistine Chapel is Michelangelo's 'Creation of Adam', illustrating God reaching out and touching the finger of Adam to give him the gift of life. It is a complex scene with many layers of symbolism, prompting many to ask what the deeper meaning is behind this breath-taking work of art.

The most direct meaning in Michelangelo's Creation of Adam is the moment when God created human life, as described in the Book of Genesis in the Christian Bible: Michelangelo chose to illustrate this moment with complete clarity, painting God reaching out and touching Adam's finger with his, to create the first great spark of life.

Many have looked into Michelangelo's composition in more detail, and found possible suggestions for further hidden meanings. One argument made convincingly by MD Frank Lynn Meshberger is that the shape of the drapery and angels surrounding God resembles that of a human brain – amazing, right? Meshberger noted surprising correlations between Michelangelo's design and the anatomy of a real brain, observing sulci in the inner and outer brain, the brain stem, basilar artery, pituitary gland and optic chasm – this astonishing level of accuracy reveals Michelangelo's deep understanding of human anatomy, and his desire to imbue this into the meaning of his art.

It has been suggested by many that the shape God and the angels create resembles that of a womb and placenta, suggesting Adam was given birth to, rather than being created by God in thin air. Some have even compared the circle of angels in the background to the surface of the placenta, and the line that unites God's outstretched arm with that of Adam with an umbilical cord.

Interestingly, it has been noted that God's presence is far more dominant than Adam's in Michelangelo's scene, which is perhaps understandable, since he is portrayed as the creator of all life, and the entire universe here. But God's arm also encircles that of a prominent female character, perhaps a mother counterpart to God's father-like role. It is almost as if Michelangelo is telling us that he understands the importance of women in childbirth and creation. If this is true, it makes a fascinatingly complex argument for equality of the sexes within the Biblical story of creation, and the vital role of women within it.

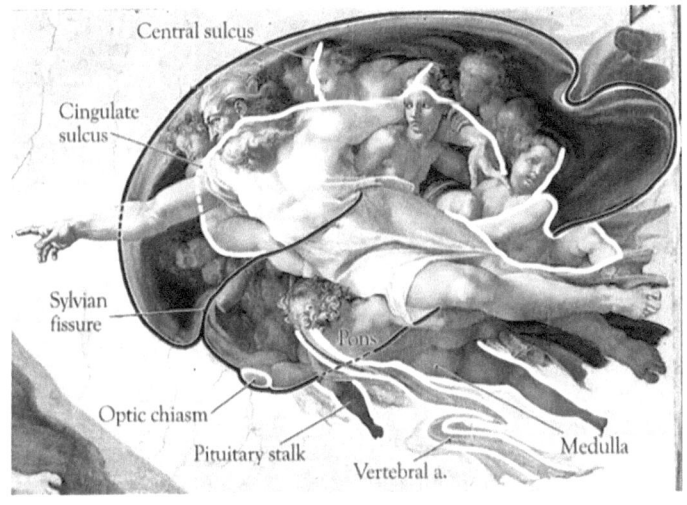

CHAPTER 1

FREE TO ACT AND A GOD-SHAPED HOLE

Over the past decade, Robert Sapolsky—a Stanford professor of biology, of neurology, and of neuro-surgery, as well as a bestselling author of popular science books—has added another line to his career: witness in murder trials. The hours waiting outside courtrooms are long, the pay beside the point. But the role allows Sapolsky to act in service of a core belief, one rooted in an epiphany he had as a 13-year-old and reinforced by everything he has learned since: That the defendants in the trials in which he testifies, a world of people who were lost before pre-K, can't be fairly judged by the court's normal standards of premeditation and intent. A life of trauma, he explains to the jury, has invariably left one part of the brain atrophied and another part enlarged. To ask, for example, why such a person, acting initially in self-defense, would continue hitting their aggressor after knocking him unconscious is to ignore neuro-logical reality. "Saying 'Why didn't he pick the right choice?' is absurd," he says. "Because there was no choice at that moment."

Where's the free will in that? For Sapolsky, the answer has seemed obvious since he was 13. He'd grown up in an Orthodox Jewish home, complete with two refrigerators and two kitchen sinks to keep kosher. But his own religious beliefs came crashing down after he read biblical commentary on a passage in Leviticus that restricts a disabled man from the priesthood. Sapolsky wore leg braces for part of his childhood, and this stricture sent him searching for explanation from a rabbi, who answered by analogy: Much like you wouldn't sacrifice a lamb with a blemish on its lip, you wouldn't present God with a priest likewise blemished. The answer struck Sapolsky as unfathomably unfair, precipitating a crisis in his young mind.

"One night at 2 o'clock I suddenly woke up and said, 'Oh, I get it. There's no such thing as God,' and then I paused a few seconds, and I said, 'and there's no free will,' and I paused, and I said, 'and this is a vast, indifferent, empty universe,'" he says. "And suddenly everything fell into place."

Born of religious angst, this realization began a lifelong interest. As undergrads at Harvard, he and a friend ran a lecture series in their dorm called "The Ethics of Free Will and Determinism," where they'd entice academic stars to spend hours arguing about what they had heard. Some of the notes he consulted while writing his book date back to this era. "That's how long all of this stuff has been percolating," he says.

Yes, Sapolsky would agree, we can do what we want, but we can't choose what it is we want to do. We are not the ultimate captains of our own ships. We have no free will. "We are nothing more or less than the cumulative biological and environmental luck, over which we had no control, that has brought us to any moment," he writes. "There's not a single crack of day-light to shoehorn in free will."

The idea of free will has challenged thinkers of all stripes for millennia, including the fourth-century theologian St. Augustine, who worked to reconcile an omniscient God— who surely knows the future—with human freedom. If God knows the future, how can we do anything but manifest that knowledge? With the dawn of the Enlightenment and the rise of Newtonian physics, another dilemma took center stage. In a universe governed by the laws of science, where every action follows from action, where cause begets cause, how can our choices be anything but another domino in an endless line of necessary consequences? If we are just matter, mustn't we behave as such?[1]

No absolute or complete freedom and free will exist, as they are constrained by both internal and external factors, such as the limits of human physiology and cognition, the physical laws, and the limitations imposed on human life by society and culture. Nevertheless, the concepts of freedom and free will are necessary for humans not only for having some purpose and meaning in life, but also because without them human life would be an unbearable ordeal.

Every human life is a story. The important question is, how much of it is written by an individual? Two related concepts are freedom and free will. The concept of free will is one of the basic elements of human life and experience.

The issue is whether one is free to make choices independent of external factors or whether genetics, prior conditioning, and preceding events and conditions causally determine one's choices and actions.

There is an undeniable perception, or perhaps illusion, that human beings have free will and choice, and that they cause their own free actions. This perception is ingrained in the human experience – from mundane choices, such as what to wear or eat, to choices that influence the direction of one's life. The future appears to be open for free will and choice, and one can guide the events in life in the desired direction. Whether real or not, human free will provides an important element in one's daily life and outlook. If free will were demonstrated to be an illusion, it would indicate that individuals are not responsible for their actions. This would have important implications for society, as the concept of free will is the central aspect in matters of moral responsibility, politics, and law.

In general terms, one can state that an individual has free will if one can choose between different alternatives, provided that the cause of the choice is attributed to the individual and not to external sources. Thus, free will can be defined as the ability of individuals to make decisions about their actions and choices that are not determined or constrained by external factors. This requires distinguishing between internal and external sources of choice, as well as between those that one is consciously aware of and those that are beyond one's conscious awareness. A more specific definition can be expressed as the ability of individuals to control their behavior in relation to moral responsibility. As the world has a strong influence on human behavior, the issue of free will is complex and open to different interpretations. However, freedom and free will are human constructs, and as such they have no reality independent of minds.[2]

Do animals have free will? Probably, the answer to that question would be agreed by most people to be a fairly obvious "no." The concept of free will is traditionally bound up with such things as our capacity to choose our own values, the sorts of lives we want to lead, the sorts of people we want to be, etc. and it seems obvious that no non-human animal lives the kind of life which could make sense of the attribution to it of such powers as these.

But in thinking about free will, it is essential, nevertheless, to consider the capacities of animals. Even if animals cannot be said to have full-blown free will, animal powers of various sorts provide a kind of essential underpinning for free will which philosophers who focus too exclusively on the human phenomenon are forever in danger of ignoring. And these simpler capacities are interesting enough to raise many philosophical issues all by themselves; indeed, I would argue that they raise the most discussed problem in this area of philosophy all by themselves. For they are, in my view, hard to accommodate within certain conceptions of the universe in which we live – what might be called mechanistic or deterministic conceptions of that universe. This makes it very useful and important to think about the simpler capacities from a philosophical perspective. Instead of asking, as philosophers constantly do, whether free will is compatible with determinism, we should first ask ourselves whether even the simpler powers which constitute what I call animal agency are consistent with it. And it might conceivably be that the answer to this question is "no," which would shed a new and interesting kind of light on the free will debate.

What do I mean by "animal agency"? We can make a start on homing in on the concept by saying that an agent is something which can act. This, though, is not yet to say anything very clear, because it simply raises the question what it is to be able to act. We sometimes use the concept of action in a very general way – we can, for example, speak of the action of inanimate things such as the wind or the waves, or of the action of a chemical agent such as oxygen or water on a material such as iron when it rusts. So, it might look as though almost everything should count as an agent, because under the right conditions, almost anything can passively impact something else just by coming in contact with it. But on the concept of action, neither the wind, nor the waves, nor oxygen, nor water, would be allowed to count as having the power to act.

We attribute to some sorts of things in the world a rather different sort of power – the power to do something or not, which is the type of power the medieval called a two-way power. For example, I now have the power to raise my arm. I could do it. But I also have the power not do it. It is up to me to settle whether my arm will go up within the next second or not. Either thing appears to be in my power at this very moment – to act or to refrain from acting.

What I do seems also to be dependent on me and on whether or not I exercise my power of action. And this gives the distinction between activity and passivity proper purchase. I am active, but the air which I move as I raise my arm is passive – because it is me and not the air that is the true source of the movement, its instigator. This isn't just a matter of the source of the movement being internal to my body.

It is a matter of what happens being up to me – a crucial idea in our conceptual scheme, the idea of an entity which has the power to make things go one way rather than another, even holding the conditions in which it finds itself fixed. And the concept of agency I want to utilize is closely associated with this idea of a two-way power – the power to do something or not. Only those things which possess two-way powers count as agents in my sense.

A very familiar way of thinking about animal nature returns the answer "no" to this question. There is a long tradition in the history of philosophy of separating ourselves off from the other animals – of trying to argue that we are nobler or better or more important than they are in some very fundamental respect.

It was always part of Christian doctrine that human beings were uniquely close to God, being made, indeed, in his image, and in the seventeenth century, Descartes gave this Christian view a metaphysical underpinning by insisting that human beings were to be distinguished completely from the other animals because only humans were possessed of souls.[3]

According to the Oxford Dictionary: The soul is the spiritual or immaterial part of a human being or animal, regarded as immortal. "The belief death is just one step in a soul's journey through the universe."

The Bible questions this concept that only humans have a soul: "For I, the Lord God, created all things, of which I have spoken, spiritually, before they were naturally upon the face of the earth" (Moses 3:5). The spirit creation involved not only people but plants and animals as well. The account in Abraham 4–5 is the Lord's blueprint of the Creation. Animals have spirits too! The "beasts" and "creeping things" and "fowls of the air" were created spiritually first... Their spirit bodies resemble their physical bodies. And they, like us, will enjoy "eternal felicity"—happiness and joy in their resurrected bodies—if they do what is required of them (Doctrine and Covenants 77:2–3). 1 Thessalonians 5:23 – Hebrews 4:12, God mentions your "whole spirit and soul and body be preserved blameless unto the coming of our Lord Jesus Christ."

In a talk in 01/31/2006 on Moral Agency, Elder D. Todd Christofferson stated: In years past, we generally used the term free agency. That is not incorrect, but more recently we have taken note that free agency does not appear as an expression in the scriptures. They talk of our being "free to choose" and "free to act" for ourselves and of our obligation to do many things of our own "free will." But the word agency appears either by itself or, in Doctrine and Covenants, section 101, verse 78, with the modifier moral: "That every man may act in doctrine and principle . . . according to the moral agency which I have given unto him, that every man may be accountable for his own sins in the day of judgment" (emphasis added). When we use the term moral agency, then, we are appropriately emphasizing the accountability that is an essential part of the divine gift of agency. We are moral beings and agents unto ourselves, free to choose but also responsible for our choices.

There's a concept that theologians often bounce around when discussing idolatry. The idea is that inside each of us is a "God-shaped hole"- a place inside of our hearts that only God can fill. If we try to put anything else in there, it won't fit (meaning, it won't fill the need we have inside of our heart/soul).

In 1670, Blaise Pascal published Pensées VII (425), which was a defense of the Christian religion. (It should be noted that this book was published after his death in 1662.) In that book, he has a quote: "What else does this craving, and this helplessness, proclaim but that there was once in man a true happiness, of which all that now remains is the empty print and trace? This he tries in vain to fill with everything around him, seeking in things that are not there the help he cannot find in those that are, though none can help, since this infinite abyss can be filled only with an infinite and immutable object; in other words, by God himself."

Since then, the concept has taken on a life of its own and the phrase "God-shaped hole," a close approximation of the concept, has been found throughout many Christian circles. (In 2002 and 2017, books were published with the a "God-Shaped Hole" in their titles.)

The "God-shaped hole" concept states that every person has a void in his soul/spirit/life that can only be filled by God. The "God-shaped hole" is the innate longing of the human heart for something outside itself, something transcendent, something "other." Ecclesiastes 3:11 refers to God's placing of "eternity in man's heart." God made humanity for His eternal purpose, and only God can fulfill our desire for eternity. All religion is based on the innate desire to "connect" with God. This desire can only be fulfilled by God, and therefore can be likened to a "God-shaped hole."

The problem, though, is that humanity ignores this hole or attempts to fill it with things other than God. Jeremiah 17:9 describes the condition of our hearts: "The heart is deceitful above all things and beyond cure. Who can understand it?" Solomon reiterates the same concept: "The hearts of men, moreover, are full of evil and there is madness in their hearts while they live…" (Ecclesiastes 9:3). The New Testament concurs: "The sinful mind is hostile to God. It does not submit to God's law, nor can it do so" (Romans 8:7). Romans 1:18-22 describes humanity ignoring what can be known about God, including presumably the "God-shaped hole," and instead worshiping anything and everything other than God.

Sadly, too many spend their lives looking for something other than God to fill their longing for meaning—business, family, sports, etc. But in pursuing these things that are not eternal, they remain unfulfilled and wonder why their lives never seem satisfactory. There is no doubt that many people pursuing things other than God achieve a measure of "happiness" for a time. But when we consider Solomon, who had all the riches, success, esteem, and power in the world—in short, all that men seek after in this life—we see that none of it fulfilled the longing for eternity. He declared it all "vanity," meaning that he sought after these things in vain because they did not satisfy. In the end he said, "Now all has been heard; here is the conclusion of the matter: Fear God and keep his commandments, for this is the whole [duty] of man" (Ecclesiastes 12:13).

As a square peg cannot fill a round hole, neither can the "God-shaped hole" inside each of us be filled by anyone or anything other than God. Only through a personal relationship with God through faith in Jesus Christ can the "God-shaped hole" be filled and the desire for eternity fulfilled. While other answers show that the concept can be supported biblically, the concept that there is a void/vacuum/hole is actually a non-biblical one.[4]

Like us, I want to suggest, many animals have two-way powers. They are of course driven to do certain of the things they do by instinct (as are we) – but this is not in the least inconsistent with the admission that they have two-way powers. Instincts govern animals, as they govern us, in a general way – setting a specific range of goals, aims and behaviors, but often leaving it up to the animal itself to settle many of the precise details of where, when and how those goals will be pursued. More complex animals have greater freedoms in this respect than less complex ones – a dog, for instance, can decide whether to urinate now, or to run after the stick which has just been thrown for it instead; a spider seems likely to be far more narrowly constrained.

But still, even a spider might be able to decide whether here or there is a better place to build its web, to take this or that route to a particular place, etc. There is evidence that certain spiders possess quite remarkable abilities. For instance, Stim Wilcox and Robert Jackson of the University of Canterbury in New Zealand (I added more of their studies to this article) have spent a lifetime trying to understand the mind of a spider and have referred to the, jumping spider, Portia's method as an "aggressive mimicry" (deceiving its prey by imitating something desirable); they stated that the spider uses "mimicry, detours, and deception."

This spider preys on other spiders and on occasion having tried and failed, they tempt the spider out of the center of its web again by means of various strategies. The Portia disappears from view for about an hour and finally reappears on a rock projection, high above the web of the target prey spider. She then lets herself down from the rock projection, and swings in on a thread to eat her prey. What seems remarkable about this account of Portia's behavior is the potential it suggests for forward planning, for spatiotemporal awareness, for the maintenance of intention over a significant amount of time, and in the absence of continuous perception of the desired object. Clearly, Portia's general goal – to catch and eat spiders – is instinctively given; but equally clearly, one could argue, the choice of means to this end in a given case is settled by Portia, on the spot, in a manner sensitive to the affordances of the environment in which she finds herself.

The Portia spider also appears to be aware that different hunting methods are required depending upon the skills of its prey and makes whatever modifications are necessary to ensure its success. For example, when attacking a spitting spider, the Portia attacks from behind—away from the nasty spit of its prey, which could immobilize a predator in less than a second. The Portia spider appears aware of the potential dangers involved in turning the tables on the enemy.

Less dangerous prey (web-spinning spiders) require a different method of attack. The Portia spider usually mimics a potential mate or other defenseless prey and waits in the center of another spider's web. The Portia spider sneaks to the middle of the web and causes vibrations of the web to get the resident spider's attention and waits patiently for the unsuspecting victim.

In their attempt at survival, these smart arachnids can travel undetected across the ground through foliage by resembling another leaf. They also have been known to mimic ants because most predators prefer spiders over ants. When employing this protective-mimicry method, the Portia walks on all eight legs in a broad path that resembles an ant following a pheromone trail. The spider pauses occasionally and raises its forelegs to mimic an ant's antennae.

The Portia spider can leap up to 50 times the length of its own body, so it's easy to see how other spiders might be unsuspecting of an attack from so great a distance. However, as the spider jumps, it leaves behind a "bungee cord" line of silk, a safety device for a missed target. In that event, the spider can always climb back up the safety net it established and try again later. This predator uses trial and error methods, seems to remember what does and doesn't work, and employs the best methods in future attacks.

Agency, then, should be regarded neither as an illusion, nor as the peculiar possession of a single species. Rather, it is a power which characterizes biological entities of a certain degree and type of complexity, an evolutionary innovation of quite extraordinary importance, which develops as creatures (plants or animals) emerge which have a range of complex and sometimes competing goals. Such creatures may need to utilize perceptually acquired information from a number of sources in order to solve problems, to which there is not necessarily any unique best answer, about how to distribute themselves and their efforts through space and time, in pursuit of their ends. Agential powers are nature's way of solving these problems; and we need to understand them, and the metaphysics they require, before we have any hope of finally resolving the question whether or not we humans could possibly have free will.[3]

One can never predict the future or future behavior with certainty, as not all the variables about the world and self are known or knowable. The perceptions and thoughts have no permanence, as they are constantly fleeting. Thus, as the future is never certain, one can develop a perception of having freedom of choice and free will. The fundamental difficulty with any choice made is that it cannot be undone; and any specific choice made leads to other choices that cannot be undone either.

In the end, no absolute or complete freedom and free will exist, as they are constrained by both internal and external factors. These include the limits of human physiology and cognition, the physical laws, the randomness of processes in nature, and the limitations imposed on human life by society and culture. The important issue is not what are the degrees of human freedom and free will, but whether one can remain human without these two notions. The concepts of freedom and free will are necessary for humans not only for having some purpose and meaning in life, but also because without them human life would be an unbearable ordeal.

Most things in life reach their natural end. In philosophy and science, however, disagreements never end due to the limits of human understanding, the ambiguity of definitions and concepts, and insufficient evidence. The debate on free will (whether it be human, plant or animal) may never end, and perhaps some ambiguity about it is preferable to the certainty that free will is an illusion, as this ambiguity leaves the question open to debate. It leaves some hope that is vital for human life.[2]

Exercising his agency, Timothy McVeigh's act of terrorism was one of the most destructive in American history. He killed 168 people (9 of them children), injured 853. More than three hundred surrounding buildings were damaged and 400 people left homeless; the blast registered 6.0 on the Richter scale fifty-miles away.

McVeigh, during his execution from a gurney, made eye contact and nodded slightly to each witness; he lay on his back, stared at the ceiling, and died with his eyes open. While silent throughout, McVeigh had requested copies to be handed to witnesses of the 1875 poem "Invictus," …Interpreted by most as a self-congratulatory poem, acclaiming himself as unconquerable, unbowed, and with a fearless visage, ending with flourish bragging about mastering his fate and captaining his soul. Screw you all, the mass murderer attempting to say one last time…

Invictus is a Poem written by British poet William Ernest Henley in 1875 which was published in 1891 in his poem collection "In Hospital". The central theme of Invictus is bravery and resilience in the face of hardships in life. The poem inspires anyone going through difficulties or anyone anticipating hardships to face it with courage and to be headstrong.

The poet was going through a really difficult phase in his life when he wrote this poem. He was in the hospital battling tuberculosis. As a child he had constantly battled tuberculosis of the bone and had his left leg amputated. He was hospitalized in 1873 when the infection in his right leg became severe.

When he wrote this poem, he was witnessing his fellow patients fighting for their lives. He distinctly talks about the past, the present and the future, referencing his endurance through past hardships, his strong will to face his current difficulties and his courage to face anything the future holds for him.

> Out of the night that covers me,
> Black as the pit from pole to pole,
> I thank whatever gods may be
> For my unconquerable soul.
>
> In the fell clutch of circumstance
> I have not winced nor cried aloud.
> Under the bludgeonings of chance
> My head is bloody, but unbowed.
>
> Beyond this place of wrath and tears
> Looms but the Horror of the shade,
> And yet the menace of the years
> Finds and shall find me unafraid.
>
> It matters not how strait the gate,
> How charged with punishments the scroll,
> I am the master of my fate,
> I am the captain of my soul.

– Was Timothy McVeigh sticking it to the thousands of people affected by this tragedy or was he confessing that he recognized a "God-shaped hole" and that he truly had been the master of his fate and the captain of his soul. If there was to be for him a passing through the veil, he would be accountable to his maker who had given all mankind free will to (morally) choose for themselves. That in 1 Corinthians 6:9 it states: "Know ye not that the unrighteous shall not inherit the kingdom of God?" A good lesson for us all.

- It appears that agential (free will) powers are nature's way of solving their challenges: Seeking food, shelter, reproduction and keeping from being eaten in an environment free of Satin's power and sin. I enjoy watching my dog, BeBe, trying to make a decision of whether she wants to stay napping on my lap, heading down the hall where she the refrigerator door is being opened or the sound of the Amazon truck coming up the driveway. Her choices are usually: 1st the truck, second the refrigerator and last napping with Walter.

- To me, Robert M. Sapolsky's book "Determined" is a wonderful journey in science and I'm grateful that he was stimulated to write it. However, I felt sorry that he had to wear leg braces for a part of his childhood, that at the age of 13 he read the passage in Leviticus that restricted a disabled from holding the priesthood, and that his rabbi was insensitive enough to infer that God rejects those of something we all have (a blemish). And: "One night at 2 o'clock he suddenly woke up and he came to the conclusions: 'Oh, I get it. There's no such thing as God,' and then paused a few seconds, and I said, 'and there's no free will,' and paused, and I said,

'and this is a vast, indifferent, empty universe,'. And
suddenly everything fell into place…"

Sapolsky's depressing hopeless closing comments in his
book "Determined" seem to me that he is sensing a "God-
shaped hole" but his experience at 13 and life studies have
suppressed these feelings: "It is the events of one second
before to a million years before that determine whether your
life and loves unfold next to bubbling streams or machines
choking you with sooty smoke. Whether at graduation
ceremonies you wear the cap and gown or bag the garbage.
Whether the thing you are viewed as deserving is a long life
of fulfillment or a long prison sentence.

There is no justifiable 'deserve.' The only possible moral
conclusion is that you are no more entitled to have your
needs and desires met than is any other human. That there
is no human who is less worthy than you to have their well-
being considered. You may think otherwise, because you
can't conceive of the threads of causality beneath the surface
that made you, because you have the luxury of deciding that
effort and self-discipline aren't made of biology, because you
have surrounded yourself with people who think the same.
But this is where the science has taken us.

And we need to accept the absurdity of hating any
person for anything they've done; ultimately, that hatred is
sadder than hating the sky for storming, hating the earth
when it quakes, hating the virus because it's good at getting
into lung cells. This is where the science has brought us as
well…

We already know enough to understand that the
endless people whose lives are less fortunate than ours don't
implicitly 'deserve' to be invisible. Ninety-nine percent of

the time I can't remotely achieve this mindset, but there is nothing to do but try, because it will be freeing."[1]

These closing comments in his book are "God Talk" to me. A different mindset about science and agency may have blossomed if he had been directed to the right Jewish Rabbi's teachings when he was 13 years of age. He would have been taught: Genesis 1:26-27: Humans are created in God's image, making them fundamentally equal, Proverbs 22:2: The rich and poor are both made by the Lord and sharing some of the New Testament teachings: Romans 3:23: All people are born under sin and fall short of God's glory. God is "no respecter of persons": Acts 10:34 & Romans 2:11. And "Thou shalt love thy neighbour as thyself: Matthew 22:39.

1– *Determined: A Science of Life without Free Will Hardcover, Sam Scott, Stanford Magazine, 10/117/2023.*

2– *Human Freedom and Free Will, Ben G. Yacobi, Journal of Philosophy of Life Vol.10, No.3 (December 2020):164-170.*

3– *Do Animals Have Free Will, Oxford Press, Helen Steward, 04/29/2015.*

4– *Got Questions: Your Questions, Biblical Answers. & Ask Question, God-shaped hole.*

CHAPTER 2

START WITH THE END IN MIND

You may not have heard the phrase "Begin with the end in mind" before. But if you have ever read Stephen Covey's best-seller "The 7 Habits of Highly Effective People", you may recognize this as the title of habit #2. The concept it conveys resonated enough with Tom Osborn that he used it as the title of his speech to University of Nebraska – Lincoln (UNL) graduates:

While I think "beginning with the end in mind" is a great philosophy to use throughout your life, it really applies right now at the beginning of our growing season. Early forage crops like small grains and alfalfa will be ready to harvest soon if they aren't already. Deciding when to begin cutting is always tricky, balancing plant maturity, labor availability, and weather. By beginning harvest with the end in mind, we can make the decision of when to cut a bit easier, at least on the maturity side. I can't help much with the weather.

Knowing what animals will end up consuming our harvested feed can make a big impact on when we want to harvest. Plants follow a general trend as they grow and mature. Early on new leaves and stems are tender and full of protein and energy. Quality is at its highest in a young plant and slowly drops as maturity increases. Alternatively, young plants are short and still growing resulting in lower yield. The amount of forage produced increases as the plant matures. The classic visual for this is a graph with plant maturity across the bottom and an x in the middle, the line sloping down is quality and the line going up is quantity. We are typically told to shoot for the middle of the x, where quality and yield are optimized, but this doesn't always happen.

The shift in yield and quality can happen quite quickly. UNL studies have shown that yields in rye and wheat increased from 12 tons per acre to 20 tons per acre by delaying harvest from boot stage to soft dough. However, the tradeoff was an 8% drop in crude protein content from 18 to 10%. A similar story can be seen in other forages like oats and alfalfa. If the middle of the x is optimal, why would we deviate for something different? This is where beginning with the end in mind comes in to play.

Growing animals like yearlings or calves need high quality feed to fuel their growth demands on top of their base metabolism. Harvesting early enough that the forage is still of high quality can provide a feed that will fulfill this demand. This will sacrifice some production, so the decision still needs to be made if a higher quality feed is worth the cost, but knowing that quality won't be wasted can assist in the decision making process.

Mature animals like cows may not need the quality a young growing animal requires. Unless in late gestation or producing milk, they only have to worry about meeting their base metabolic demands. If the hay we are producing is destined for dry or early gestation cows, we don't need super high quality. In fact, providing too high of quality could end up backfiring by putting on too much condition and causing issues with breed-back next year. In this scenario, quantity trumps quality, so harvesting later and going for a lower quality hay is best.

As we look toward summer annual options, this decision gets even more complicated. Deciding what sorghum, millet, or Sudan grass variety or hybrid to plant depends on not only where the feed is destined, but how we plan to harvest and store it as well. Forage sorghums and thicker stemmed millets take longer to dry down, but produce the most yield. They are best suited for silage, while thinner stemmed sorghum/Sudan hybrids and millets are ideal for hay. If you plan to harvest by grazing, a variety that is thin stemmed and has regrowth potential is often preferred, making Sudan grass one of our best options. Beginning with the end in mind isn't earth shattering, but it does help provide clarity and direction when decisions need to be made. Whether planning a summer forage or harvesting now, look ahead to how a forage will be used to make better decisions in the present.[1]

Seneca, an epic Stoic philosopher, wrote in his work On The Tranquility Of The Mind: "Let all your efforts be directed to something, let it keep that end in view." This work is dated somewhere between 49 to 62 AD but Seneca's assertion is as valid now as it was then. The idea suggests that we program our own lives and in order to be effective at working towards anything we need to "begin with the end in mind."

Beginning with an ending really does have its merits. One of those being the fixed point it provides us with to work towards. This point is something we can test against and check in with. We can measure any decision against whether the outcome will move us closer or further away. The ending can help orient our actions and efforts in the present. An ending is a real destination, it's tangible and concrete and we all know the benefits of having one. So why don't we begin with an end more often, what's so hard about it? Here are some possible explanations:

For every ending we choose we turn our backs on an innumerable number of alternatives. This idea can debilitate some people into never picking a specific point to work towards. People who struggle with this fact of life may also find more general, everyday choices hard to make for exactly the same reason.

Fixing an endpoint and working towards that one goal can feel like a confining and absolute act. In some ways, it puts the pressure on as it doesn't allow for much flexibility. You may feel torn between the two and the truth is that sometimes it's nicer to think we can do everything and be anything. Living this way means we don't set any goals in concrete though because flexibility and freedom feels better in the short term. In the long term though it doesn't always work out as it could leave you achieving very little or traveling in circles.

You're not clear about what the endpoint is. The destination you're trying to get to or the goal you're trying

WALTER R. HOGE, DVM

to achieve to is hazy. It lacks a form that you can fully invest your time and energy in working towards. You're not clear about why you're heading where you are. If you don't know what you want that's never going to change.

Some of us live lives where perfection is the only option. It makes beginning with an end hard because if we don't get there we feel like we've failed. By setting an end before you begin you have no excuses, you would clearly know what you're working towards. However, if you never set in stone where you were going you can't feel bad about never getting there. Instead, you can chalk it up to keeping your options open and never deal with the discomfort of failure.

It's all well and good knowing that endpoints are helpful and to some extent necessary. It's also great to know how they can keep us on track along the journey towards whatever achievement we have in mind. Some of us may struggle to set these endpoints. This is when finding some clarity around why has its benefits. If you're struggling to begin with an end, in work or in your personal life, there's probably a good reason. Take the opportunity to learn something about yourself and figure out why.

Is it because of any or all of the reasons above? Or is it for completely different reasons? When you've figured out why you can't begin with an end you can make conscious choices and move forward. Maybe you'll end up being able to find the courage and clarity to set an endpoint and state your intentions to yourself and to the world. Whether you get there or not is down to you but at least you'll know which way you're heading and where you're trying to get to.[2]

The idea, "Begin with the end in mind", resonates with what the Preacher wrote in Ecclesiastes 7:8-9 some two thousand years ago. The Preacher, now seemingly advanced in years has reflected back in Ecclesiastes all that he had done. At the end of the day, the Preacher says that the end is better than the beginning and it is better to be patient than haughty — that is proud. The comparison talks about what one puts into a task and likewise the results of the task. He's saying that generally speaking, when one sets out to do something, if he or she invests a lot of time working towards an honorable goal, and for this reason the goal, when obtained is most certainly a better state of affairs than when one started towards that goal (Psalms 126:5-6).

But at the same time, the Preacher is offering a warning too: patience is better than pride. This is a warning against looking for quick results to build up one's self. Rather than taking shortcuts, one should invest the proper time and energy into a task and be patient so that the results are robust rather than shoddy. The Preacher also gives warning against being hot tempered, because anger of this fool makes one a fool. The Preacher is probably speaking about those that get ahead quickly. Those who use dubious schemes to advance themselves quickly frustrate another who is trying to do things the right way. Rather than become hot headed, one should keep his or her cool in the matter, for this is best (Proverbs 14:29, Proverbs 16:32).

Hebrews 12:1-3, describes a race. Hebrews says that one should put off things that entangle and run with perseverance the race that is marked out. Following the commandments of God helps keep us on course. It is of value to remind ourselves that the light of Christ is available 24/7, for all of us, to help encourage, strengthen and guide us along the way. The runner in the race Hebrews is describing is fixing his eyes on Jesus' example as how we can live a joyful happy life. Jesus himself has already persevered and atoned for our sins, born the cross and despised its shame, and through this he received glory. For Jesus, the beginning of the task was not easy, but the end result was glory.

For all of us life is full of challenges, but if we run with perseverance — that is not take shortcuts — and by enduring hardships we gain understanding that they occur for our own personal growth.

At the end of the race, one will be rewarded for his or her faithfulness and repentant attitude. Rewards come during successes and recovery from failures during our life's race and our goal is to endure to the end and be one again with our Father in Heaven.

We should heed the words of the Preacher, know the end is better than the beginning, but patience is better than pride. Lord, help me run the race with the end in mind![3]

In 1969 Richard L. Evans related: One warm summer night, Wendy and I were having dinner on our patio when a pesky bee kept buzzing around us. though I repeatedly waved a napkin at the bee, he persisted and was fascinated with our butter. We finally gave up trying to shoo him away and watched him land on the butter and gorge himself.

Moments later he was dead. In a matter of minutes this energetic bee progressed from temptation to indulgence and then to death. he succumbed to a distraction that trapped and then destroyed.

The lesson is obvious. Your ultimate safety lies in never taking even the first enticing step in a direction you do not want to go. Do you really want to end up where that first wrong step will lead you? That bee did not want to die. So be careful. Ask yourself when you are taking a first step. "Do I really want the end result of his choice I'm tempted to make?" Every addiction begins with drinking or smoking or watching something that leads to danger and a loss of agency. What may seem like a harmless flirtation can result in a tragic end. Avoid unnecessary tragedies in your life by refusing to take the first step down a forbidden path. If I were talking with you, I would repeat that last sentence.

On the other hand, beginning with the end in mind can lead to positive outcomes. I think of a grandson who, upon graduating from high school, asked how many years of schooling it would take to become a heart surgeon. When I told him that it would take about fourteen more years, he said, "Oh, that's too long, Grandfather." I then asked him how old he would be in fourteen years if he did not pursue his dream of becoming a heart surgeon. He got the message.

When he finished his training at the Mayo Clinic, it had indeed taken him fourteen years to become a heart surgeon. Because he pursued his education with the end in mind, he achieved his dream.

Beginning with the end in mind can help in almost any situation. As one simple example, whenever I anticipate greeting a dignitary who will be meeting with the First Presidency, I review pertinent details such as my most recent visit to his or her country to help me engage in a meaningful conversation with our guest. I want him or her to feel completely welcome and to leave feeling that life is better because of our time together. So, I picture, plan, and prepare for that desired outcome.

As you begin with the end in mind, you will accomplish more and avoid unnecessary disasters.[4]

There is this observation from an unnamed source: "There is an old man up there ahead of you that you ought to know. He looks somewhat like you, talks like you, walks like you. He has your nose, your eyes, your chin: and whether he loves you or hates you, respects you or despises you, whether he is angry or comfortable, whether he is miserable or happy, depends on you. For you made him. He is you, grown older."

This has both caution and promise, depending upon which direction we choose to take. "We live forward, we understand backwards," said William James. And yet we are not altogether at a loss to know, along broad lines, where any road will lead. There are many who have traveled almost every road that we might choose to take; there are many who have done most things that we might choose to do, and we can look to the principles that have been proved and the results that have been realized in the lives that others have lived.

Every young person, for example, can know that patience, preparation, learning, working are essential for a fullness of life. Any observer, of the present or the past, may know that cleanliness of body, of mind and morals is kindly and peacefully comfortable; that uncleanness is coarsening and corrosive; that standards are essential; that personal responsibility is real; that law sustains life; that there are consequences for every act; that "wickedness never was happiness"; that the commandments are founded on eternal facts.

If we live one way, we get one result— if we live another way, we get another result. We ought to be smart enough, realistic enough, observant and alert enough to know this, forward as well as backward.

"There is an old man up there ahead of you that you ought to know.... whether he is miserable or happy, depends on you. For you made him. He is you, grown older."5

"Although none of us can go back and make a brand-new start, anyone can start from now and make a brand-new ending." *Carol Bard*

1– *University of Nebraska – Lincoln, Begin with the End in Mind, Ben Beckman – Beef systems Extension Educator, 2023.*

2– *Forbes, Why Is It Hard To Start With The End In Mind?, Carley Sime, 01/29/2019.*

3– *Ecclesiastes 7:8-9, The End in Mind, Blaize-Modified, 07/05/2011.*

4– *Heart of the Matter, What 100 Years Of Living Have Taught Me, Russell M. Nelson, pages 15-17, 2023.*

5– *Rotary Club Bulletin of Graham, Texas; Hibbert Lectures at Oxford, Richard L. Evens, Improvement Era, Sept. 1969, Pg. 63, Author of "There is an old man up there ahead of you" - Unknown.*

CHAPTER 3

COLLAPSING DOGS, GOATS AND FOLKS

During my small animal clinical studies in veterinary school at Purdue University, an intern placed a young dog onto the floor asking us to hold still, observe the behavior, and make no signs of recognition that the puppy was in the room. The dog explored the area, seemed to be normal and after a short time the intern placed a bowl of food on the floor. The puppy headed full speed towards the food and dropped to the floor as if he had been shot dead. In a few seconds it seemed to awaken, staggered as it got up, ate the food in the bowl and proceeded exploring the room. I observed the event one other time, involving a client, during my practice as a companion animal veterinarian.

This condition has been identified as narcolepsy and is most commonly seen in dogs, cats, and a genetic line in goats. It is a disorder of the nervous system, affecting primarily young dogs and cats. A narcoleptic episode involves sudden collapse and loss of movement. The pet literally seems to fall asleep, rapid closed eye movements

(REM) may occur and muscles become slack. But the dog may still be aware of his surroundings.

Narcolepsy is often linked to another neurologic disorder called cataplexy that results in temporary muscle paralysis and loss of reflexes. Episodes last a few seconds or several minutes and often occur when the pet is eating, playing, or excited. Often, the dog will abruptly come out of an episode after auditory or physical stimulation. Episodes last a few seconds or several minutes and often occur when the pet is eating, playing, or excited. Neither is a fatal disease, but both merit attention.

The genetic line of goats that collapse do not have narcolepsy or cataplexy. They're known as Myotonic goats but they go by a number of common names, including: wooden leg goats, Tennessee fainting goats, stiff leg goats, and nervous goats.

They get their name from a genetic condition called myotonia congenita, which causes their muscles to briefly stiffen after they are startled. Myotonia congenita is not unique to goats or livestock and can also affect human beings, though not as a response to fear. To say that the goats are fainting is a misnomer—the animals never actually lose consciousness.

Most animals that experience fear receive a chemical rush that triggers a "fight or flight" response. One hypothesis for why fainting goats "lock-up" when frightened is a cell mutation that inhibits them from receiving this muscle-moving chemical. In other words, instead of responding normally, their muscles seize up.

Because myotonia congenita is a recessive gene, goats that are crossbred with other breeds typically do not display fainting behaviors. The breed is one of only a few types of goats native to North America and, as their name might indicate, they are commonly found in Tennessee and neighboring states in the South.[1]

Stanford University professor Emmanuel Mignot has a dog, named Watson, he adopted from Vermont to replace another dog that was being used for studies on narcolepsy. As director of Stanford's Center for Sleep Sciences and Medicine, founded by the legendary sleep researcher William Dement, Mignot helped oversee the country's first and largest pack of narcolepsy research dogs. The dogs – about 80 of them at the program's peak – were mostly Dobermans and Labradors, collected over the years mostly via word-of-mouth.

Mignot states: "Narcolepsy in dogs is vanishingly rare. Mignot estimates that about one in a million dogs have the disease compared to one in 2,000 humans. In 1999, Mignot identified the genetic cause of canine narcolepsy: a mutation that blocks a response to hypocretin, a brain chemical that keeps us awake.

Watson has a form of narcolepsy that has one of two causes and becomes apparent when he's overly excited and then collapses. Mignot and others believe another, "sporadic" form of narcolepsy may be caused by an immune reaction, perhaps to the flu. He believes dogs may experience this type as well.

Mignot noted that he hopes that narcoleptic dog research – dormant for the last decade or so – might have its own revival to answer new questions about sleep disease.

Discussing Watson's disease prior to being sent to Stanford, Dr. Mignot mentioned: "I received an email from a veterinarian in Vermont, telling me they had a dog with narcolepsy. In this case, an owner, seeing that the dog was collapsing and falling asleep all the time, didn't want to keep him. So, he had returned the dog to the breeder, who took it to the vet. They didn't really know what to do with the dog.

It's very cute. You see him fading, like "Oof, I fall asleep" and he kind of crumples, you know? Then he lifts his head again, like he nods, trying to stay awake. And he looks at you with his eyes half closed and you have the feeling like he's telling you "I love you," but in fact he's falling asleep."

Falling asleep a lot is one aspect of narcolepsy. But another symptom that can be present is cataplexy. When Watson gets excited, sometimes he becomes completely paralyzed. That happens with good food, but it has to be really good food, like a piece of chicken, or filet mignon. He gets excited and then --boom! -- he's paralyzed. Sometimes it's just the back legs and he stumbles. Or sometimes he falls on the floor and can't move for a few seconds.

In humans (who have narcolepsy) it can happen when patients are laughing or joking, but with dogs it's anything that he's very happy about. For example, it's not uncommon that (I come home from work and) he's running around, so happy to see me and then – boom! -- he collapses and he can't move for a few seconds or minutes. That's called cataplexy. It's a symptom that's classic of narcolepsy.

Like going on the beach. We often go to the beach and he runs around and loves to run around and very often, when he's too happy – poof! – he collapses on the sand. And he's paralyzed for a few seconds to a minute sometimes.

Cataplexy doesn't appear to be painful or stressful. When Watson's down, you can sense sometimes there's frustration, like his nose is in front of a piece of food, and he's trying to fight it. But it lasts for only a few seconds. The best cure is to have him well rested. He has a normal life. It's not severe enough that he needs to be treated.

Narcolepsy is a lot more stressful for people than for dogs. With humans, if you can nap at any time the disease is much less severe. I know a few patients who don't get treated and have special lifestyle where they wake up, work for an hour and a half or so, then take a nap for a half an hour, work a bit more, and so on. If you can live like this, you can almost have a normal life. But in our society, it's usually impossible. That's why narcolepsy is a terrible disease."

Stanford no longer maintains a pack of narcoleptic dogs for research purposes. However, scientists think there's still mysteries around narcolepsy that have not been solved. Thanks to the dogs, we found the cause of narcolepsy was this lack of chemical in the brain, called hypocretin – a chemical produced by cells in the brain. When it's not there you have narcolepsy.

And sometimes this happens because of a genetic mutation. But other times it's spontaneous? We think that in these cases, it's an immune disease, triggered by the flu. People develop a reaction to the flu that is abnormal and instead of just fighting flu there is damage to the cells that produce this chemical, hypocretin, and destroy them. Then you have narcolepsy. But we still don't understand this process very well.

Some of the dogs we have probably developed narcolepsy the same way. I wouldn't be surprised if we discover something new again that helps us understand how the immune system is killing the hypocretin.

With Watson, I don't know if it's the genetic form with the mutation, or if it's the sporadic kind. I have blood samples from all the dogs who were in the colony. It'll be interesting to sequence all these dogs that have sporadic form and see if we can find something else that will eliminate the human disease."[2]

Several years ago, I was at work having a pleasant visit in our exam room with a client in her mid-eighties. We were laughing about a couple of things when she suddenly went limp, was non responsive and my first thoughts were that she had a heart attack or stroke. My staff and I worked with her for a few minutes and called 911.

While waiting for the paramedics her husband came into Camden Pet Hospital and was summoned into the room. He explained to us that his wife had a neurological disease that under conditions of stress she would become limp and non-responsive. He advised me that if we would relax for a few minutes she would wake up and be fine. And, she did.

During another visit I calmly, trying to not getting her to laugh, discussed this condition with her. She mentioned that she is completely aware what is going on during these attacks but cannot respond until the affected muscles gain their strength.

I latter spoke with her daughter about her mother's narcolepsy and cataplexy. She told me that she had no idea her mother had the disease. I was very surprised, but suspected she knew her mother slept a lot but her parents had never discussed the condition with her. I also spent some time trying to imagine how her parents kept the house so quiet, void of stress and kept laughter down to a chuckle?

As for Dr. Mignot, his dog Watson and his narcolepsy research at Stanford University: "Emmanuel Mignot, MD, PhD, the Craig Reynolds Professor of Sleep Medicine, is the winner of a 2023 Breakthrough Prize in Life Sciences. He will share the $3 million prize with Masashi Yanagisawa, MD, PhD, of the University of Tsukuba for discovering the causes of narcolepsy and paving the way for new treatments for sleep disorders."

Mignot's statement: "I became interested in narcolepsy because I thought it was a key to understanding sleep, and because it had this human dimension of trying to help patients with this disease that nobody cared about. When I started studying narcolepsy, people thought it was very rare. Nobody knew about it."

"For so many years, the neurological mechanisms that cause narcolepsy were a complete mystery to the medical community," said Lloyd Minor, MD, dean of the Stanford School of Medicine. "Dr. Mignot's research not only unearthed the protein at the center of this mystery but also led to effective treatments and therapies for people suffering from the condition. Through his brilliant work, Dr. Mignot forever changed the field of sleep medicine and, in doing so, opened the door for more discoveries across a variety of neurodegenerative diseases."

1– *This Swing Is Just Too Much For Fainting Goat, National Geographic, Sarah Gibbins, 2017.*

2– *Interview with Stanford University Professor Emmanuel Mignot about his narcoleptic dog Watson and their studies looking for a cure for human narcolepsy.*

CHAPTER 4

WONDERFUL SPIDERS

Famously Spider-Man can do whatever a spider can. But how true is that, exactly? How accurate are Spider-Man's powers compared his real-life counterparts?

Arachnologist Rod Crawford, curator at the Burke Museum in Seattle points out that in certain Spider-Man movies he squirts silk out from his hands. Real spiders only produce silk from their spinnerets, which are appendages at the tail end of the abdomen. So, if a human carried a spider's silk production ability, you would normally expect it to come out of the human's butt."

Spider-Man's super strength is based on the idea that a spider can lift many times its own weight. Therefore, if a human possessed the abilities of a spider, they too could lift many times their own weight.

But Crawford is sceptical of that idea. As an object grows larger, so too does the strain and demands on that object. Strength does not scale directly with size. According to the square-cube law, the smaller you are the easier it is to lift large objects because the large object itself simply does not weigh very much. The larger you are the harder it is to lift large objects because the weight of the large object increases a great deal faster than your own strength.

The Square-cube law is a mathematical principle first described by Galileo Galilei as "the ratio of two volumes is greater than the ratio of their surfaces." In other words, as an animal increases in size, its volume will grow faster than its surface area, so larger animals need much larger limbs to support their weight. If we were to merely scale up an elephant by several orders of magnitude, the square-cube law holds that it would collapse — its mass would increase by a power of three, while its limbs would increase in size by a power of two.

Spiders have about as much strength as insects of the same size range, and a spider in a web is able to lift a prey item that weighs a few times more than the spider. But in an absolute sense that item is still extremely light.

Some spiders are good at jumping, some aren't. Also, spider jumping is done in a quite different manner from the jumping of a being like us that has internal bones in our legs that are surrounded by muscle. Spider legs do not have extensor muscles at all. So, when they extend the leg in order to jump, that is not done by a muscle, it's done by hydraulic pressure of blood. A spider that's jumping increases the blood pressure in jumping legs to such an extent that if the spider had a doctor that doctor would go through the roof about it.[1]

Spider corpses turned into robots sounds like the far-fetched plotline for another Spider-Man movie. But researchers from Rice University have created just that— dead wolf spiders that can be used as machines to pick up and put down objects. Researchers have dubbed the use of biotic materials as robotic components "necrobotics." They say this area of research could be used to create biodegradable grippers for very small objects.

The research began in 2019, when the scientists noticed a dead spider curled up in their lab. Wondering why spiders always die with their legs in that position, they searched and discovered that spiders have a hydraulic pressure system that controls their limbs. The hydraulic mechanism allows some spider to be good jumpers.

Spiders do not have antagonistic muscle pairs, like biceps and triceps in humans. They only have flexor muscles, which allow their legs to curl in, and they extend them outward by hydraulic pressure. When they die, they lose the ability to actively pressurize their bodies.

To create their gripper, researchers stuck a needle into internal valves in the spiders' hydraulic chamber, created a seal with superglue and attached a syringe to the other end. By puffing small amounts of air through the syringe, the scientists could extend and retract the spider's legs.

The dead spiders could pick up more than 130 percent of their own body weight and last through 1,000 open-close cycles. Without any kind of coating on the corpse, the spiders only remained functional for two days because dehydration made their joints brittle. The researchers experimented with a beeswax coating and found it could slow the loss of the spiders' hydration.

The Rice team says necrobotic grippers could have multiple applications, including for the assembly of things like microelectronics and for collecting specimens. Because the necrobotic gripper has inherent compliance and camouflaging capabilities, they envision that they can deploy it in scientific fieldwork. For example, to capture and collect small insects and other live specimens without damaging them.[2]

Spider-Man's reflexes are super-fast, as befitting certain types of spiders. Some spiders are extremely quick. There is a ground spider found only in North America which, in terms of body lengths per seconds, can run in relative terms twice as fast as a cheetah. However, if it was scaled up to human size it couldn't run at all, because of square-cube law.

There is no single explanation for Spider-Man's ability to stick to and climb walls. The explanation for the original comic book Spider-Man, for instance, was that he could bond himself to surfaces through an electrostatic force. Any spider can climb a rough brick wall because they have claws. But jumping spiders and some other groups have special microscopic hairs on the tips of their legs that are able to cling to smooth surfaces. The hairs of a spider contain hundreds of thousands of even smaller hairs called setules, which can exploit van der Waals forces – the attraction of intermolecular forces between molecules – to create a temporary molecular bond with a surface. Scientists have concluded that this bond is so strong that a spider could conceivably carry 173 times its body weight while attached to a surface.

Spider-Man's webbing is ridiculously strong. In the 2017's Spider-Man: Homecoming, where it's proven tough enough to prevent a ferry from splitting in two; or 2004's Spider-Man 2, where it's stretched to breaking point slowing down a runaway train. And real-life spider silk is not too dissimilar.

A typical spider thread is only a few microns thick and yet for its size it is considerably stronger than something like a typical steel cable. It is probably the strongest natural fiber known. This is why scientists are attempting to artificially reproduce spider silk for use in bike helmets and single-use plastics.[1]

The next time you brush aside a spiderweb, you might want to meditate on its delicate strength—if human-size, it would be tough enough to snag a jetliner. Now, scientists know just how these silken strands get their power: through thousands of even smaller strands that stick together to form this critter's clingy trap.

To find out how most spider silk is five times stronger than steel, scientists analyzed the silk that venomous brown recluse spiders use to create their ground webs and hold their eggs, using an atomic force microscope. They found that each strand—which is 1000 times thinner than a human hair—is actually made up of thousands of nanostrands, only 20 millionths of a millimeter in diameter. Just like a tiny cable, each silk fiber is entirely composed of parallel nanostrands, which they measured to be at least 1 micron long. That may not sound very lengthy, but on a nanoscale, it's at least 50 times as long as these fibers are wide—and researchers believe they could stretch even further.

The idea that nanofibers make up spider silk has been proposed before, but until now, there was no evidence to suggest nanostrands comprised the entire makeup of a silk fiber. The team's secret weapon was the unique silk of the brown recluse spider, which, unlike most, is a flat ribbon as opposed to a cylindrical fiber, making it easier to examine under the lens of a powerful microscope.

The new discovery builds on a finding the team made last year, which demonstrated how the brown recluse spider reinforces its main silk strands with a special looping technique. Equipped with a tiny sewing machine–like spinneret, the spider weaves about 20 microloops into every millimeter of silk it ejects, which strengthens their sticky spool and prevents it from collapsing.

Researchers say even though the flat ribbons and looping technique are not shared by all spiders, their study of brown recluse silk may be a window to exploring the stringy fibers of other species. Such studies could pave the way for creating new materials that could be used in medicine and engineering. But synthetic spider silk has been notoriously difficult to create. In the meantime, researchers hope their work will help us unreel one of the toughest materials of the natural world.[3]

People have been cultivating silkworms for thousands of years, unwinding their cocoons to provide material for textiles. But their silk breaks easily. Spiders have the opposite problem: They make incredible silks, but the arachnids are hard to cultivate. One hundred silkworms can hang around peaceably in a small space, whereas 100 confined spiders will attack one another, until only one or two are left alive.

In an attempt to harness the best of both animals, researchers have tried for years to genetically engineer silkworms to make spider fibers. But spider silk proteins are large, and the correspondingly large genes have been difficult to insert in the genomes of other animals.

Biotechnologists worked with a relatively small spider silk protein. It's found in an orb-weaving spider from East Asia. The scientists used CRISPR to insert the spider's gene in place of the gene in silkworms that codes for their primary silk protein. But the scientists retained some silkworm sequences in their gene construct in order to ensure the worm's internal machinery could still work with the spider protein.

The transgenic silkworms produce fibers with high strength (a measure of how much stress a material can take without deforming) and high toughness (a measure of how much energy it can absorb through stretching before rupturing). The fibers were almost as tough as the strongest natural spider silk, and about six times tougher than Kevlar. Kevlar is a type of aramid (organic polymer) fiber. It is woven into textile materials and is extremely strong and lightweight, with resistance toward corrosion and heat. It is used in vast applications such as aerospace engineering (such as the body of the aircraft), body armor, bulletproof vests, car brakes, and boats.

To commercially produce the spider silk fibers there will need to be cross-breed research-grade silkworms with commercial strains that are used for large-scale silk cultivation. The fibers, which are biodegradable, might find first use in surgical sutures.

It could be challenging to protect intellectual property rights when commercializing the spider silk because it would likely entail distributing transgenic silkworm eggs to many farmers. It also remains to be seen whether the inserted genes will persist when the silkworms are bred.

Next, plans are made to see whether they can engineer silkworms to make spider silks that are even stronger and stretchier. Scientists are thinking about designing silk proteins that incorporate nonnatural amino acids, which has "boundless potential" to enable silks with totally new properties—perhaps one not only tougher than Kevlar, but stronger, too.[4]

The sight of Spider-Man using his webbing to swing through a city isn't as far-fetched as you may think either. Spiders do descend from high points to low points on threads. They don't do any kind of Tarzan-like vine swing, because they don't have any way of launching themselves. However, if a spider is descending on a thread and there's any kind of a wind blowing, the spider can be moved by the wind in a horizontal direction to land on something that's not vertically below a starting point.

One of Spider-Man's most famous powers is his spider-sense, which gives him the ability to sense danger before it happens –represented by a tingling feeling at the back of his skull. This sudden inspiration recognizing danger is a subjective thing and Crawford is skeptical of the idea of spiders being alerted to danger before it happens. That sounds like premonition. And he doesn't believe there's any research that demonstrates premonition in spiders.

Real spider senses are attuned to their local environment, but do have their limits. Spiders have hairs that are extremely sensitive to air vibrations, including very specific frequencies of what we would call sounds. They also have what we call a chemotaxis sense, which you might describe as smell by touching. Only a few spiders can detect airborne odors at all.

And as for their sight, that varies on the kind of spider. Jumping spiders have some of the best vision in the animal kingdom. It's almost as good as a human's. However, your typical house spider's eyes cannot form recognizable images at all.[1]

Remember where your primary support web of life comes from. Whether on earth or in the eternities it begins and ends with family. Its fibers must be ever tended to with loving care keeping it strong enough to resist the changing storms that come our way.

The "natural man" may find himself longing for the support of his primary web. Like the prodigal son, who needed to rebuild and restore his life's web, we will need to constantly repair and restore our web and help others care for theirs. It may not be easy, but as Christ has shown – It is worth it.

Psychologist David Premack's relates a case study of a fiercely addicted smoker who pulled to the curb in front of a public library one day to pick up his kids. "He rummaged in the glove compartment for his cigarettes without success. He looked under the seats, but could not find the damn smokes. It was starting to rain. The kids would be out in a second. But wait—there was a store not far away. He could zip over there and be back in just a few minutes. It wasn't raining hard. The kids wouldn't get too wet.

Then something shifted in this man. He thought, Dear Heaven, I am the kind of father who would let his kids stand in the rain while he chased a drug. The insight was powerful enough to break through years of denial. And that was it, he never smoked again."

Sounds easy. However, all the imaginable sins man may concoct in his devious mind, are ever with them in the back of his mind and he needs to keep faith, hope and charity in the fore front of his mind. It's too easy to fall pray in sins like the alcoholic saying: "Once an alcoholic, always an alcoholic" exists because recovery is not an easy process, and it can sometimes take years to find a methodology that works and is sustainable for an individual; there are often relapses that take place on the road to recovery.

Remember, if we stay spiritually tuned in with the Spirit, we too can possess one of Spider-Man's most famous powers. His spider-sense, which gives him the ability to sense danger before it happens. However, this premonition may not be represented by a tingling feeling at the back of our skull. It can be felt personally in many ways reassuring us we are on the right path.

To forget the divine source of our support will leave us struggling and helpless. A Danish fable tells of a spider that slid down a single strand of web from the high rafters of a barn to a lower level. In that new space, she spun her web outward from that strong, single line. She caught flies, grew fat, and prospered.

Self-sufficiency and conceit lulled her into forgetfulness of where her true support and strength lay. One day, wandering her realm, she noticed the thread still stretching into the unseen spaces above her. "What is that for?" she asked, and in a fit of impatience she snapped it off. And her web collapsed and fell to the ground. *Harry Emerson Fosdick book, Twelve Tests of Character*

However, no matter what we've accomplished—no matter how much we have grown—there will always be unanswered questions that need searching out. Looking heavenward to our eternal Father will bring us comfort and peace—and life. *Music & The Spoken Word 1999*

1– *No Way Home: An arachnologist critiques Spider-Man's powers, BBC Science Focus, Stephen Kelly, 12/14/2021.*

2– *Scientists Use Dead Spiders as Claw Machines, Advanced Science, Rice University, Margaret Osborne, 08/01/2022.*

3– *Spider silk is five times stronger than steel—now, scientists know why Thousands of tiny nanostrands make up larger silken "cables", By Courtney Miceli, 11/20/2018.*

4– *Worms with spider genes spin silk tougher than bulletproof Kevlar, Science, Katherine Bourzac, 09/20/2023.*

CHAPTER 5

FREEZING WITHOUT DYING

During one of our annual anniversary cruises, Shauna and I visited Jewell Gardens, just out of the town of Skagway Alaska. There are three acres of beautiful organic gardens. Thinking about my several years of failing to grow rhubarb in California - it was unbelievable how large their rhubarb grew. I also noticed the bushes in the gardens were loaded with red and black banded caterpillars called wooly bear.

We had the opportunity to choose the color and item we wanted to make and participated in a glassblowing experience we will always remember. In a couple of weeks following the cruise we received our glass creations safely at our doorstep.

The Arctic Woolly Bear Caterpillar (Pyrharctia Isabella) can last the polar heights of the Arctic Circle, Greenland, and Canada because it can alternate between feeding, freezing, and thawing. There is sugar in the blood of Arctic wooly bears that function like antifreeze and safeguard the cells in frozen temperatures. The caterpillar is also one of the more ubiquitous and more impressively adaptable creatures found in the Northeastern United States. These black, red, and fuzzy caterpillars emerge in the fall and explode in numbers around October. When winter finally comes in November, the insect buries under only the top layer of leaf litter and characteristically curls up with its bristles facing outwards. In this curled-up state, the Woolly Bear Caterpillar performs a number of striking biological processes. To prepare for winter, they convert their glycogen stores into glycerol and sorbitol (alcohols) which then make up 5% of the insect's body mass. These alcohols are cryoprotectants, or antifreeze proteins (AFP), and they reduce the freezing point of the caterpillar's blood to 14°F as well as prevent ice formation over the outside of the animal up to -22°F. Despite this, the insects are hard to the touch when the temperature dips below 7°F and the glycerol and sorbitol act to prevent cell damage from this freezing. In late March, the caterpillar thaws and spins a cocoon under the leaf litter. One month later, the caterpillar emerges from the winter as an Isabella Tiger Moth.[1]

Permafrost — ground that has been frozen solid for two years or more — can preserve snapshots of life (and death) from millennia ago. For instance, a small bird carcass found in Siberian permafrost in 2020 was 46,000 years old but looked like it [had] died just a few days before.

A frozen and mummified cave bear, also found in Siberia in 2020 and dating to about 39,000 years ago, still had a fleshy black nose and much of its fur. Retaining a lifelike appearance after spending thousands of years in ice is impressive. But some types of plants and animals locked in ancient permafrost have managed to do something even more astonishing; return to life from a frozen state.

In 2012, scientists described how they regenerated 30,000-year-old plants from immature fruit tissue that had been frozen in Siberian permafrost. Two years later, researchers regrew Antarctic moss that had been icebound in Antarctica for 1,500 years. In 2018 tiny worms called nematodes were recovered and revived from ancient permafrost in two Siberian locations: at one site the rocks were around 32,000 years old, and in the other they were approximately 42,000 years old.

Researchers previously found that modern rotifers could be frozen at minus 4 degrees Fahrenheit (minus 20 degrees Celsius) and then revived up to 10 years later. They are multicellular microscopic wheeled animals, so-named for the wheel-like ring of tiny hairs that circle their mouths, and have been around in freshwater for about 50 million years.

Now, scientists have resuscitated rotifers that froze in ancient Siberian permafrost for thousands of years. Once thawed, these ancient rotifers began reproducing asexually through parthenogenesis, creating clones that were their genetic duplicates.

Rotifers evolved to use cryptobiosis because most of them live in watery habitats that often freeze or dry up. They suspend their metabolism and accumulate certain compounds like chaperone proteins that help them to recover from cryptobiosis when the conditions improve. Rotifers also have mechanisms for repairing DNA damage and for protecting their cells against harmful molecules called reactive oxygen species.

However, it doesn't mean that humans will be capable of duplicating rotifers' deep-freeze sleep and recovery anytime soon. The more complex the organism, the trickier it is to preserve it alive frozen. For mammals, it's not currently possible.[2]

Mammalian sperm are among the first cells to be successfully cryopreserved, and over the last seven decades the use of cryopreserved semen for artificial insemination has come to play a crucial role in animal agriculture. For most animal species, however, a large population of sperm are incapacitated after cooling to and warming from liquid nitrogen temperatures. Thus, to achieve equivalent artificial insemination fertility rates, several times more cryopreserved bull sperm are needed.

Although artificial insemination (AI) in pigs with frozen or fresh semen is common, the fertility of cooled semen remains about 50% of fresh semen. After the insemination of super ovulated ewes, pregnancy rates and fertility characteristics with frozen–thawed ram semen are reduced from fresh semen by 20%. The long history of advancements in sperm cryopreservation in livestock has facilitated modern genetic strategies in breeding programs but has also been at the forefront in the assessment and mitigation of cryopreservation-induced damage, including osmotic, oxidative, and epigenetic damage that has expanded to somatic cell cryopreservation research.

Beyond agriculture, human cryopreservation has provided flexibility in fertility options not only for couples but also for those undergoing iatrogenic treatments such as cancer therapy or transgender women undergoing gender-affirming surgery.[3]

Cryopreservation is an established laboratory technique used to store cells and other biological material at a temperature close to that of liquid nitrogen (–196°C). It provides researchers with a backup should growing cells be lost due to contamination and helps to minimize the occurrence of genetic drift by allowing early passage cells to be brought into use when current cultures have been grown for an extended time.

Cryopreservation media typically comprises the growth media, a cryoprotectant such as DMSO or glycerol, and a source of protein (usually serum) may be used.

Freezing cells slowly is essential to prevent intracellular ice formation and can be achieved using a freezing container that provides a freezing rate of 1°C/minute until the cells have been frozen at -80°C.

Leaving cells at -80°C for long periods can result in cell death and cells should be stored in the vapor phase of liquid nitrogen to prevent liquid from entering the tubes.

Once the cells have been removed from liquid nitrogen storage, the cryovial should be placed in a 37°C water bath until the contents are just thawed.[4]

Researchers have for the first time successfully frozen and recovered an entire mammalian brain. The cryogenically preserved brain belonged to a rabbit, and using an innovative technique called Aldehyde-stabilized cryopreservation (ASC), researchers were able to return the animal's brain to near-perfect condition. Using a combination of ultrafast chemical fixation and cryogenic storage, it is the first demonstration that near perfect, long-term structural preservation of an intact mammalian brain is achievable.

The team filled the vascular system of the rabbit brain with chemicals that prevent decay and allow it to be cooled to -211 degrees Fahrenheit (-135°C). When thawed, the brain was found to have all of its synapses, cell membranes, and intracellular structures intact. Current cryopreservation methods aren't ideal, they lead to dehydration and the destruction of neural connections. While the rabbit's brain can't be revived yet, either, the researchers' success suggests all neural components responsible for forming one's personal identity, including memory and personality, can be preserved.

The same research team tested their ASC freezing technique on a larger pig brain which is more similar to the human brain. They are currently awaiting the results of that experiment.[5]

Thousands of donated organs are discarded every year. As soon as one becomes available, doctors race to find a compatible recipient—but transplantation time lines are measured in hours, and many organs still can't be used. Now researchers have successfully preserved rat kidneys for 100 days before thawing and transplanting them into other rats.

Scientists have cryogenically preserved organs for decades via vitrification: cooling them so quickly that ice cannot form and rupture cells. Then thawing them rapidly enough to avoid damage has proved nearly impossible. If the outside heats faster than the middle, you get thermal stress—like when you drop an ice cube in water and you hear it crack. You could basically put a crack right through the middle of the organ and make it not function.

For the new study, just before vitrification (process of changing something glass like hard) the team flooded the rat kidneys' vasculature with iron oxide nanoparticles and a newly developed cryoprotective solution that can preserve the organs at extremely low temperatures. After 100 days, they thawed the organs with an alternating magnetic field, which caused the nanoparticles to oscillate and evenly warm the tissue. The researchers then flushed the nanoparticles and cryoprotective solution out of the organs before replacing the rats' native kidneys with these transplants. The recipients were able to live without medical support.

Only one previous study successfully rewarmed and transplanted a vitrified organ in any animal, and the rabbit kidney in question had been vitrified for roughly 10 minutes—and it performed poorly after transplantation. Drastically extending the preservation period and developing a new method for warming has not been reported as being accomplished before.

Human organs are bigger than rat organs, but there is optimism this technology will translate because of how the nanoparticles uniformly heat an organ from within. This study potentially changes the field of transplantation. 100 days is a long time to match an organ transplant. Hopefully, human organ trials will be soon in coming. Long-term organ banking would be invaluable for the 100,000 people on the organ transplant waiting list.[6]

Antifreeze proteins (AFPs) are specific proteins, glycopeptides, and peptides made by different organisms to allow cells to survive in sub-zero conditions. AFPs function by reducing the water's freezing point and avoiding ice crystals' growth in the frozen stage. Their capability in modifying ice growth leads to the stabilization of ice crystals within a given temperature range and the inhibition of ice recrystallization that decreases the drip loss during thawing.

The ability of organisms to tolerate cold conditions is a natural phenomenon in nature. The development of AFPs reveals a quintessence to comprehend this self-protection circumstance. Over the last decade, our understanding on the utilization of AFP have confirmed the promising usages of this protein with its specific function in different medical and industrial fields. Developments in both structural and physicochemical biological and genetic approaches significantly contribute and allow us to obtain an unprecedented perception towards the mechanisms of membrane protection and ice-binding of AFP. The useful applications of AFPs have been proven in numerous investigations. However, the time-consuming purification process of AFPs has limited the huge usage and functionality of these beneficial biomolecules in various applications.

AFPs are one of the main proteins that remain functional in cold temperatures naturally encompass bony fish, insects, plantae, fungi, Nematoda, amphibia, bacteria, yeast and diatoms. Anti-freeze glycopeptides proteins (AFGP) are produced by various organisms, categorized into five different classes (depending on their sources and structural features). Arctic and Antarctic organisms have been identified to have or express these AFPs in different types and structures. Besides possessing various structures, they could be categorized based on their capability in binding to ice and preventing or slowing down the ice growth and/or ice recrystallization. Potential uses for anti-freeze proteins in the near future are:

Food:
  – Applied as recombinant protein to improve milk fermentation, especially for the storage of frozen yogurt and ice cream.

Industrial:
  – Screened for proteolytic and biolytic activities to obtain a heat-stable protein.
  – Applied as recombinant protein to use in frozen food such as meat.

Medicine:
  – Cryopreservation of rat organs, mammalian cells, red blood cells and subcutaneous tumor cells.

Agriculture:
  – As biofertilizer to increase plant growth at cold temperature.
  – Inhibition of ice nucleating activity in Erwinia herbicola (a bacterium).[7]

The palm-sized wood frog amphibian was hibernating in a box outside Brian Barnes' Fairbanks home a few decades ago. Barnes, director of the Institute of Arctic Biology, and his students were in his living room checking a temperature gauge he recently plucked from the "frog corral." When he plugged the device into his computer, a graph spilled across the screen. The temperature at frog level, under a few inches of snow and moss, had dipped to 10 degrees Fahrenheit in December.

The senses of opinion concluded that this particular frog whose belly the temperature recorder had been stuck to was toast. None of the researchers in the room doubted the diagnosis. According to Lower 48 and Canada studies, wood frogs could not survive temperatures below about 20 degrees.

Barnes' lab tests, performed on Alaska wood frogs, showed the same thing: 10 degrees is just too cold for a wood frog. If its blanket of forest litter and snow isn't thick enough to keep it warmer than 20 degrees, it will, in theory, die.

Theory took a hit a few days later. As the frogs thawed in Barnes' garage, they began twitching, then hopping around. All five frogs groggily woke in mid-December, perhaps wondering which way to the breeding pond. The resurrection proved the Alaska version of wood frog is a little different from its relatives in the Lower 48.

Wood frogs, which take on the temperature of their environment, survive as far north as the Brooks Range because their bodies are able to freeze and thaw without bursting. The species ranges all the way Down to Alabama.

As a wood frog's body freezes, its liver converts glycogen to sugary glucose. All its vital systems are flooded with the sweet liquid, which helps cells resist drying. Though its cells are protected, a hibernating wood frog is frozen like a little green ice sculpture, including its heart and brain and eyeballs. But these living ice cubes have a limit as to how cold they can get. To avoid it, wood frogs seek a snug winter nest when fall temperatures start biting.

The previous September, Barnes' students had tracked four wood frogs with the aid of tiny transmitters glued to the frogs' backs. When the frogs settled late in the month, the students followed them. One frog dug into loose sand next to a horse trailer. Another burrowed six inches into moss near the shore of a pond.

Three months later, the students returned to check the temperature within the frog's chosen wintering spots. Though the air temperature above had once fallen below minus 30, the frog in the sand by the horse trailer never got colder than 27 above. The one that chose to tunnel into the moss didn't experience temperatures colder than 31.

The warmth of the frogs' resting places was due to the blanketing effect of moss, leaves and 18 inches of snow that slowed the escape of the Earth's warmth. The five frogs that wintered in the corral at Barnes' home had only a thin cover of snow because the box was under a tree, and also had a bottom that insulated it from the relatively warm ground. The frogs lived to hop again after being exposed to a temperature of 10 degrees, a feat that was previously unheard of.

The surprising survival of the Fairbanks Five may be attributable to the roller-coaster ride of temperature changes endured by wild wood frogs. In the lab, frogs perished at 18 degrees when the temperature dropped steadily. Exposure to temperatures jumping above and below freezing during fall may trigger the successful release of added glucose from a frog's liver.

According to the Alaska Dept. of Fish and Game, the blood sugar acts as an antifreeze that protects the cells, even though most of the water in the frog's body outside the cells does freeze. In a person, a blood sugar level of 90 micrograms per 100 milliliters of blood is normal. In freezing wood frogs, the blood sugar level is 450 times higher, which would kill a person many times over. The frogs survive in part because their metabolism has essentially shut down.[8]

Cryonics is one extreme of cryopreservation where the whole body is frozen in the hope that one day it will be possible to revive it. On a smaller scale in day-to-day medicine, freezing is an extremely useful technique for storing living cells, such as blood cells, bone marrow, sperm and embryos, at ultra-low temperatures.

But scientists agree that preserving and reawakening the complete human body is a remote possibility which would take massive breakthroughs in technology. However, scientists believe you can never say never in science even though there is little chance of it happening based on current knowledge. Taking tissues from healthy people to be stored for future use was one thing but taking a diseased body, freezing it safely - including the complex structure of the brain - and reactivating it is a far, far more difficult task.

We are not even at the stage of cryopreserving organs yet, so doing it with a whole body would be a huge challenge. Organs themselves are very complicated, containing different types of cells, blood vessels and an inter-cellular structure - which would all need to be preserved. The first step will be to demonstrate that human organs can be cryopreserved for transplantation. But at the moment the equipment to make that happen is not available.

After death, patients have to be acted on quickly, volunteers trained in cryonics take care of the body, starts the process of freezing and arranges for it to be shipped to the country where it is to be stored. At this stage, dry ice is used to keep the body at a low temperature. Bodies are cryogenically preserved in liquid nitrogen at extremely low temperatures.

Once at the storage facility, patients are infused with cryoprotectants (like antifreeze) to prevent ice crystal formation - which would kill cells - before the temperature is slowly lowered and they are preserved in liquid nitrogen at extremely low temperatures of below -130C.

The low temperatures are needed to allow the cells to survive dehydration after death. Uncontrolled dehydration and freezing is lethal to living cells, so it has to be done carefully.

The eventual aim is that one day they will be rewarmed and revived, but there is no evidence or guarantee that they can be.[9]

Let's see:

- We have all types of plants and animals that have survived frozen in cold temperatures for thousands of years by using anti-freeze proteins and anti-freeze glycopeptides.
- The Wood Frog that can release enough glucose from its liver to act as anti-freeze to survive subzero conditions. Their body levels of glucose are 450 times higher than normally found in a human.
- A rabbit's brain has been frozen in perfect condition – but it can't be brought back to life.
- A rat's kidney has been frozen for 100 days, thawed without damage and functioned normal when transplanted back into the rat. In the near future larger human organs harvested for transplant may become more readily available and viable.

- Some suspect that they can be frozen upon death and revived after developing new technology to fix and repair whatever ails them. No one knows if they are successful if the central nervous system will function. Maybe a kiss from a loved one's princess or prince charming (if they are still alive) during the thawing process may yield surprising results. It worked in fairy tales and the kiss is not even needed for a Wood Frog to successfully thaw intact brain and all each spring.

- When my children were all still living at home, we stayed a couple of days in a hotel in Lake Tahoe with an unheated outdoor swimming pool. I got on my swimming suite and without success dared my "chicken little" kids to follow my advice by jumping into the pool. After the initial cold-water shock, I proceeded to swim for several minutes before hypothermia began to set in.

Being a tough guy, I ignored the signs of mild hypothermia which meant my body temperature was between 95 F and 89.6 F. Soon, not only was I shivering and my teeth chattering; I don't recall other symptoms of exhaustion, clumsiness, slow movements and reactions, sleepiness, weak pulse fast heart rate, rapid breathing, pale skin color, confusion and poor judgment/loss of awareness, excessive urination and trouble speaking – setting in.

What I do remember from this experience was how long it took for the uncomfortable shivering and chattering teeth to subside. Even with a hot shower I couldn't stop shaking. Cryopreserving of my body upon death will never be written into my will – the dreams of a beautiful fairy princess placing a kiss on my cheek and giving me a reborn life would not make up for the nightmares I would have for the rest of my life thinking about my memories of hypothermia. I'm holding out for the promise of resurrection!

1– *Wooly Bear Caterpillars, Institute of Agriculture and Natural Resources, Nebraska Extension, Dodge County.*

2– *24,000-year-old 'zombies' revived and cloned from Arctic permafrost, News (from Live Science), Mindy Weisberger, 06/07/2021.*

3– *Animals, Cryopreservation of Semen in Domestic Animals: A Review of Current Challenges, Applications, and Prospective Strategies, Mohsen Sharafi et al., 2022 Dec; 12(23): 3271.*

4– *Top Tips for Freezing and Thawing Cells to Maintain Viability, Emma Easthope, 02/19/2020.*

5– *Cryogenics: Entire Rabbit Brain Successfully Frozen and Revived For First Time, By Samantha Mathewson, 02/11/2016.*

6– *After 'Absurdly Long' 100-Day Freeze, Rat Kidneys Were Successfully Transplanted Nanoparticles can allow long-term freezing of transplant organs, Scientific American, Timmy Broderick, 09/01/2023 Issue.*

7– *Antifreeze Proteins and Their Practical Utilization in Industry, Medicine, and Agriculture - Biomolecules. 2020 Dec; 10(12): 1649.*

8– *Report of frog's death greatly exaggerated, Ned Rozell, UAF News Information - U of Alaska, 01/05/2023.*

9– *What does cryopreservation do to human bodies? BBC News, Philippa Roxby, 11/18/2016.*

CHAPTER 6

GREED AND EGGS

During January 2023 officers at the San Diego Customs and Border Protection Office had seen an increase in the number of attempts to move eggs across the US-Mexico border. CNN reported the Director of field operations Jennifer De La O reported: "The San Diego Field Office has recently noticed an increase in the number of eggs intercepted at our ports of entry. Uncooked eggs are prohibited entrance from Mexico into the U.S. Failure to declare agriculture items can result in penalties of up to $10,000."

Bringing uncooked eggs from Mexico into the US is illegal because of the risk of bird flu and Newcastle disease, contagious viruses that infect birds, according to Customs and Border Protection. The rise in attempted egg smuggling is due to the spiking cost of eggs in the US. A massive outbreak of deadly avian flu among American chicken flocks has caused egg prices to skyrocket, climbing 11.1% from November to December and 59.9% annually, according to the Bureau of Labor Statistics.

For the most part, travelers bringing eggs have declared the eggs while crossing the border. When that happens, the person can abandon the product without consequence. Agriculture specialists will collect and then destroy the eggs (and other prohibited food/ag products). If travelers do not declare their eggs and the products are discovered during inspection, the eggs are seized and the travelers given a $300 penalty.

According to the Pan American Health Organization, Epidemiological Alerts & Updates on Avian Influenza: The virus also known as 'bird flu', is a disease primarily affecting birds and is caused by a virus of the Orthomyxoviridae family. According to subtype it may be classified as high or low pathogenicity. Most of the influenza viruses circulating in birds are not zoonotic. However, some strains have the ability to infect humans, posing a threat to public health. The main risk factor is the direct or indirect exposure to infected animals or environments and surfaces contaminated by feces.

The most common way for the virus to enter a territory is through migratory wild birds. The main risk factor for transmission from birds to humans is direct or indirect contact with infected animals or with environments and surfaces contaminated by feces. Plucking, handling infected poultry carcasses, and preparing poultry for consumption, especially in domestic settings, may also be risk factors.

When avian influenza is transmitted to humans, symptoms in people can range from mild upper respiratory tract infection (fever and cough) to severe pneumonia, acute respiratory distress syndrome (difficulty breathing), shock, and even death.

Along with milk, eggs contain the highest biological value (or gold standard) for protein. One egg has about only 72 calories, but 6 grams of high-quality protein, 5 grams of fat, and 1.6 grams of saturated fat, along with iron, vitamins, minerals, and carotenoids. The egg is also contains the disease-fighting nutrients like lutein and zeaxanthin. These carotenoids may reduce the risk of age-related macular degeneration, the leading cause of blindness in older adults. Hard-boiled eggs are an excellent source of protein. The protein in hard-boiled eggs also works alongside vitamin D to promote prenatal development. These elements support a baby's teeth, bones, and general growth throughout pregnancy. Choline is important for cellular maintenance and growth, and hard-boiled eggs are the top source of it in the U.S. diet. Brain development and memory may be enhanced by the choline content of eggs. Lutein and zeaxanthin, which are found in boiled eggs, have antioxidant and anti-inflammatory properties that help maintain your eye health. Hard-boiled eggs are also a source of vitamin A, vitamin D, calcium, and iron.

Eggs are perishable and must be stored in the refrigerator or freezer. Many factors can affect how long eggs last. When properly handled and stored, eggs rarely spoil. However, if you keep them too long, they are likely to dry up.

Refrigeration is required by the United States Department of Agriculture for shell eggs and egg products, while other countries may not require refrigeration. Eggs in the shell can be stored for 4-5 weeks beyond pack date and out of the shell 2-4 days and hard-boiled eggs 1 week. Freezer storage is not recommended for eggs in the shell and for out of the shell they can be stored for up to 1 year.

Century eggs, also known under a wide variety of names, are a Chinese egg-based culinary dish made by preserving duck, chicken, or quail eggs in a mixture of clay, ash, salt, quicklime, and rice hulls for several weeks to several months, depending on the method of processing. Through the process, the yolk becomes a dark green to grey color, with a creamy consistency and strong flavor due to the hydrogen sulfide and ammonia present, while the white becomes a dark brown, translucent jelly with a salty flavor.

The method for creating century eggs likely came about through the need to preserve eggs in times of plenty by coating them in alkaline clay, which is similar to methods of egg preservation in some Western cultures. The clay hardens around the egg and results in the curing and creation of century eggs instead of spoiled eggs.

The century egg has at least four centuries of history behind its production. Its discovery was said to have occurred around 600 years ago in Hunan during the Ming Dynasty, when a homeowner discovered duck eggs in a shallow pool of slaked lime that was used for mortar during construction of his home two months before. Upon tasting the eggs, he set out to produce more – this time with the addition of salt to improve their flavor – resulting in the present recipe of the century egg.

To check the freshness of the century eggs, you just need a large bowl of cold tap water. Simply drop the century eggs into the water bowl. If the eggs sink to the bottom of the bowl, they are not bad and are safe to eat. However, if the eggs float, discard them as they have gone bad.

In 1848 with the Gold Rush, San Francisco started the year with a mere thousand souls, but over the next twelve months the population rose to twenty-five thousand. The city experienced scarcities of women and of food, particularly protein. Scaling up farms to provide eggs for the local population proved harder than it seemed. Nobody could get large groups of chickens to survive there, and the technical solutions to this problem were decades off. Without chickens, of course, there could be no eggs. And without eggs, there could be no cakes, morning scrambles, pancakes, puddings, or muffins.

As gold poured into the city, the prices for fresh eggs skyrocketed. Out in the field, a single chicken egg might sell for $3, while in the city that same egg fetched the still exorbitant price of $1. Even without accounting for inflation, $12 to $36 per dozen eggs is ridiculously expensive. If we account for inflation, the miners paid something astounding—more like $427 to $1,282 per dozen. This explains the origins of Hangtown Fry rather well. According to legend, a guy who had struck gold wandered into the El Dorado Hotel in the mining supply camp of Hangtown (so nicknamed for its penchant for stringing up criminals). He threw down a bag of gold and demanded the most expensive meal the chef could make— which turned out to be oysters and eggs. If someone could bring good fresh eggs to San Francisco Bay, he would more than make his fortune.[1]

The Farallon Islands are the site of the largest seabird colony in the United States outside of Alaska and Hawaii, as well as an important sea lion rookery. This abundance of fresh meat and eggs attracted ships to replenish supplies and Russian sealers, who were the first to collect the abundant common murre eggs.

When control of California passed from Mexico to the United States, it was not long before the economic potential of the islands became apparent. In 1849 a recent immigrant to San Francisco, "Dr. Robinson", sailed to the islands to collect the eggs, and despite losing half of his cargo, was able to make enough money to found a pharmacy and to form the Pacific Egg Company (the name changed over its history and is usually referred to as the Egg Company). The Egg Company strove to assert its claim to South East Farallon (SEFI) and the adjoining West End (or Maintop Island). It surveyed the islands, obtained a school warrant, and constructed buildings, paths, and landing facilities.

Egg collection was a seasonal occupation, from mid-May until July. The eggs of murres were preferred over those of other species, their eggs being the largest and most common ones available. Western gull eggs were also occasionally taken, having a comparable flavor, but they were smaller than murre eggs and more fragile (an important factor given the choppy seas between the Farallon Islands and San Francisco). Individual eggers collected from certain areas. Prior to collecting the workers would progress through a colony destroying every egg they could find, thus, returning to the site on subsequent days, they could be certain the eggs they collected were fresh. Eggers had to work quickly as the murres would flush and immediately the gulls would move in to snatch the unguarded eggs.

The Egg Company attracted rivals, due to the amount of money to be made from the trade. Many fishermen collected eggs on the smaller and more treacherous North Farallon's (which were not claimed by the Egg Company), but others attempted to egg on the main islands. The company's claims to exclusive ownership of the island were dealt a further blow by an executive order issued by President

James Buchanan in 1859 which claimed the islands for the federal government in order to build a lighthouse (which had already been built in 1855). The then lighthouse superintendent of the area, Ira Rankin, did not attempt to push the Egg Company off the island and instead asserted their right to collect over that of the other companies. In 1863, when a company of men, led by a David Batchelder sailed to the islands, Rankin sent a boat of armed men to remove them from the island, seizing several weapons. Batchelder returned a few weeks later and, reinforced, tried again to remove the Egg Company. Rankin again sent forces to evict him and his men from the island.

Batchelder returned once more to the Farallon's, on June 2, 1863. Rankin's forces again encountered them moored off North Landing, but Batchelder convinced them that he was intending to egg the North Farallon's, not SEFI. Rankin's men left for San Francisco. With the government cutter gone, three rowboats with twenty-seven armed men attempted a landing on the morning of June 4. As Batchelder's men landed, they were fired upon by men from the Egg Company. Batchelder's men returned fire. The defenders had the advantage, having been able to pick their positions ahead of time, and after twenty minutes Batchelder's men retreated. One man was killed on each side, and four of Batchelder's men were wounded.

The aftermath of the conflict left the Egg Company in sole control of the islands. David Batchelder was convicted of murder, but he was acquitted on a technicality. The presence of the eggers on the island was tolerated for another twenty years, but they were finally evicted in 1881. *Wikipedia*

The Farallon egg trade greed lasted for a half century, with tragic ecological consequences for the birds. Estimates vary from source to source, but at the beginning of the egg rush, the company likely shipped around 900,000 eggs per year. Fifty years later, that number was closer to 150,000 eggs shipped, a sixth as many. The unchecked smashing and stealing of murre eggs had a predictable effect, decreasing the murre population by about 95 percent.

Later environmental degradation—multiple oil spills, shipping lanes, falling numbers of tasty sardines, to say nothing of an underwater nuclear waste dump—further diminished the number of murres to a mere 6,000 by the 1950s. Since then, thanks to conservation efforts, numbers have greatly recovered, hitting 100,000 in 2000 and 250,000 to 300,000 in 2020.

Humans have done far worse in pursuit of eggs. Before Doc Robinson retrieved the first boatload in the Farallon's, before the Gold Rush entirely, the great auk flourished. A large, docile, penguin-looking bird, the great auk was a member of the common murre's biological family. Like murres, great auks congregated in large groups—a move that would turn out to be foolish—to lay their eggs on the bare rock of sea islands. Black with white bellies like the murre, this oversized, flightless cousin bred on rocks off the coast of Greenland, Newfoundland, Iceland, Massachusetts, and Scotland.

They had the minor misfortune of moving and breeding slowly—females laid only one egg a year—and the greater misfortune of soft feathers, tasty flesh, and fat that made a fine fuel oil. Laws going back to the 1550s tried to protect the birds, but they proved too easy to catch and too useful.

One of the sadder passages is the 1794 description of an auk hunt by Aaron Thomas of the HMS Boston:

"If you come for their Feathers, you do not give yourself the trouble of killing them, but lay hold of one and pluck the best of the Feathers. You then turn the poor Penguin adrift, with his skin half naked and torn off, to perish at his leisure. This is not a very humane method but it is the common practice. While you abide on this island you are in the constant practice of horrid cruelties for you not only skin them alive, but you burn them alive also to cook their Bodies with. You take a kettle with you into which you put a Penguin or two, you kindle a fire under it, and this fire is absolutely made of the unfortunate Penguins themselves. Their bodies being oily soon produce a Flame; there is no wood on the island."

By 1800, many of the great auk habitats had been destroyed. The scarcity of great auks made their eggs more valuable to oologists, who sent collectors out to snatch eggs and skins, which further decimated their populations. In 1844, three Icelandic hunters visited Geirfuglasker, a coastal island, to secure some specimens for a merchant. On June 3, they found the last known nesting pair of great auks, strangled them, and deliberately smashed the last egg with a boot. One of the hunters later described the scene to a researcher: "I took him by the neck and he flapped his wings. He made no cry. I strangled him."[1]

Greed is the insatiable desire to acquire more, is a normally distributed trait in the population that can be measured well with a number of well-validated scales. There are good, bad and ugly sides to scoring high on greed: Good in the sense that greedy individuals tend to work harder, have more sexual partners and enjoy higher family incomes, which may trickle down to others; bad in the sense that greedy individuals tend to harm others by taking more of a scarce good, by being tempted more by immoral behaviors and by being more corrupt; ugly in the sense that greedy individuals tend to be less happy and less satisfied with life, distrusting other people more and being more envious.

This raises the questions what makes people greedy. A large-scale survey among 120,000 Dutch employees found that dispositional greed was higher for people working in extractive industries, real estate, banking and insurance, and lower for those in education, healthcare and government sectors. This could be self-selection and/ or these jobs incentivizing greedy behaviors. The latter is supported by the finding that economics education makes people greedier. Another factor might be the economic situation in people's childhood. Several studies found that growing up rich is related to greed in adulthood. What could be done to counteract the bad and ugly aspects of greed? Initial findings suggest that mindful parenting may inhibit greediness, and future research should examine this further.[2]

The seven deadly sins, also known as the capital vices or cardinal sins, is a grouping and classification of vices within Christian teachings. Although they are not directly mentioned in the Bible, there are parallels with the seven things God is said to dislike in the Book of Proverbs. Behaviors or habits are classified under this category if they directly give rise to other immoralities. According to the standard list, they are pride, greed, wrath, envy, lust, gluttony and sloth, which are contrary to the seven capital virtues. These sins are often thought to be abuses or excessive versions of one's natural faculties or passions (for example, gluttony abuses one's desire to eat).

Greed (Latin: avaritia), also known as avarice, cupidity, or covetousness, is a sin of desire like lust and gluttony. However, greed is applied to an artificial, rapacious desire as well as the pursuit of material possessions. Thomas Aquinas wrote: "Greed is a sin against God, just as all mortal sins, in as much as man condemns things eternal for the sake of temporal things." In Dante's Purgatory, the penitents are bound and laid face down on the ground for having concentrated excessively on earthly thoughts.

Hoarding of materials or objects, theft, and robbery, especially by means of violence, trickery, or manipulation of authority, are all actions that may be inspired by greed. Such misdeeds can include simony, where one attempts to purchase or sell sacraments, including Holy Orders and, therefore, positions of authority in the Church hierarchy (Wikipedia).

All suffering is caused by ignorance. People inflict pain on others in the selfish pursuit of their happiness or satisfaction. Yet true happiness comes from a sense of inner peace and contentment, which in turn must be achieved through the cultivation of altruism, of love and compassion and elimination of ignorance, selfishness and greed (Dalai Lama).

C. S. Lewis explained this teaching of the Savior: "The moment you have a self at all, there is a possibility of putting yourself first—wanting to be the centre—wanting to be God, in fact. That was the sin of Satan: and that was the sin he taught the human race. Some people think the fall of man had something to do with sex, but that is a mistake. … What Satan put into the heads of our remote ancestors was the idea that they could 'be like gods'—could set up on their own as if they had created themselves—be their own masters— invent some sort of happiness for themselves outside God, apart from God. And out of that hopeless attempt has come … the long terrible story of man trying to find something other than God which will make him happy."

A selfish (greedy) person is more interested in pleasing man—especially himself—than in pleasing God. He looks only to his own needs and desires. He walks "in his own way, and after the image of his own god, whose image is in the likeness of the world" (D&C 1:16). Such a person becomes disconnected from the covenant promises of God (see D&C 1:15) and from the mortal friendship and assistance we all need in these tumultuous times. In contrast, if we love and serve one another as the Savior taught, we remain connected to our covenants and to our associates (D.H. Oaks, Unselfish Service, April 2009).

The avaricious (greedy) man is like the barren sandy ground of the desert which sucks in all the rain and dew with greediness, but yields no fruitful herbs or plants for the benefit of others (Zeno, 336-264 B.C.).

1– *When California Went to War Over Eggs, Smithsonian Magazine, Lizzie Stark, 03/29/2023.*
2– *Current Opinion in Psychology, The Good, Bad & Ugly of Dispositional Greed, Volume 46, Aug. 2022.*

CHAPTER 7

SNAKE VENOM

Sometime in 2006, when my ex-boyfriend failed to show up for dinner, I assumed something was wrong or perhaps he'd forgotten. About a week later, calling to apologize, he told me he'd had an overdose, accidentally injecting a lethal cocktail of venom from three snakes. A lot has been written about Steve Ludwin, widely known as the man who injects snake venom, and lately his life has turned into a non-stop frenzy of international journalists and film crews revealing in the seeming sheer insanity of it.

Steve was once my great love; an animal lover, vegan and musician who wrote songs for Placebo and Ash, and played the Reading festival with Nirvana. In between tours and recordings, he dabbled with snake venom. In his latest incarnation as a self-taught snake expert, molding himself into the role of a lifetime, he appears as a kind of living specimen and star in a short film at the Natural History Museum's exhibition, Venom: Killer and Cure.

Since 1988, he's been shooting, swallowing and scratching venom into his skin from some of the world's deadliest snakes for 30 years. "Snakes are f...... everywhere.

The symbol for medicine is two snakes. They're ingrained in our brain and DNA," he tells me, proudly insisting that he hasn't been ill for decades and has developed "a superhuman immune system".

"When I was 17," he says, "I knew I was going to inject snake venom in the future. I felt like Richard Dreyfuss in Close Encounters of the Third Kind, when he had that feeling 'this means something'. It took many years and accidents of messing around with it to finally make sense." He looks down at his arms, showing the maze of track marks. "I look like a junkie. You can see all the incisions."

Steve stated, "This is what intrigues me about snake venom, that scientists say there are compounds in certain venoms that help its victims accept and relax into death. I felt that first-hand." After injecting himself with three different snake venoms, the next morning, "my arm was all red and doughy with a sack of liquid hanging from it and I could see the blood vessels appear. It was like something out of Evil Dead. It's evolution telling you to stay away. Why do you think monkeys, dogs and everyone is instinctively scared of snakes?"

When he finally went to the hospital, the NHS doctors had never treated a snakebite victim, let alone someone with the venom of three different snakes coursing through their bloodstream. "They didn't know what to do," Steve says, when he had to tell the stunned A&E nurses, he deliberately injected himself. The doctors put him on the phone to a renowned snake expert, who Steve recalls telling: "'I used a Northern Pacific rattlesnake, an eyelash viper and a green tree viper from Asia.' And he just said: 'Well, you're screwed. There isn't an anti-venom because you used three different species.' Then he said: 'You're probably going to die or, at best, lose your arm.'"

The doctors suggested "cutting his arm wide open in a fasciotomy" to release the pressure. "I said: 'F… that, I'd rather die.' The snakes that I used had a hemotoxin, which destroys red blood cells, and that's why people's legs and limbs fall off in Central America."

They gave him the anti-venom CroFab to target the rattlesnake venom that most likely caused all the problems. After three days in intensive care with no improvement Steve, pulling out his IV, discharged himself. Contrary to all their dire predictions, his hand, aside from the bruising, was back to normal a week later. "The doctors were shocked when I went back. They'd never seen a recovery like it. I thought: 'Cool, this sh..'s working.'"[1]

Snake venom was a well-known arrow poison. Since snake venom is digestible, it could be safely used for hunting because the venom did not make game harmful to eat, but the venom in the bloodstream of an enemy brought a painful death or a never-healing wound. Numerous poisonous snakes exist around the Mediterranean and in Africa and Asia.

According to the Greek and Roman writers, archers steeped their arrows in serpents' venom and according to the ancient Greek geographer Strabo, the arrow poison concocted by the Soanes of the Caucasus was so noxious that its mere odor was injurious. Strabo also reported that people of what is now Kenya dipped their arrows 'in the gall of serpents', while the Roman historian Silius Italicus described the snake venom arrows used by the archers of Libya, Morocco, Egypt, and Sudan. Ancient Chinese sources show that arrow poisons were also in use in China at early dates. In the Americas, Native Americans used snake, frog, and plant poisons on projectiles for hunting and warfare.

Complex recipes for envenomed arrows are recorded in Greek and Latin texts. One of the most dreaded arrow drugs was concocted by the Scythians, who combined snake venom and bacteriological agents from rotting dung, human blood, and putrefying viper carcasses bloated with feces. Even in the case of a superficial arrow wound, the toxins would begin taking effect within an hour. Envenomation accompanied by shock, necrosis, and suppuration of the wound would be followed by gangrene and tetanus and an agonizing death.

Different snake venoms tipped the arrows encountered by the army of Alexander the Great in his conquest of India in 327–325 BC. According to the historians they smeared their arrows and swords with an unknown snake poison. Most modern historians assume cobra poison, but the ancient historians' detailed description of the gruesome deaths suffered by Alexander's men points to the deadly Russell's viper. Even the slightly wounded went immediately numb and experienced stabbing pain and wracking convulsions. Their skin became cold and livid and they vomited bile. Black froth exuded from the wounds and then purple-green gangrene spread rapidly, followed by death. Death from cobra venom is relatively painless, from respiratory paralysis, but the Russell's viper causes numbness, vomiting, severe pain, black blood, gangrene, and death – as described by Alexander's history.[2]

Of the nearly 3,000 species of snakes in the world, there are about 300 which are poisonous. Rattlesnakes, cobras, and sea snakes have a powerful venom which is not only harmful and sometimes deadly to humans, but also helpful as it has been used to treat inflammation caused by arthritis and cancer as well as pain relief.

Activated by the saliva glands, the venom contains proteins which injected into a prey will paralyze the muscles to the point where small animals will die fairly quickly. However, larger animals such as humans will mostly endure the effects of the venom with some dying depending on the dose and if treatment is not obtained quickly.

There are roughly sixteen different chemicals found in most snake venom with variations depending on the species. The three types that may be fatal to humans are neurotoxins that affect the nervous system, hemotoxin that destroys blood vessels, and cytotoxin that damages the cells and tissues of the body.

The threat to human life comes not only from the amount of venom that is injected, but also from the location. Swelling and pain are common from the bite itself, but the effects of the poison may include dizziness, nausea, sore throat, vomiting and shortness of breath. Darkening of the bite wound and pain and swelling of the area can result in necrosis that harms the victim for years after the attack. In serious cases, snake venom can lead to hypotension, convulsions, coma and finally a heart attack and death.

The time elapsed before the neurotoxin (called alpha Cobratoxin) begins affecting the body can vary from minutes to a few hours after the bite. At first, the venom will cause weakness as a consequence of blocking nerve transmission.

The first real symptoms of paralysis will be palpebral ptosis (drooping of the eyelids) and external ophthalmoplegia, which is also an eye movement disorder. The reason for this is that the ocular muscles are more susceptible to the blockage of nerve transmissions in comparison with other muscles of the body. The next muscles affected are the facial and neck muscles followed by the respiratory muscles and the limbs, then the victim begins having trouble breathing and death may soon follow.

Although the symptoms of snake venom can be serious, if not fatal in large doses, in small doses it has therapeutic qualities for treating certain conditions. Snake venom has been used for medical purposes for around 3,000 years. Today, snake venom is used to counteract the effects of being bitten by a snake, some medicines, research and the venom supply comes from snake farms around the world raising poisonous snakes and milking their venom.

Near the turn of the 19th century, the venom from cobras was used to create an anti-cobra serum used to treat thousands of victims yearly who otherwise may have died or been permanently scarred from the poisonous bites. Multi-purpose venoms have become common place and the venom can be stored dehydrated and has many medical uses. With research centers around the world producing new anti-venom drugs, particularly cobra, they have saved innumerable victims with remarkably few side effects.

The use of snake venom to treat medical conditions goes back many years, but it was just after World War II that the uses for certain venoms became better know. For example, the venom from the Brazilian viper dilates blood vessels and causes the victim to slow down in their reactions and ultimately collapse. But when used in very small doses, it can actually treat high blood pressure effectively.

One of the most interesting avenues of research for snake venom is its treatment for cancer patients. Because chemotherapy can be harsh and destructive, scientists are looking at certain types of snake venom that can attack the blood vessels that feed cancer cells, slowing their growth and eventually destroying the cancer.

In addition, there is research using snake venom that affects the nervous system to be used in treating conditions such as Alzheimer's disease, dementia, and other conditions in which brain cells are dying. In low doses, certain types of snake venom can actually help in the formation of new blood vessels in the brain that help support brain cells which in turn stave off the effects of debilitating conditions that affect the brain itself. Furthermore, it has been reported that such venom treatments in small doses can be used to support the circulatory system which in turn treats heart disease, diabetes, erectile dysfunction, and more.[3]

If you were bitten by a poisonous snake, the venom would travel from the fangs and into your bloodstream within seconds. Snake bites can be dangerous and kills 81,000 to 138,000 people worldwide every year. But if you decided to drink the venom, the story would take a different turn. Snake venom is not the same as poison. The protein-based toxins of snake venom will need to get into your bloodstream to cause substantial damage. If you swallowed it, your stomach acids and digestive enzymes would likely break up the proteins. It could be as if you never took a sip.

However, drinking a shot of venom might not give you the same painful results as pouring it on your open wound.

But it may not be harmless. Some could still make its way through your digestive system and into your bloodstream. If it did, you would likely experience some of the hemotoxic and cardiotoxic effects from loss of the blood's ability to clot resulting internal bleeding, damaged kidneys, changing the heart's normal rhythm or a heart attack from increased potassium in the blood. If neurotoxic venom is ingested it may directly effect your nervous system. This could lead to reduced eye movement, droopy eyelids and difficulty talking, swallowing, breathing and it may leave you unable to breathe without external support. Mycotoxins present in venom could significantly damage your muscle cells or cause death of tissue (necrosis) resulting in severe pain and toxemia.[4]

There are reports of rare and unusual addictions among drug users, such as using snake and scorpion venom and wasp stings to get high. However, the literature with regard to use of snake venom is limited to few case reports/case series. Most of these cases have been described among patients who have been using opioids. Presented is a case of snake venom use as a substitute for opioids.

A 33-year-old, male presented with history of substance use for the past 15 years. He started smoking cigarettes and taking alcohol at the age of 18 years. He became dependent on alcohol and tobacco by the age of 24 years. From the age of 25 years, in addition, he started taking opioids in the form of raw opium and puppy (poppy?) husk and became dependent on the same over the next 1 year. Over the years, he had been using all the substances concurrently. He had made a few attempts to abstain from the substances but would experience relapse after 1–2 months. Use of substances was associated with marked psychosocial dysfunction, financial difficulties, and physical complications in the form of fatty liver.

A few months before presentation to our center, he learned from his friends about the intoxicating effects of snake venom, who would also at times use snake venom as a substitute to opioids. Out of curiosity, he also tried it as a cheaper substitute for opioid and alcohol. Initially, with the help of the nomadic snake charmers, he subjected himself to the snake bite (possibly cobra, but patient was not sure) over his tip of the tongue. The snake bite was associated with jerky movements of the body, blurring of vision, and unresponsiveness, i.e. "blackout" as per the patient for 1 h. However, after waking up he experienced a heightened arousal and sense of well-being, which lasted for 3–4 weeks, which according to the patient was more intense than the state of high experienced till that time with any dose of alcohol or opioids.

According to patient, during these 3–4 weeks, he did not have any craving for alcohol and opioids and did not consume the same. His smoking continued in the similar manner. After 3–4 weeks, the sense of well-being started to decline, he started to remain irritable, lethargic, and started having craving for drugs. Following this, he again went for a snake bite. He again had the similar experience lasting for 3–4 weeks. After this, he started indulging in the snake bite every 3–4 weeks, so as to experience the sense of well-being and high associated with the snake bite. Over the period, his use of opioids and alcohol reduced and most use of these would be seen after 1–2 weeks of snake bite.

On exploration, patient further disclosed that subjecting self to snake bite was common in his ethnic community (Northwestern part of Rajasthan, India), either as a substitute to other substances of abuse, or is used concomitantly with other substances to experience the feeling of ecstasy. According to the patient, often snake charmers give this kind of bite only to those people who are known to them and best to his knowledge no person had lost their life after the snake bite.

There are few case reports in the literature about snake venom use. A thorough PubMed search and searching of cross references yielded four reports of use of snake venom for recreational purposes. All these reports are from India. Most of these cases have been described in patients using opioids as was seen in our patient. The snakes used for such bites have been identified as cobra, krait, or green-colored snakes seen on the trees. Our patient also described that the snake was possibly cobra. One of the patients, in a previous report described snake-dens, where different types of snakes are graded as mild, moderate, and severe form, based on the type of intoxication provided.

The bites have been reported to be taken on the feet or tongue. As was our patient, previously reported cases have also described the experience of snake bite to be associated with happiness, grandiosity, and excessive sleepiness.[5]

Convinced his miraculous recovery was down to his self-immunization, Rock Singer Steve Ludwin became more fervent. He cheerfully admits mixing black mamba, cobra and puff-adder venom like the ingredients of an exotic cocktail and then, dizzied on pain and adrenaline, skateboarding through London traffic. "It made me feel invincible," he says. "I was living like a madman. It got to the point where I was injecting almost daily, my legs, all over my body because you don't want to do a lot of damage in one area as it could destroy nerves."

He had literally turned himself into a science experiment, but there was a point to his madness. "For the past four years, I've been flying to Copenhagen to give blood and last year I had a bone-marrow operation. They drilled into my lower spine to take out bone marrow. It took me two months to recover." Researchers at the University of Copenhagen have recently created an artificial library of antibodies, the Ludwin Library, generated by Steve's immune system in response to the toxic injections, to develop the first human-derived anti-venom.

"What most people don't realize is that anti-venom has been taken from horses' blood for more than 100 years and sometimes snakebite victims die anyway, because their bodies reject it. When I walked into one of those blood farms and saw about 60 horses with holes in their necks being injected with venom, and with massive bags draining out blood, I was very emotional, knowing what they were going through."

The World Health Organization considers venomous snakebites among the most neglected tropical diseases, killing more than 125,000 people a year. Anti-venom is very expensive. Pharmaceutical companies see it as a developing-world problem and have slowed the production, so snake fatalities are rising. These Danish scientists will solve that problem quickly by using technology and having found an idiot like me who spent decades injecting himself.[1]

I've been thinking about how Steve Ludwin's contribution as a rock star will probably be smothered by the potential real contribution to society from his donation of blood and bone marrow to Researchers at the University of Copenhagen. Also, how they have recently created an artificial library of antibodies in his name, the Ludwin Library, generated by Steve's immune system in response to the toxic injections, to develop the first human-derived anti-venom.

I recently reached into my *Museum of Shame* and removed a box containing one last vial of a medication called Cobroxin that states on the drug insert, "Cobroxin is a solution of highly purified fraction of cobra venom in which the neurotoxic principle has been concentrated to more than twice its original potency. And from which most hemotoxic and proteolytic constituents have been removed. Cobroxin is a potent analgesic for use in intractable pain, especially that due to malignant disease. Highly favorable results have been reported in most cases for which it has been used. Cobroxin has the outstanding advantage that it is not habit forming and does not produce the undesirable by-effects associated with the opioids. Lot#158, expiration date 8/74."

Cobroxin was mostly used at Camden Pet Hospital to treat acral lick granulomas on the top of the forelegs of dogs. These are caused from excess licking and chewing in one area. I think of it as when a child starts itching an insect bite or chicken pox. The more you scratch the area – the more you want to scratch it. The skin becomes reddened, moist, thickened, infected and eventually develops into a hardened mass.

In dogs, these were mostly caused by skin irritation and allergies caused by fleas. The dog would scratch, chew and lick mostly in convenient areas on its body particularly near where their mouth rests when lying down. Clients would complain about hearing their dogs licking and chewing the area throughout the night. Some dogs chewed enough to wear down their front teeth from their hair acting as an abrasive agent on the incisors.

Attempts to prevent licking by placing products, like bitter apple, on the area usually increased their determination to lick. Cool baths, injecting steroids under the granuloma, antibiotics, wraps and oral steroids usually kept the dog from licking and chewing the area for at least a short time. The Cobroxin was used to inject under the sore like steroids. The thought was that the cobra venom would help by deadening nerves in the area. The development of good flea control products has resulted in few acral lick granulomas needing treatment.

No, I'm not being tempted to open my outdated vial of Cobroxin, sucking up some of it into an out- dated glass syringe and injecting it into the tip of my tongue in hopes that I would feel what a study mentioned. "Previously reported cases have also described the experience of snake bite to be associated with happiness, grandiosity, and excessive sleepiness." I was being thoughtful about whether the advances in the use of cobra venom will be used for arthritis, cancer or other painful experiences us old folks will have come our way if God chooses to let us linger a little longer on His planet.

1– *The Observer, Snakes, Poison pass: Rock singer Steve Ludwin who became immune to snake venom, Britt Collins, 2018.*

2– *Ancient Warfare and Toxicology, Snake Venom in Biological Warfare, A. Mayor, in Encyclopedia of Toxicology (Third Edition), 2014.*

3– *Medical use of Snake Venom, Enjoy Vietnam, October 2016.*

4– *scishow, Can You Drink Snake Venom? + others.*

5– *Snake Venom Use as a Substitute for Opioids, Aseem Mehra et al, Indian J Psychol Med., 2018.*

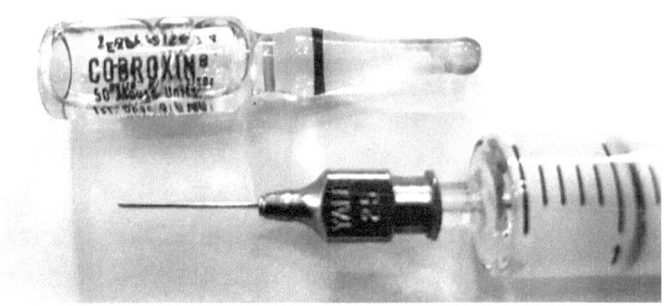

CHAPTER 8

CAPONS AND MINK MAKE A STINK

In the 50's and early 60's during Easter time or winning them at the annual September Eastern Idaho State Fair in my home town in Blackfoot Idaho, my family would raise chickens or ducks. Mother and I also made a chicken egg incubator, purchased fertile eggs from our local chicken hatchery and with a little luck hatched and raised chickens. I don't remember what happened to these birds but I know that non were ever butchered or eaten where we lived.

Dr. Jack Hylton established Camden Pet Hospital in 1969 after spending many years practicing primarily as a traveling to the farm large animal veterinarian. The new hospital cared for primarily companion/comfort pets which included animals ranging from reptiles to primates. His hobbies included raising and racing greyhounds and pigeons.

He would often see pet roosters that were filling the measure of their creation by crowing at the crack of dawn and welcoming one and all that there was coming their way another wonderful day in the neighborhood. Often owners and neighbors did not appreciate the early wake up calls and came to Dr. Hylton for help. Informing the owner that his treatment "should do the trick", He would inject a small pellet of medication under the skin in the rooster's neck.

I learned that the medication was a feminizing hormone called DES (Diethylstilbestrol) and would neuter the rooster, like removing the gonads (sex organs) in dogs and cats, to prevent unwanted male sexual behavior. The neutered rooster is called a capon.

Passing by Dunlap Hatchery on Cleveland Blvd. in Caldwell Idaho in the 2020's I noticed a sign that said free rooster chicks. I also noticed near the same area a wild mink crossing Middleton Road where a canal crosses under the road. Growing up in Idaho, I don't remember the Blackfoot chicken hatchery having a free chick sign and in my out of doors experiences had never seen a mink.

In the chicken egg production and meat industry if a home can't be found for the male chicks they are killed. The sex of day-old chicks is determined at the hatchery. Sexing chicks (determining whether they are a hen or a rooster) requires considerable skill and is done at this very early stage to determine their fate.

If strong and healthy, the female chicks are transferred to a site where they are grown to a suitable size and then moved to a laying or meat production facility. They are raised in what could be a cage, free-range or barn set up. Male chicks are considered an unwanted byproduct of egg production and are killed and disposed of shortly after chick sexing at just one day old.

Male chicks are killed for two reasons: they cannot lay eggs and they are not suitable for chicken-meat production. This is because layer hens — and therefore their chicks — are a different breed of poultry to chickens that are bred and raised for meat production. Layer hens are bred to produce eggs whereas meat chickens are bred to grow large breast muscle and legs.

Chick hatcheries breed one or the other type of chick depending on which poultry industry they supply — egg or meat. At the layer hen hatcheries supplying the egg industry with layer hens, the eggs are developed in industrial incubators. Once hatched, the newborn chicks pass down a production line to be sexed and sorted. Sick or weak female chicks and all male chicks are separated from the healthy female chicks and then killed.

The Model Code of Practice for the Welfare of Animals: Domestic Poultry states that all culled or surplus newly hatched chicks that are destined for disposal must be treated as humanely as those that will be retained or sold. The Code states that these chicks must be killed promptly by carbon dioxide gassing or maceration. Chicks must then be carefully inspected to ensure they are all are dead.

Maceration is done in a manner to ensure that chicks are killed within a second and, when carried out effectively and competently, this method may be considered more humane than gassing with high concentrations of carbon dioxide. This is because carbon dioxide at high concentrations is aversive to poultry and the method results in prolonged suffering prior to death.

The RSPCA continues to urge the egg industry to invest in alternatives that remove the need for male chick culling and avoid the potential pain and suffering with current killing methods. Technologies such as hormone level analysis of egg fluid, the use of spectrophotometry or cameras, and fluorescence spectroscopy have all demonstrated sex determination of eggs is possible. Sex determination of eggs during the first few days of incubation allows for sexing prior to the embryo developing a sensory nervous system and potential pain perception. Once egg sexing has occurred, male chick eggs can be removed from incubation and used for other purposes such as processing into animal feed or utilized in laboratories.[1]

Neutering or castrating a rooster is known as "caponizing." This process produces what is called a "capon." (A castrated horse is a gelding, a castrated male cow is a steer, and a castrated rooster is a capon.) Caponizing used to be a very common practice, back when most people raised their own chickens.

The meat from a rooster can be very stringy and pungent, but the meat from a capon is much more tender. Incidentally, this is the same reason that male cows are turned into steers. Caponizing was invented by Romans, in order to get around a law regarding fattening hens. A caponized rooster will get much fatter than an intact rooster. Capons can be twice as plump as normal roosters.

The practice of caponizing let farmers put their male chicks to good use. Although each flock can only have one rooster in order to keep the peace, an unlimited number of capons can be reared together without risk of fighting. Capons were often preferred over hens, because all hens were laying hens, and therefore tended to be quite lean. The meat from a capon was tender and plentiful.

Caponizing needs to be performed before the chicken enters puberty. Instructions on an old Sears Roebuck caponizing tool set recommended caponizing be performed when chicks are between six weeks and three months old. A rooster's testicles are high up in the body, near the back. The procedure of caponizing is a relatively minor surgical procedure. It is traditionally performed without anesthetic.

Large scale commercial producers of capons often choose chemical methods instead. An estrogen implant is inserted under the skin of the male chick. This suppresses the chick's natural testosterone, without the need for a major surgical procedure. It should be noted that the surgical method is considered by many to be inhumane. Whereas the hormonal method is potentially unsafe for human consumption, due to the artificially large amount of estrogen which is present in the meat.

Even if you buy pre-sexed chicks, there is no guarantee they will all be female. The sexing process is only between 95-98% accurate. This means that every year, some people end up with male chicks by accident. Male chicks are cute. Male chickens, once they have matured into roosters, can become a real hassle. Contrary to what the cartoons would have us believe, roosters actually crow all the time. And it is loud! This is why most urban areas' laws about keeping chickens specify "Hens Only."

Roosters are a valuable addition to the flock. Aside from being entertaining and beautiful, a rooster will literally give his life to save his hens. Having a rooster around can help prevent losses due to dogs, cats, snakes, hawks, and a number of other culprits.

There are some circumstances where you would want to neuter a rooster. As with dogs and cats, the rooster's behavior is dictated by his hormones. No testicles, no hormones. No hormones, no obnoxious rooster behavior. A neutered rooster is a much more calm and docile addition to your family. Although he may not be as protective of the flock, he may also be much more tolerable to you![2]

The requirements for all-female or all-male litters is not limited to laboratory models. For example, it would also be extremely advantageous for agriculture, with the layer hen industry representing a prominent example. Approximately 6 to 7 billion male chicks are culled worldwide per year, generating a well-known and highly controversial ethical issue. Conversely, in pest control, reducing or controlling the female mosquito population, the vector for the malaria parasite, found in over 100 countries including large parts of Africa and Asia, would be extremely advantageous, and similarly for the eradication of invasive pest species such as rodents in island countries such as New Zealand. In these examples, a genetic method of producing all-male litters in a controlled laboratory and factory environment for sterilization, prior to release in the wild, would eliminate or reduce the population size. One alternative method of controlling malaria spread would be to repurpose engineered gene drives in order to produce single-sex progeny.

The production of all-female or all-male litters by genetic methods is feasible because in some species, males and females differ in their sex-chromosome complement. Eutherian (includes all placentals and excludes the marsupials and monotremes) female mammals, such as mice and humans, are homogametic, producing only

X-chromosome–carrying gametes. Eutherian male mammals are heterogametic, producing mature sperm that, with rare exceptions, carry either the X or Y chromosome. Early studies on differences of sex determination (DSDs) showed that in eutherian mammals, sex determination is not regulated by the number of X chromosomes. Instead, it is driven by the presence of the Y chromosome via a locus originally coined the Y-linked testis-determining factor, which is expressed in Sertoli cell precursors. It is important to note that Y-linked testis-determining factor mode of sex determination is not the primary method of sex determination for all mammals. For example, the platypus, a prototherian mammal, does not have a Y linked gene.

Conversely, in many bird species, including chickens, females are heterogametic and carry a single Z and a single W chromosome. Males are homogametic and carry 2 Z chromosomes. Avian sex determination is controlled by the dosage of a Z-linked gene. Female birds carry 1 copy, whilst males have 2 copies.[3]

In some farmers' ideal world, cows would birth only females, sows would bear no boars, and chicks would all grow up to be hens. Such sex ratios would stop them from killing millions of male animals, which don't produce eggs or milk.

Now, scientists are a step closer to this reality. Researchers have harnessed the gene editor CRISPR to produce litters of mice all of one sex. That's a potential boon to agriculture and may offer a more immediate advantage in scientific research. The impact for lab animals may be huge. If we could prevent the generation of the unstudied sex, the number (saved) would be in the hundreds of thousands.

That could alleviate some ethical dilemmas. The choice is made before the animal is born and the new technology will eliminate this unpleasant and inefficient reality.[4]

According to the Department of Environment Conservation, mink have a long, thin body and neck, short legs, and a 6-8 inch bushy tail. Male mink generally are larger than females and may exceed two feet in length. The fur is dark brown on the back, blending into a slightly lighter shade on the belly. A distinguishing mink characteristic is the small white patch of fur on the chin of all animals. Mink fur is very soft and lustrous. The dense underfur is protected by oily guard hairs that tend to waterproof the coat. Like other members of the weasel family, such as weasels, ferrets, and skunks, mink possess a pair of anal scent glands. The liquid in these glands has a strong smell and probably is used for communication or defense purposes.

In the late 1980s, central and western New York trappers were surveyed to determine the types of habitats where mink were caught. The results are: 62% stream, 9% marsh, 10% lake, and 12% beaver ponds. Mink generally are solitary animals, with males and females associating only during the late winter breeding season. Female mink are sexually mature at one year of age. Pregnant female mink may establish den sites in cavities of tree roots, rock piles, brush piles and log jams or beaver lodges. Research in North America shows that the most widely used den sites are bank burrows of other animals, particularly muskrats.

Mink are primarily nocturnal with most activity spent feeding. Their list of prey species is varied. Food items include small mammals, fish, birds and amphibians. Mammals such as muskrats, rabbits and small rodents lead the list as the most important food for mink. Waterfowl, small marsh-nesting birds, and crayfish. In Idaho, wild mink have been reported seen in most wild areas containing streams, marshes, lakes or beaver ponds.

More than 85% of pelts used in the world's fur trade come from small, family-run farms. Approximately 275 mink farms in 23 states across the USA produce about 3 million pelts annually, with a value of more than $300 million USD (2013). Wisconsin is the leading mink-producing state, generating well over 1 million pelts. Other important producers are Utah, Idaho, Oregon and Minnesota.

Mink are vaccinated for several diseases including canine distemper, a type of parvovirus and rabies. According to the mink industry, about 95% of the approximately two-million-plus farmed mink in the U.S were vaccinated against SARS-CoV-2 with the Zoetis vaccine in summer through fall 2021. The Zoetis vaccine is still considered experimental, though the company is hoping to get it USDA-licensed for use in mink as the USDA has declined to approve any domestic cat or dog COVID-19 vaccines, deeming them epidemiologically unnecessary.

In 2020 authorities in the Netherlands began to gas tens of thousands of mink, most of them pups born do to COVID-19 (SARS-CoV-2) viral spread to farms that raise the animals for fur, and the Dutch government was concerned that infected mink could become a viral reservoir that could cause new outbreaks in humans.

But there are also other public health concerns. Genetic and epidemiological sleuthing has shown that at least two farm workers had caught the virus from mink – at the time, the only patients anywhere known to have become infected by animals. COV-19 can infect other animals, including cats, dogs, tigers, hamsters, ferrets, and macaques, but there are no known cases of transmission from these species back into the human population.

Also in 2020, animal rights activists released 2,000 mink and vandalized fur farms in Northern Utah and Southern Idaho. According to the director of the Fur Commission USA, most of the mink stayed near their nesting boxes and all the mink released tested negative for coronavirus and 90 percent were recaptured. When the animals are released, they don't want to leave the farm. The mink may go to the roads if they hear traffic because traffic noises sound the same has a tractor that feeds them. So, they may head to the road where they get hit by vehicles.

Also, in 2020, Rep. Rosa DeLauro, D-Conn. Presented a bipartisan proposal to ban the farming of mink fur in the United States in an effort to stem possible mutations of the coronavirus, something researchers have said can be accelerated when the virus spreads among animals.

Ryan Moyle, whose family have the largest mink operation in Idaho (at least prior to the arrival of COVID-19), of Magic Valley was convinced the federal bill that would ban his industry nationwide has more to do with placating animal rights activists than accomplishing its stated goal of avoiding potential COVID-19 mutations. He noted that a COVID-19 vaccine has already been developed for animals including mink and Moyle anticipates he'll have access to the animal vaccine soon which should resolve the issue.

As a precaution against COVID-19, Moyle had already closed three of the family's five mink farms and reduced his mink numbers by 90%. He downsized his operation and moved all their breeding stock to one farm that was operated by family members with no employees on the farm. The decision was made before the vaccine became available.

Moyle, a third-generation mink farmer, said Idaho ranks among the top three mink producing states in the U.S., and the first mink farm in the world opened in Franklin, Idaho. Idaho is also unique in that the Idaho State Department of Agriculture has its own certification program for mink farms.

His family got its start in the industry back in the 1930s, when Moyle's great-grandmother gave her son, Rodney Moyle, money she had in a coffee can — intended to cover her eventual funeral expenses — so he could buy his first five mink for breeding. That endeavor lifted the family out of poverty, Moyle explained.

Currently (2022) mink farms feed a paste of fish, chicken (including the neck and head), cow, pig, and other leftover meats from the animal agriculture industry. It is placed on top of their wire-topped cages daily for them to feed on.

In the 1950's mink breeders reported to the Federal Department of Agriculture, Bureau of Animal Husbandry, that their entire farms were stricken with an unaccountable disease. They lost their hair, they were fat and puffy, you could put your finger in the skin and dimple it and the skin would not come back. The affected mink did not reproduce. Cysts developed in breasts, ovaries and kidneys. The mink had become sterile.

At the time, stilbestrol was used in cockerels to make capons out of roosters. As explained by a spokesman of the local Board of Health, the principle is to prevent testicles from developing.

A spokesman for the poultry division of the University of Hawaii, College of Agriculture, said that no cancer has been found in chicken, turkey or cattle using stilbesterol. As for mink, he said, one is dealing with an entirely different species. The amount of stilbestrol inducing cancer in mice during an experiment was minute. He said when the amount is transposed to larger animals, it is negligible.

He said that stilbestrol has been used for 10 years by the poultry industry. If there is any ill effect, the harm would have been more evident on fowls, or human beings who have eaten chicken with stilbestrol.

After 10 years, if there were adverse effects, he said there should be a lot of men going around with feminine characteristics—high-pitched voice, loss of hair, etc.

Two local poultry supply dealers who sold stilbestrol pellets, that were placed under the skin in the necks of roosters, said that the Federal Pure Food and Drug Administration looked into this matter and approved the use or stilbestrol. One of them explained that fowls with stilbestrol were not too be marketed before six to eight weeks have passed from the time the pellets were placed in chickens. It takes four to eight weeks for the stilbestrol to be absorbed.

An entirely different picture is given, in an article which appeared in the New York Mirror and was inserted in the Congressional Record by Rep. Usher L. Burdick (N.L.). The article written by Joan Dickinson and entitled "You

Are Science's New Guinea Pig," says in part: Dr. William E. Smith of the Cancer Prevention Committee, and one of the country's foremost cancer research authorities, warned the present Congress of another great hazard—the widespread practice of using stilbestrol pellets to fatten and tenderize poultry and livestock Stilbestrol is a hormone, known to be cancer-inciting, and so potent and dangerous that under the drug law it cannot be purchased without a physician's prescription. Its use is banned in, Canada. Dr. Smith notified Representative (James J.) Delaney that it is urgent that any bill to amend the food laws should include chemicals given to animals destined for use as foods.[5]

Who would have believed that a Dunlap Hatchery free rooster chicks sign and the chance siting of a wild (or farmed one released by a rights activist group) mink in the Nampa/Caldwell area of Idaho, years ago had ancestors that crossed interesting paths involving DES being used to make capons out of roosters? The event resulted in the demise of the male chicken industry and threatened the mink farming business? Things I do know:

1– The reason that Dr. Hylton used the DES (Diethylstilbesterol) pellets (he placed into the necks of roosters to help stop them from crowing) sparingly was because they were not readily available. Caponizing of roosters with DES was found to be unsafe and DES eventually became unavailable because of the potentially dangerous side effects to both man and animals. Hormone induced Capons used for consumption was stopped and the rooster became of little economic value - except one per flock as protector and a sperm donor.

2– In an ideal world, cows would birth only females, sows would bear no boars, and chicks would all grow up to be hens. Such sex ratios would stop producers from killing millions of male animals, which don't produce eggs or milk. Is there going to be a future need for us guys? Will we go the way of the rooster?

3– The mink industry was saved from destruction in the 1950's leaving little use for the rooster and virtually stopping the use of DES. However, consumer displeasure has been building over the use of farm mink for fur. Especially from the large companion animal market living in 70 percent (90.5 million) of US households with a pet - which includes 63 million dogs and 45 million cats.

4– With the COVID-19 pandemic there have been millions of mink killed as a result of the disease.

Betting that mink farming will not be banned near-term in Europe or the U.S. the pharmaceutical industry of Zoetis and Ceva are developing vaccines to help keep a potentially failing mink industry afloat from a virus that threatens human and wildlife health, for negligible and shrinking revenues.

The mink biologics business is a high-risk, low-reward gamble. With mink fur rejected on ethical grounds as a luxury fashion item by most of modern society, with mink pelts selling at below the cost of production for most of the past decade, and with so many documented public health and animal welfare concerns, mink industry sutlers (a person who followed an army and sold provisions to the soldiers) may be clearly on the wrong side of history.[6]

Leaving God out of the equation, "There is nothing permanent except change." -Heraclitus

1– *Advances and challenges in genetic technologies to produce single-sex litters, Charlotte Douglas & James M. A. Turner, RSPCA.*

2– *8 Ways to Stop a Rooster From Crowing Excessively, by Nicole Cosgrove, Last updated: Jan 13 2022.*

3– *Advances and challenges in genetic technologies to produce single-sex litters, Charlotte Douglas, James M. A. Turner, University of Michigan Medical School, UNITED STATES. Published: July 23, 2020.*

4– *Gene editing produces all-male or all-female litters of mice, CRISPR approach shows promise for curbing culling of lab animals, chicks, version appeared in Science Vol 374-Issue 6573, Elizabeth Pennisi, 2021.*

5– *Center for Labor Education & Research, University of Hawaii - West Oahu: Honolulu Record, Volume 10 No. 4, Thursday, August 22, 1957 p. 1.*

6– *Rethinking Mink: The Sutlers Who Enable Mink Farming Must Be Shamed (Part I), The Moral Race to the Bottom by Zoetis Animal Health and Ceva Santé Animale, Jim Keen, DVM, PhD, 2021-22.*

CHAPTER 9

BRAIN CONTROL

Considered by some cultures to be an art, the sport of bullfighting torments, attacks and eventually kills bulls. The practice is portrayed by many to be a fair fight between man and animal, and a spectacle of skill and physical strength. In reality though, the bull is subjected to immense physical pain and psychological stress, and the event almost always ends in their death.

Bullfighting is a sport responsible for taking the lives of 250,000 bulls every year. There are different forms of bullfighting. The most prevalent form today is Spanish-style bullfighting — "corrida de toros." During one of these events six fights take place. Each of these fights ends in the death of a bull.

Before the event even begins, each bull grows substantially weaker as he is subjected to physical and psychological abuse. Common practices include beating the bull, giving the animal tranquilizers and laxatives, and rubbing petroleum on his eyes to blur his vision, and having heavy weights hung around his neck. The aim of these practices is to deplete the bulls' physical strength so that the bullfighters are able to finish them off in the arena.

Across the three main acts of the fight itself, the bull is tormented and repeatedly stabbed in the neck. The final act ends with the matador stabbing the bull between the shoulder blades with the aim of severing the bull's spinal cord. The paralyzed but potentially still conscious bull has his ears and tail cut off, and victory is declared.

The principal bullfighter, known as the matador, is the one responsible for killing the bull. Before he does this, his "cuadrilla," more or less his team of assistants, attacks and torments the bull. There are two main roles within the cuadrilla, known as picadores and banderilleros. Each has their own part to play in weakening the bull before the final performance of the matador.

The mounted picadores enter the ring at the beginning of the first act, each armed with a lance. The bull is tormented to encourage him to charge at one rider's horse, giving one of the picadores the chance to spear the bull in his neck or shoulder. Next to enter the arena are the banderilleros. These men are on foot and are responsible for preparing the bull for the matador's kill. This involves piercing the bull's neck with four wooden darts, forcing him to lower his neck to make the matador's target more accessible.

Finally, the matador enters, the bullfighter responsible for slaying the bull. As the most senior in the bullfighting team, the role of the matador is respected and considered to be highly skilled. While performing a series of dance-like movements with a brightly colored cape, the matador aims to torment the bull, enticing him to charge so that the kill can be made.

The precise origins of bullfighting are difficult to trace but the practice is known to have roots that go as far back as 2000 B.C. Bullfighting as we know it today began in the 18th century. As the sport became increasingly ingrained in Spanish culture, the role of the matador became regarded as an honorable profession.

Bullfighting was such an integral part of Spanish culture that attending a bullfight was at one time seen as an expected part of visiting the country. In recent years, however, as the barbarism of the events has been more widely recognized, bullfighting has become less popular with the public. Between 2007 and 2019, before the impact of COVID-19, the number of bullfights held in Spain decreased by over 2,000 — more than 50 percent.

Bullfighting is far from the fair fight that it is portrayed by supporters to be. Bulls are physically and mentally tormented before entering what is a stressful environment, then tormented again, stabbed multiple times and eventually killed.

As dangerous as they can be, bulls are naturally prey animals. When they attack the bullfighter, they're not doing so as a predator but instead as a prey animal who perceives themselves to be in danger. A bull charging at a matador's cape has been stressed and tormented to the point that they have no choice but to attempt to remove the stressful object from their environment. The bull is exhibiting an instinctive response to a highly stressful situation, not a desire to fight.

In each stage of the event the bull experiences intense fear and physical pain. They are also subjected to exhaustion, dehydration and eventually a slow and painful death.

The aim of the matador is always to kill the bull, and a fight is only considered successful if it ends in the bull's death. During the final act of the event, the matador is given a time of 10 minutes during which to stab the bull between the shoulder blades, severing his spinal cord. The move has to be performed in a specific way, meaning that the matador often misses and stabs the bull without killing him. If the matador is unsuccessful within the first 10 minutes, he may be given an additional five minutes. In the event that he is still unsuccessful, other members of the team enter the arena and kill the bull, who is often then butchered and sold as meat.

In the rare event that the bull kills or severely injures the matador, the bull is killed by another member of the cuadrilla. Although a dangerous practice for the people involved, the risks to their personal safety are somewhat limited by the bull's weakened state. In 2016, Victor Barrio became the first matador to be killed by a bull in over 30 years. The bullfighter died of a punctured lung and severed aorta after the bull's horn penetrated his chest. Prior to this, the last fighter to be killed in the ring was Jose Cubero in 1985.

The sport has been outlawed in many countries across the world but is still legal in some including Spain, France, Ecuador, Mexico, and Portugal. Animal advocates want to see the sport abolished, but resistance comes from those who are more concerned about the cultural and economic impact of banning the practice than the suffering it causes.

Regions of Spain have attempted to impose local bans on bullfighting, but in 2016 were barred from doing so by the Spanish Constitutional Court. Bullfighting is considered by some to be such an integral part of Spanish heritage that there is substantial resistance to its demise. Despite this, the number of people attending bullfights in Spain is falling, especially among younger generations.

Since the early 1500s, bullfighting has been a popular sport in Mexico, with children as young as six years old allowed to train towards participation. Although bullfighting is still legal in Mexico as a whole, regions of the country have placed bans on the practice. Mexico City extended what had been a temporary ban on the sport, dealing a significant blow to the country's bullfighting industry.

Many countries have banned the practice including Canada, Cuba, Italy, Denmark and the United Kingdom. Bullfighting laws vary across the U.S., with all forms of the sport banned in some states but exceptions still existing in others. In Florida, for example, all styles of bullfighting have been outlawed. In states such as Texas, however, "bloodless" bullfighting events can still be legally held.

Traditional in Portugal, bloodless bullfights involve the bull being mentally tormented in the ring, but not physically injured or killed. A bloodless bullfight ends when the cavaleiro is successful in grabbing the bull by the horns, as opposed to killing him. The emotional torment, however, remains and the bulls are sent to slaughter after their ordeal. Blood may not be shed in public, but the practice in most cases still ends in the animal's death.[1]

For detailed descriptions of changes going on physiologically and mentally inside a bull during a bull fight, I recommend reading: *Quality of Death in Fighting Bulls during Bullfights: Neurobiology and Physiological Responses, Animals (Basel) MDPI, NIH- Nation Library of Medicine, 10/11/2021.*

My family went to a bull fight in Mazatlan, Mexico in 2000. My oldest child (25 years of age) remembered a young fighter getting gored, and they were stabbing and poking the bull to make it mad. It was bleeding pretty good. My second oldest child remembered the fighter being gored in the rear end, thrown high in the air and taken from the ring. He thought the man was dead. However, he returned later in the fight to kill the bull. My third oldest child remembered that the bull died, and she was not expecting that. She had no idea that the whole point was to tire the bull out and then kill him with a sword. My fourth oldest child remembered the fighter had his pants split up the back. No response from my youngest child. I remember most a spectator yelling about how the bull was suffering, the fighter was unskilled and him running into the ring trying to distract the bull from the injured bull fighter.

One day in the summer of 1963, Spanish neurologist José Delgado stepped into a bullring outside Córdoba and prepared to perform an audacious experiment. Armed only with an experimental radio transmitter, he prepared to face off with an angry Spanish fighting bull, bred specifically for strength and aggression. Delgado waved a flag to set the bull charging, but before the ton of galloping muscle and sharp horns could reach him, he pressed a button on his remote control. Immediately the bull stopped in its tracks, shook its head in confusion, then calmly trotted away. Eyewitnesses to the event were stunned, for Delgado had apparently defeated the bull's innate aggression using only a set of tiny electrodes implanted in its brain. It was the most dramatic – and disturbing – demonstration in a pioneering but controversial career that would earn Delgado the title "the father of mind control."

This charging bull experiment that put Delgado's name on the map originated in a conversation with a Córdoba bull breeder, who argued that while Delgado's electrodes might work in cats, monkeys, or even humans, they could not stop a fighting bull, which was specifically bred for aggression. Delgado accepted the challenge and with the breeder's permission he and his team anesthetized a bull and fitted it with stimoreceiver equipment he had invented. The next day the bull was back to normal and ready for the experiment. As Delgado climbed into the ring, the breeder asked him if he had taken bull-fighting lessons in preparation. Delgado, who had grown up in the heart of bullfighting country, responded with mock outrage that of course he knew how to fight a bull!

José Manuel Rodriguez Delgado was born August 8, 1915 in the town of Ronda, Spain and received his doctorate of medicine just as the Spanish Civil War broke out in 1936. During the war he served as a stretcher-bearer and medic for the Republican forces, being captured and held in a Nationalist concentration camp for 5 months. He later was forced to redo his doctorate, receiving a Ph.D. in physiology in 1940. Initially Delgado wanted to be an ophthalmologist like his father, but became fascinated by the many mysteries of the brain, after reading the works of Nobel Prize-winning Spanish neurologist Ramon y Cajal.

In 1948 Delgado won a fellowship at Yale University working under an American neurologist John Fulton, whose experiments with severing the frontal brain lobes of chimpanzees had led to the development of the lobotomy for the treatment of mental illness. Delgado was horrified by such extreme methods, and instead gravitated towards the work of Walter Hess and Wilder Penfield, who had shown that by applying a mild electrical current to different regions of the brain they could elicit all sorts of responses, from involuntary limb movements to tastes, smells, and sounds, to emotions such as fear, aggression, and euphoria.

The equipment used in these early experiments, which involved wires snaking out of subjects' scalps into bulky external monitors, was cumbersome, restrictive, and increased the chances of infection. Delgado, a technical as well as a medical genius, thus invented what he called a "stimoreceiver," a miniaturized radio transmitter the size of a quarter which could be completely implanted beneath the scalp, power being supplied through an electromagnetic coil transmitting through the skin. Delgado also invented a "chemitrode" which delivered controlled amounts of drugs into the brain via radio command.

Delgado's main interest lay in using implanted electrodes to help regulate strong emotions, especially aggression. He next turned his attention to the treatment of epilepsy and schizophrenia, setting up shop in a psychiatric hospital in Rhode Island. Here the results of deep-brain stimulation were varied and often alarming,

A paper expressing his views about his work was presented at the 1972 Congressional hearings on, CIA secrete mind control studies, stated: *"We need a program of psychosurgery for political control of our society. The purpose is physical control of the mind. Everyone who deviates from the given norm can be surgically manipulated. The individual may think that the most important reality is his own existence, but this is only his personal point of view. This lacks historical perspective Man does not have the right to develop his own mind. This kind of liberal orientation has great appeal. We must electrically control the brain. Someday armies and generals will be controlled by electric stimulation of the brain."*

Despite the storms of controversy surrounding his views about his work, the neurostimulation technology Delgado pioneered never yielded the results he had hoped – and his critics feared. The brain, it turns out, is far more complicated than Delgado and his contemporaries assumed, and scientists as yet still haven't fully cracked its complicated neural code.

At this time in history, the drug Chlorpromazine was being given to schizophrenic patients for the first time with success that would spawn the neuropsychopharmacology revolution. Delgado positioned himself between the burgeoning disapproval of mutilating surgical lobotomies and the belief that direct electrical or chemical stimulation of specific brain areas was scientifically and clinically superior to oral administration of drugs whose effects on the brain were inevitably mitigated by metabolism in the liver, obstruction by the blood-brain barrier and uncertain distribution throughout the brain. Delgado was not entirely alone in these beliefs.

Researchers have had some success in using deep-brain stimulation to treat conditions such as Parkinson's, epilepsy, and paralysis, and chronic pain, and promising studies are underway to use it in the treatment of depression, anxiety, other mood disorders and the development of the heart pacemaker came about partly from Delgado's "stimoreceiver" research.[2]

Brain–machine interfaces (BMIs) enable direct electrical communication between the brain and external systems. They allow brain activity to control devices such as prostheses and computer programs, or to modulate nerve or muscle function to compensate for dysfunctional endogenous pathways.

Collectively, BMIs have the potential to help individuals with paralysis or neurological disorders to regain function. However, recording from deep-brain regions currently requires surgery to implant probes, so less invasive methods for interfacing bioelectronic devices with neurons are required.

Conventional BMIs use detection methods such as electroencephalography and electrocorticography, which measure local field potentials from ensembles of neurons at the surface of the scalp or on the dura mater (a meningeal layer that covers the brain), as well as intracortical probes that can measure single-neuron activity from deeper regions. However, intracortical probes require craniotomy and cause mechanical disruptions to the brain tissue. These probes also induce inflammation and fibrosis, which degrade device performance within weeks. These deleterious effects can be attributed to the large mismatch in mechanical stiffness between the implant and brain tissue. Any surgery that penetrates the blood–brain barrier poses a risk for infection, so less invasive methods to deliver devices into deep-brain regions are crucial.

The newly developed vascular system BMIs have the potential delivery route because it mirrors the structure of the neuronal networks that it supports and most neurons are within 10 to 20 μm of a capillary. The vascular network can be accessed through an incision in locations such as the jugular vein or carotid artery, which are used by neurosurgeons to implant self-expanding stents in the brain to treat conditions such as cerebral atherosclerosis. These endovascular probes might form the foundation for machine interfaces throughout the body.[3]

Brent McClusky wrote: I thought I was accustomed to seeing violence, having spent my life immersed in hyper-realistic war movies and blowing the heads off of enemies in killing-based video games. But while in Spain, I entered the stadium of my first bullfight with a great deal of naivety. I didn't understand the tradition; I had never been exposed to the specific form of violence portrayed in bullfights. Though I had been inoculated to a great deal of violence throughout my life, this new stimulus had a profound effect on my conscience.

But within an hour, my psyche had been transformed. By the end of a experiencing a bull fight, my shackles of empathy had been loosed. My concern for the bulls was completely gone. I rejoiced when the matadors triumphed. I even joined the crowd in thunderous applause and shared nods of approval with complete strangers.

I had just voluntarily subjected myself to systematic desensitization—a form of behavioral therapy that, when used in a clinical setting and administered by a licensed professional, can help clients rid themselves of debilitating phobias. This method, developed by Joseph Wolpe in the 1950's, works by having clients set up a hierarchy of fears, ordered from least to greatest, and then systematically working through them until the fear response is gone.

This study also noted that exposure to scenes of violence over periods of time systematically desensitizes us by not only decreasing our ability to empathize, but also by fostering an attitude that lends itself to recreating these scenes in real life. Dr. Linda Castillo, professor of psychology at Texan A&M University, said, "It is clear from decades of research that repeated exposure to scenes of violence, whether it is via media or video games, does have some impact on a person's physiological reactions to new scenes of violence. Systematic desensitization to violence affects empathy we feel for others. And, it is empathy that moves us to help others. Systematic desensitization is a means for coping with a conflict of your paradigm. There's always a turning point in someone's mind when it comes to violence."

It was, in fact, empathy, the ability to understand and connect with another being's feelings and situation, that acted as the catalyst to my systematic desensitization during the bullfight. My empathy for the bull led to feelings of revulsion over how I perceived it was being treated. And like all subjugates of this method, I had to make a choice. The process only works if the participants willingly submit themselves to it. While I could have objected to the bullfight, walked away or even closed my eyes, I instead chose to watch with morbid fascination. I knew I didn't like what was happening, but the more I saw, the less I cared.[4]

Severing brain frontal lobes, placing electrodes deep into brain tissue, controlling an aggressive fighting bull with the push of a button, medications that can be taken orally or injected to help control neurological pathologies and the recently discovered use of very small vascular probes to establish brain-machine interfaces (BMIs) that mirrors the structure of the neuronal networks. It appears that Jose Delgado's vision of controlling various portions of the brain with electric probes needed to wait until technology could catch up. However, Brent McClusky's experience leads me to believe bull fights do have a type of "mind control" at least on certain parts of the brain.

If the statistics on attendance at bull fights continue the present trend, there may be a day when such fights will be far and in between even in Spain. Likewise, the day may come when Jose Delgado's title of "the father of mind control" may be forgotten. His new name may become known as "the father of Brain-Machine Interfaces (BMIs)."

I found interest in the extensive biography, *Jose Delgado: A Case Study Science, Hubris, Nemesis and Redemption, By Barry Blackwell, Neuropsychopharmacology, 2014,* that included direct quotes from Delgado's and history of attempts to understand and medicate the brain. It gave me more insight into Delgado's work and not only who he is often perceived in the eyes of those "in the know."

As for my family's visit to a bull ring in Mazatlan, Mexico in 2000: I wish Jose Delgado had of been there dressed in a policeman's uniform, holding his hand in front of him like a traffic control officer and yelling "DETENER"(stop). I'm quite sure if I asked their impressions of the event – all of

WALTER R. HOGE, DVM

us would have remembered Dr. Delgado demonstration of his "stimoreceiver."

1– *Is Bullfighting Cruel to the Bull?, Explainer, Rachel Graham, 09/30/2022.*

2– *That Time a Scientist Stopped a Charging Bullfighting Bull using Mind Control for Science!' Today I Found Out (Feed Your Brain), Gilles Messier, 06/24/20022.*

3– *Neural implants without brain surgery, Science, 20 Jul 2023 pp. 268-269.*

4– *How Does One Enjoy a Bullfight?, Brent.*

CHAPTER 10

WEEDS

Striga, commonly known as witchweed, is a genus of parasitic plants that occur naturally in parts of Africa, Asia, and Australia. It is currently classified in the family Orobanchaceae, although older classifications place it in the Scrophulariaceae. Some species are serious pathogens of cereal crops, with the greatest effects being in savanna agriculture in Africa. It also causes considerable crop losses in other regions, including other tropical and subtropical crops in its native range and in the Americas.

Witchweeds are characterized by bright-green stems and leaves and small, brightly colored and attractive flowers. They are obligate hemiparasites of roots and require a living host for germination and initial development, though they can then survive on their own. The number of species is uncertain, but may exceed 40 by some counts.

Although most species of Striga are not pathogens that affect human agriculture, some species have devastating effects upon crops, particularly those planted by subsistence farmers. Crops most commonly affected are maize (corn), sorghum, rice and sugarcane.

Witchweed parasitizes maize, millet, sorghum, sugarcane, rice, legumes, and a range of weedy grasses. It is capable of significantly reducing yields, in some cases wiping out the entire crop. Host plant symptoms, such as stunting, wilting, and chlorosis, are similar to those seen from severe drought damage, nutrient deficiency, and vascular disease.

Each plant is capable of producing between 90,000 and 500,000 seeds, which may remain viable in the soil for over 10 years. Most seeds produced are not viable. An annual plant, witchweed overwinters in the seed stage. Its seeds germinate in the presence of host root exudate, and develop haustoria (highly modified stem or root of a parasitic plant or a specialized branch or tube originating from a hairlike filament "hypha" or a fungus). The haustorium penetrates the root cells of a host and absorbs nutrients and water. Host root exudate contain strigolactones, signaling molecules that promote Striga seed germination. A bell-like swelling forms where the parasitic roots attach to the roots of the host. The pathogen develops underground, where it may spend the next four to seven weeks before emergence, when it rapidly flowers and produces seeds. Witchweed seeds spread readily via wind and water, and in soil via animal vectors. The chief means of dispersal, however, is through human activity, by means of machinery, tools, and clothing.

Once germination is stimulated, the Striga seed sends out an initial root to probe the soil for the host root. The initial root secretes an oxidizing enzyme that digests the host root surface, releasing quinones. If the quinone product is at the appropriate concentrations, a haustorium will develop from the initial root. The haustorium grows toward the host root until it makes contact with the root surface, establishing parasitic contact in relatively short order. Within 12 hours of initial haustorium growth, the haustorium recognizes the host root and begins rapid cell division and elongation. The haustorium forms a wedge shape and uses mechanical force and chemical digestion to penetrate the host root, pushing the host cells out of the way. Within 48–72 hours, the haustorium has penetrated the host root cortex. Finger-like structures on the haustorium, called oscula (from Latin osculum, "little mouth") penetrate the host xylem through pits in the membrane. The oscula then swell to secure their position within the xylem membrane. Striga sieve tubes develop along with the oscula. Shortly after the host xylem is penetrated, Striga sieve tubes develop and approach the host phloem within eight cells. This eight-cell layer allows for nonspecific nutrient transport from the host to the Striga seedling. Within 24 hours after tapping the host xylem and phloem, the Striga cotyledons emerge from the seed.

Soil temperature, air temperature, photoperiod, soil type, and soil nutrient and moisture levels do not greatly deter the development of witchweed. These findings, while limited to the Carolinas in the United States, seem to suggest that the pathogen could successfully infect the massive corn crops of the American Midwest. *Wikipedia*

Weeds are plants that have never learned to grow in rows. They are very independent plants they are the entrepreneurs of the plant world. It doesn't matter to them whether they are liked or not, they grow where they please, and when they please. These might seem like desirable traits, but we don't appreciate them in weeds, because they are just weeds.

Some weeds have beautiful blooms. Actually, some weeds have been upgraded to the status of "wild flowers." Their blooms are in all of the colors that flowers use for their blooms. Also, the foliage of some weeds are very attractive. Yes, some weeds are more beautiful than their more domesticated cousins, but they are still just weeds.

While not as productive as more domesticated plants, weeds do provide some products that humans use. Even the lowly dandelion has been made into wine. Other weeds end up in salads, and even in some medications. Weeds can provide beneficial products for their natural enemy, humans, but they are still just weeds.

So, if they are strong, persistent, innovative, attractive and productive, why are they so universally disliked? The answer is quite simple, they won't conform. Now this is where the plight of the weed gets complicated. Humans have always admired, celebrated, and have even built monuments to the non-conformists in their mist. So, if humans love a non-conformist, why don't they love weeds?

The answer is quite simple there is a time to be a non-conformist, and a time to conform. Actually, it is the refusal to conform, along with the inability to learn to grow in rows, that makes a weed, a weed. A rose in a house yard can be a plant in which its owner takes great pride, but a rose in a wheat field is a weed. A stalk of corn in a field of corn can be a part of something very productive, but a stalk of corn, no matter how big it is, is just a weed in the front lawn of a suburban home.

What this all means, is that the difference between beautiful and useful plants and weeds, is just a matter of time and place. The difference between being fed, cultivated, trained and encouraged, or being destroyed by whatever means possible is determined by when and where.

The same is true of people. Most of life's best accomplishments come as a result of group effort. Feeding the world is possible because of large fields of plants that have learned to grow in rows or groups. It is true that all inventions start as an idea in the mind of one person, usually a non-conformist. However, it takes the cooperative effort of many people to produce the invention in large enough quantities to make it economically feasible.

So, if you are willing to live the dangerous, but adventurous life of the non-conformist, go for it. However, you might find it more rewarding, at least in the work part of your life, to cooperate with your employer and fellow employees. Non-conformists in the work place, like weeds in a wheat field, tend to have a short work life.[1]

Management of witchweed is difficult because the majority of its life cycle takes place below ground. If it is not detected before emergence, it is too late to reduce crop losses. To prevent witchweed from spreading it is necessary to plant uncontaminated seeds and to clean soil and plant debris off of machinery, shoes, clothing, and tools before entering fields. If populations are low, hand weeding before seeds are produced is an option.

Striga in the United States has been controlled through the use of several management strategies, including quarantines imposed on affected areas, control of movement of farm equipment between infected and uninfected areas, herbicide application, and imposed "suicidal germination". For the latter, in fields not yet planted in crops, seeds present in the soil are induced to germinate by injecting Ethylene gas, which mimics the natural physiological response tied to host recognition. Because no host roots are available, the seedlings die. Unfortunately, each mature Striga plant can produce tens of thousands of tiny seeds, which may remain dormant in the soil for many years. Thus, such treatments do not remove all seeds from the soil. Moreover, this method is expensive and not generally available to farmers in developing nations of Africa and Asia. *Wikipedia*

Hand weeding seems to be a straightforward approach to interrupt the growth cycle of Striga (witch weed) and is easy to practice and understand. Nevertheless, it is not very effective, and farmers are reluctant to employ it, since Striga plants become large enough to be uprooted only after the first weeding for the crop, and it is extremely time-consuming at high densities. Nevertheless, hand weeding remains an integral part of an integrated Striga spp. control approach to minimize mature plants and diminish the seedbank.

Intercropping of cereals with legumes such as cowpea, peanut, mungbean, soybean and others have been shown to reduce the number of Striga spp. plants that mature in an infested field. Intercrops can act as trap crops, stimulating suicidal Striga spp. germination or altering the microclimate of the crop's canopy and soil surface to interfere with Striga spp. germination and development. This push–pull technology has been used to effectively manage Striga in sorghum and maize-based cropping systems where maize is intercropped with a stem borer–repellent plant, *Desmodium* spp., and an attractant host plant, is planted as a trap plant around the field. Though it is novel, adoption of the push–pull system is constrained, because *Desmodium* spp. is a fodder (cattle feed) crop that cannot be directly used as food.

"Push/Pull agricultural methods to control stemborer moths are also used to help control witchweed:

"Push": The "push" in the intercropping scheme is provided by the plants that emit volatile chemicals (kairomones) which repel stemborer moths and drive them away from the main crop (maize or sorghum). These semiochemicals are also produced in grasses such as maize when they are damaged by insect herbivores, which may explain why they are repellent to stemborers.

Being a low-growing plant, *Desmodium* (silver leaf) does not interfere with the growth of crops, but can suppress weeds and help improve soil quality by increasing soil organic matter content, fixing nitrogen, and stabilizing soils from erosion. It also serves as a highly nutritious animal feed and effectively suppresses striga weeds through an allelopathic mechanism.

"Pull": The approach relies on a combination of companion crops to be planted around and among maize or sorghum. Both domestic and wild grasses can help to protect the crops by attracting and trapping the stemborers. The grasses are planted in the border around the maize and sorghum fields where invading adult moths become attracted to chemicals emitted by the grasses themselves. Instead of landing on the maize or sorghum plants, the insects head for what appears to be a tastier meal. These grasses provide the "pull" in the "push–pull" strategy. They also serve as a haven for the borers' natural enemies.[2]

Senior at Purdue University, Cameron Matthews, has been involved in agriculture his whole life. he grew up on a hobby farm in east-central Indians, and as a teenager began raising show cattle and pigs and growing mums to sell. He planned to major in biochemistry at Purdue, with the intention of specializing in plant breeding in graduate school. But there was just one problem. "I'm too social for biochemistry," he says, laughing. Wanting hands-on work, he reached out to several professors in the College of Agriculture about research opportunities. Gebisa Ejeta, Distinguished Professor of Agronomy and executive director of the Purdue Center for Global Food Security, responded. Would Matthews be interested in studying striga (witchweed), a parasitic plant that affects sorghum crops?

Cameron Matthews likes to compare striga to a leech. It attaches itself to plants like sorghum and siphons off their nutrients. Ejecta had identified a gene that makes sorghum produce less strigolactone, a chemical compound that causes striga to germinate near another plant's roots. Less strigolactone means less striga, which means stronger sorghum. Matthews is now working to help characterize a second phase of striga resistance that keep striga from growing into a full plant.

"A lot of sorghum is grown in Africa because sorghum provides grain for feed (farmers) families and also grass or biomaterial to feed livestock," says Matthews, who conducted full-time research during the summer as part of a Summer College of Agriculture Research Fellowship project.[3]

What this all means, is that the difference between beautiful and useful plants and weeds, is just a matter of time and place. The difference between being fed, cultivated, trained and encouraged, or being destroyed by whatever means possible is determined by when and where.

The same is true of people. Most of life's best accomplishments come as a result of group effort. Feeding the world is possible because of large fields of plants that have learned to grow in rows or groups. It is true that all inventions start as an idea in the mind of one person, usually a non-conformist. However, it takes the cooperative effort of many people to produce the invention in large enough quantities to make it economically feasible.[1]

…Declare unto us the parable of the tares of the field. He that soweth the good seed is the Son of man; The field is the world; the good seed are the children of the kingdom; but the tares are the children of the wicked one; The enemy that sowed them is the devil; the harvest is the end of the world; and the reapers are the angels. *Matthew 13:36-43*

1– *Weeds, The Dooley Letter, Donald R. Dooley, Volume 9-#5, May 1994.*

2– *Weed Sci. 2018; 66(4): 516–524.*

3– *Undergraduate Research, A Study of Outcomes, by Emily Natchar, Purdue University Envision, 2023.*

CHAPTER 11

BAVARIAN BOARS

Pigs are one of the smartest animals in the animal kingdom. Most ratings of the smartest 15 animals in the world list pigs at number 6 or 7 and dogs at 9 or 10. I've worked mostly with dogs, cats, and rabbits during my professional career as a veterinarian. With the experiences I've had with them and my numerous pets, I can believe these ratings. Dogs are smart, cats set the rules and rabbits don't say much; but, none of them were consciencely clean or tried to carry on an almost intelligent grunting conversation like the pigs I've owned. And, that's not all – pigs are a very important part of our human existence and not just for eating. In many respects pigs are in some real important ways one of "man's best friends.

Clinically gene-edited pigs are leading the way to be used for human organ transplants in the near future. In 2022 the University of Maryland transplanted a genetically modified pig heart into a man that lived for two months before the heart failed. But pigs offer more than just a potential source for organ donation. Since the late twentieth century, scientists have been using pigs in a number of medical fields.

Recently, research developed the ability to re-grow human leg muscles using implants made of pig bladder tissue. Michael Swindle, retired veterinary researcher and author of "Swine in the Laboratory" stated, "It just so happens that, despite our differences, many of the pig's biological systems are very similar to our own. They are what's known as a translational research model, so if (something) works in the pig, then it has a high possibility of working in the human." Because of these similarities, scientists have long used pigs to test interventional catheter devices and methods of cardiovascular surgery, as well as to understand how people develop atherosclerosis and get heart attacks. Tissues derived from pig hearts have been used to replace defective heart valves in humans, lasting upwards of 15 years in the human body. Pigs are omnivores like humans and are used to study digestion, metabolic processes and oral absorption studies of drugs. Human insulin is very similar to pig's and diabetics who needed daily insulin injections relied on pork insulin until the 1980's. The pig's skin can be used for plastic surgery and wound repair, and their kidneys are similar to ours and used for research.

Feral swine (also called wild pigs, Eurasian boar, or feral hogs) are a harmful and destructive invasive species. They are not native to North America. Early explorers and settlers first brought feral swine into the United States in the 1500s as a source of food. The number of feral swine grew further after that; they were introduced repeatedly in different areas of the country and also started crossbreeding with escaped domestic pigs.

Feral swine can carry at least 30 diseases and nearly 40 types of parasites that may affect people, pets, livestock, and wildlife. Some diseases, such as pseudorabies, are fatal to cats and dogs that may be exposed from direct contact with a feral swine carcass. Feral swine can also transmit foodborne illnesses, such as E. coli, toxoplasmosis, and trichinosis. In some areas, feral swine have been the cause of elevated waterborne bacteria levels in streams and irrigation canals, which is another risk for human health.

When in roadways or at airports, feral swine can collide with vehicles and aircraft, putting the safety of drivers, pilots, and passengers at risk. Other public safety risks arise when feral swine are in urban and suburban areas. As they become less afraid of people over time, they have shown aggression toward golfers, picnickers, and others.

Feral swine damage crops and destroy fields (reducing crop yield) with their feeding, rooting, trampling, and wallowing behaviors. They usually target sugar cane, corn, grain sorghum, wheat, oats, peanuts, and rice, among others. Vegetable and fruit crops, such as lettuce, spinach, melons, and pumpkins, are also attractive to them. Feral swine can also impact the regeneration of forests. By consuming seeds, nuts, and seedlings and damaging land, they keep new trees from growing and can stunt the growth of existing trees. Feral swine can spread diseases to livestock.

Feral swine are omnivorous, meaning they eat just about anything. They can kill calves and lambs, and adult livestock are vulnerable to predation while giving birth. In addition, feral swine degrade pasture grasses; eat, contaminate, and destroy livestock feed; and damage farm property, such as fences, water systems, irrigation ditches, troughs, and levees.

Feral swine will destroy nests and eat the eggs of alligators, other reptiles, and ground-nesting birds, such as quail, turkey, and shorebirds. And because feral swine prefer wet environments, they compete with native wildlife for scarce water resources during dry seasons. Feral swine can also have negative effects on threatened and endangered species and their habitats. Lastly, feral swine can spread diseases to wildlife, some of which can be fatal. The damage they cause also tends to increase mosquito habitat; this, in turn, can increase the prevalence of avian malaria and avian pox, which threaten the health of native birds.

Feral swine can multiply faster than any other large mammal; females begin breeding at about 8 months and can produce 2 litters of 4–12 piglets every 12–15 months. *USDA, 2020*

In Europe, especially in Bavaria, Germany, the meat of the hairy, tusked wild boar (Sus scrofa) is one of the most popular forms of game meat, making those pigs particularly prized prey among hunters in that part of the world. Yet, for many years, scientists have known that these hogs have a unique affliction that is both a mystery and something of a menace. In short, a significant portion of the German wild boar population — more than 1 in 3, in certain locales, according to some testing — is radioactive.

German hunters who kill a wild boar are supposed to submit it to authorities for testing. Often, the meat of the pig is deemed too radioactive for human consumption and must be destroyed. The situation has led many hunters to stop harvesting wild boars altogether, giving rise to a new problem: The proliferation of these feral pigs.

Since about 1986, researchers believed that they understood why pigs lit up the Geiger counter on radioactivity. They tended to register for high levels of a certain radioactive isotope known as cesium-137 — an isotope associated with nuclear reactors, among other things. And in 1986, one particular nuclear reactor emitted a whole bunch of cesium-137 into the atmosphere.

That reactor? Chernobyl, the Ukrainian nuclear power plant that suffered an explosion and partial meltdown of its core, resulting in the worst nuclear disaster in history. Thanks to prevailing winds and weather patterns, cesium-137 fallout drifted several hundred miles across Europe.

For many years thereafter, plenty of wild European animals besides pigs were deemed to be contaminated by that fallout, especially in the vicinity of Chernobyl. You wouldn't have wanted to eat any of those creatures unless you were prepared to absorb unsafe levels of radiation and accept the health risks that might entail. Over time, though, as the cesium-137 from Chernobyl dispersed, the radiation levels of most animals within the massive fallout zone dropped to less-than-dangerous levels.

Curiously, that didn't happen with wild boars. The stomach and tissue samples of the boars that researchers tested still continued to exhibit unsafe levels of cesium isotopes. Why were these pigs still so radioactive when other animals in the same habitats were not? It was a conundrum, one so profound and mystifying that it came to be known in some scientific circles as the "wild boar paradox."[1]

On September 13th of 1987 a nuclear incident occurred in Goiania Brazil. The accident was caused primarily because of radioactive contamination of an abandoned piece of hospital equipment. The incident is considered one of the top 10 nuclear disasters to date, as it is classified as a level 5 accident.

When the Goiania Institute of Radiotherapy relocated, they left behind many old hospital machines and supplies that would not play a role at their new location. An old teletherapy unit containing Cs-137 was one of the machines left in the abandoned building. Rummaging through the abandoned building, two men found the machine and sold it to a local junkyard. When employees at the junkyard dismantled the machine, the remaining Cs-137 was released. "Cesium 137 is a radioactive isotope of cesium which is prevalent due to its spontaneous production, which occurs as a result of nuclear fission of other radioactive materials." Employees at the junkyard were fascinated by the blue powder that glowed in the dark that was hiding in the machine and unaware of its many dangers and its repercussions, they distributed it to family and friends.

As the Cs-137 spread around Goiania, individuals began getting sick and many were suffering from acute radiation poisoning. "112,000 people were examined for radioactive contamination with 249 having significant levels of radioactive material in or on their body." With the widespread contamination of Cs-137, experts from the United States and the Soviet Union traveled to Brazil to help "in a radiation accident now proving to be the most serious of its kind in the Western Hemisphere." According to scientists, the government of Goiania was not prompt in its response to the emergency and did not properly recognize the magnitude of the problem. However, with the help of other authorities, the situation was contained, as contaminated areas were swept of radioactive waste and patients were properly treated.

This particular incident created widespread awareness throughout Brazil, as it reminded citizens of the many dangers that could arise due to the nuclear reactor near Rio de Janeiro, as well as the many pieces of equipment in the country that contains radioactive material.[2]

The chemical similarities of lithium, sodium, potassium, rubidium, and cesium are grouped together and called the alkali metals. They all react violently with water!

Lithium is a mood stabilizer, and is used to treat depression, alcoholism, ADHD and ADD, aggression, PTSD, Alzheimer's disease, and to improve memory. Sodium may increase blood pressure, while potassium is used to treat hypertension (it's in "Lite Salt", potassium chloride), for those who must restrict sodium intake. Both potassium and sodium are involved in neural conduction (which helps explain why Potassium is used in lethal injections to stop the heart). Rubidium behaves biologically like potassium, and is used in nuclear medicine to visualize brain tumors, while cesium causes hyperirritability, but it is so seldom encountered that people rarely experience its effects. The radioactive Cs-137 isotope occurs naturally or from nuclear fission of other radioactive materials. Because cesium behaves like potassium, it is readily absorbed in the body, but also readily excreted.

All five are metallic, silver to gray in color, and Li, Na, and K are: solid at room temperature, less dense than water and float on the surface while they react. Alkali metals are soft and easily cut. Beyond similar reactions with water, all alkali metals undergo analogous reactions with oxygen and hydrogen from the atmosphere.

Each member of the chemical family of alkali metals has physical and chemical properties very similar to all the others and in most cases all alkali metals behave the same with regard to the formulas of their compounds. *Chemical and Biological Properties of Element Groups - Chemistry LibreTexts*

Cesium is a naturally-occurring element found in rocks, soil, and dust at low concentrations. Natural cesium is present in the environment in only one stable form, as the isotope 133Cs. Pure cesium metal is silvery white in color and very soft, but pure cesium is not expected to be found in the environment. Pure cesium metal reacts violently with air and water, resulting in an explosion-like reaction. Cesium compounds do not react violently with air or water and are generally very soluble in water. Cesium is not mined or produced in the United States and very little is imported from other countries. There are relatively few commercial uses for cesium metal and its compounds.

Radioactive forms of cesium are produced by the fission of uranium in fuel elements (fuel rods) during the normal operation of nuclear power plants, or when nuclear weapons are exploded. Radioactive forms of cesium are unstable and eventually change into other more stable elements through the process of radioactive decay. The two most important radioactive isotopes of cesium are 134Cs and 137Cs.

Both stable and radioactive cesium are the same element and behave in a similar manner chemically and in the body. Cesium compounds can travel long distances in the air before being brought back to the earth by rainfall and gravitational settling. In water and moist soils, most cesium compounds are very soluble. Cesium binds strongly to most soils and does not travel far below the surface of the soil. Consequently, cesium is not readily available for uptake by vegetation through roots. However, radioactive cesium can enter plants upon falling onto the surface of leaves.

Radioactive cesium has been detected in surface water and in many types of food. This includes breast milk and pasteurized milk. The amount of radioactive cesium in food and milk is highly dependent upon several factors. The most important factor is whether or not there has been recent fallout from a nuclear explosion such as a weapons test or an accident that has occurred at a nuclear power plant. However, atmospheric testing of nuclear weapons was halted many years ago, and there have only been two major reactor accidents at nuclear plants where radiocesium was released in significant amounts. The two accidents occurred in Windscale, England in 1957 and Chernobyl, Russia in 1986. Cesium only contributed a small fraction of the total radioactivity released following these events.

The radiological impacts in Europe from 137Cs and 134Cs released from the Chernobyl accident, however, were great. These included environmental dispersion of radiocesium and uptake in reindeer, caribou, and livestock.

Stable and radioactive cesium can enter your body from the food you eat or the water you drink, from the air you breathe, or from contact with your skin. When you eat, drink, breathe, or touch things containing cesium compounds that can easily be dissolved in water, cesium enters your blood and is carried to all parts of your body. Cesium is like potassium; it enters cells and helps to maintain a balance of electrical charges between the inside and the outside of cells so that cells can perform tasks that depend on those electrical charges. Cells like muscle cells and nerve cells require changing electrical charges in order to function properly and allow you to think and move.

Once cesium enters your body, your kidneys begin to remove it from the blood; some cesium is quickly released from your body in the urine. A small portion is also released in the feces. Some of the cesium that your body absorbs can remain in your body for weeks or months, but is slowly eliminated from your body through the urine and feces.[3]

Whoever thinks of truffles usually has a culinary delicacy in mind. Wild boars are also truffle lovers, but they love other species than their human counterparts: Deer truffles, which, however, are not real truffles at all. Their fruiting bodies represent only a convergent development among the ascomycetes (tubular fungi). The Deer Truffle, is one of the most important ectomycorrhizal fungal genera in temperate and subarctic forest ecosystems. But it is also one of the least documented in public databases.

The current systematics is based mainly on macromorphology and does not differ significantly from that proposed in 1831. Very recent phylogenetic treatises of the genus are based mainly on some non-European species. The most common European species are still poorly documented.

For humans, deer truffles are inedible or not tasty, especially older fruiting bodies are not edible. They are mycorrhizal fungi that form symbiotic relationships with various tree species. However, the visible deer truffles are only the fruiting bodies of the fungal mycelium, which grows year-round. Unlike the fruiting bodies of other mushroom species that grow above ground only seasonally (especially in the fall), the fruiting bodies of deer truffles grow year-round.

The fruiting bodies consist of a relatively hard, rubbery bark and are filled with spores when mature. The rind usually has a wart-like texture and is light brown in color. The color and consistency of the spore material varies as the truffle matures. The initially light gray solid mass inside turns darker and darker as it matures. When fully ripe, the truffle is loose, powdery and deep purple inside. Since their fruiting bodies grow underground for this purpose, the commercial interest is very low. Accordingly, little is known about the biology of these fungal species.

There also seems to be no interest in deer truffles from the scientific community so far. This is surprising since deer truffle fungi enters into a symbiosis with tree roots (spruce, pine and beech) with the purpose of exchanging (nutrients) substances with one another. It is probably the most abundant and widespread of all truffles in the world, fruiting nearly the whole year. The fruiting bodies accumulate radioactivity cesium-137, leading to Cs-137 contamination of wild pigs.

The fruiting body spores develop just under the soil and it clearly relies on animal vectors for excavation and dispersal However, there is history of long-distance dispersal of the genus and current spore trajectories suggest that the spores can also be dispersed passively in the air. This is because the spores can remain airborne long enough to be dispersed over long distances by the wind.

Deer truffles are eaten by soil invertebrates (especially ants, beetle larvae, nematodes, annelid worms). These seem to prefer the outer rind of the fruiting bodies, the spore mass is less often attacked. In addition to wild boars, vertebrates also include roe deer and red deer and fallow deer, badger, squirrels, mice and various American small mammals are known to be consumers of deer truffles. This diet is called mycophagy.

It is possible that the passage through the digestive tract of animals is necessary for spore germination of the deer truffles.[4]

So, why were feral pigs in Germany still so radioactive when other animals in the same habitats were not? Eventually, scientists thought they had it figured out. Researchers were able to conclusively link wild boars' excessive radioactivity to their diet. It turns out that feral pigs go hog-wild for the deer truffles that are growing a few inches below ground level and tend to absorb high levels of radioactive cesium. Boars rely on the truffles as a major food source at certain times of the year.

But even though wild boars like to root out those radioactive truffles, more than 30 years after the Chernobyl disaster, researchers still should have seen some declines in the wild pigs' contamination levels.

Recently, that answer was determined: the cesium-137 that the truffles absorbed wasn't simply coming from Chernobyl, but from a much older source. Researchers in Germany and Austria concluded that a sizable portion of the cesium contamination was the result of years of

20th-century nuclear weapons tests, according to a study published in Environmental Science & Technology in 2023. These tests dated at least as far back as the 1960s, but the fallout from those decades-old weapons was still accounting for anywhere from 10 to nearly 70 percent of the radioactive contamination that scientists were finding in the wild boar population.

Although various international bans and agreements have curbed the testing of such weapons of mass destruction, it will be a while yet before cesium contamination ceases to be a problem for wild boars — and the people who like to eat them. Cesium penetrates the ground at an exceedingly slow rate, so slowly that researchers surmise the deer truffles have mostly absorbed just the "old" cesium from weapons testing.

Meanwhile, the "new" cesium from Chernobyl is only recently reaching the underground depths where deer truffles grow. So, between the lingering residuals of nuclear tests and the Chernobyl disaster, Bavaria's boars will continue to remain under watch, a potential vector for nuclear contamination for as long as pigs continue to root for those truffles.

Hunters who don't wish to expose themselves or their customers to radioactive danger will need to keep submitting their wild hogs for testing for the foreseeable future. Make no mistake: It may still be several years before this "new" cesium abates enough that lovers of wild boar meat will be able to pig out — without fear of fallout.[1]

Boars have many symbolic meanings, including courage, ferocity, war, sustenance, fertility, and prosperity. In Greek mythology, boars are associated with Artemis, the goddess of hunting, mountains, and forests, and are sometimes sent by her to punish humans. Boars are also known for their strength, destructiveness, and ferocity. In Celtic mythology, the boar is a universal symbol of strength and fertility, and appears on the helmets of warriors. In Japan, boars are respected and feared for their courage and tendency to charge and attack. Boars are also symbols of recklessness, fertility, and prosperity.

Cesium is like potassium; it enters cells and helps to maintain a balance of electrical charges between the inside and the outside of cells so that cells can perform tasks that depend on those electrical charges. Cells like muscle cells and nerve cells require changing electrical charges in order to function properly and allow you to think and move.

Once cesium enters your body, your kidneys begin to remove it from the blood; some cesium is quickly released from your body in the urine. A small portion is also released in the feces. Some of the cesium that your body absorbs can remain in your body for weeks or months, but is slowly eliminated from your body through the urine and feces.

Deer truffles are probably the most abundant and widespread of all truffles in the world, fruiting nearly the whole year. Cesium binds strongly to most soils and does not travel far below the surface of the soil. The fruiting bodies of the deer truffles are accumulating radioactivity (Cs-137) that is penetrating into the ground at an exceedingly slow rate from "old" cesium left from weapons testing.

Meanwhile, the "new" cesium from Chernobyl is only recently reaching the underground depths where deer truffles grow. So, between the lingering residuals of nuclear tests and the Chernobyl disaster, Bavaria's boars

WALTER R. HOGE, DVM

will continue to remain under watch, a potential vector for nuclear contamination for as long as pigs continue to root for those truffles.

So Bavarian boars are eating the deer truffles that concentrate cesium, the boar absorbs it into its body, most of the cesium is rapidly excreted from its kidneys and poop, and scattered throughout the environment during the pig's search for food and shelter. My conclusion is that the sows and boars are diluting the environment of potentially dangerous radioactive Cs-137 concentration and reducing the risk of animal and human radiation sickness.

I say – hooray for the pig. No wonder it is included in mythology and considered to be one of the most intelligent animals on the planet. Do you suppose eating the deer truffles is its way of serving mankind like our dog at home is supposed to be doing? Or is it just mother nature showing another of her many skills?

Hopefully, the Germans can figure out a way to control the prolific reproduction capacities of the pig – it looks like they aren't going to be eating a lot of them for a long time. I find it distasteful to hunt down and slaughter the poor beasts. After all, the last name of my recent ancestors was Hogg – keeper of the pigs…

The name Hogg is traceable to the abbreveations of the personal name Roger. It is the name of a popular English born saint. Saint Roger was born in Lincoln and traveled to France in order to study for the priesthood. He achieved international renown as a preacher and his feast was celebrated on July 7th.

The personal name of Roger was frequently abbreviated to the pet-form Hogg as a term of endearment and affection. Secondly, this name can derive from a nickname source, from an object particularly associated with the individual. In this case, the name derives from an Old English term 'Hogg' which denoted 'a pig'. By extension therefore, the name came to denote one who kept pigs. The name shows regestry as early as 1273…

1– *Why Are Wild Pigs in Germany So Radioactive?,
Discover Magazine, Stephen C. George, 01/25/2024.*

2– *Goiania Nuclear Accident, Brazil 1987, Stanford University, Meg Gerli, 03/24/2018.*

3– *Agency for Toxic Substances and Disease Registry (ATSDR). 2004. Toxicological profile for cesium, Atlanta, GA: U.S. Department of Health and Human Services, Public Health Service, 2004.*

4– *umweltanalysen.com, Deer Truffles, Cesium 137 Contamination, July 2008.*

CHAPTER 12

THE FUNGUS ERGOT
(CLAVICEPS PURPUREA)

Since humans first began cultivating cereal grains such as wheat, rye, barley, and oats, they have been susceptible to ergot (Claviceps purpurea) poisoning. This fungus has devastated crops and European societies for many centuries.

Most commonly attacking rye, ergot infects and replaces the cereal grain with a dark fungal body called a "sclerotium." When made into bread or otherwise ingested (e.g. barley beer), it causes ergotism, also known as "St. Anthony's Fire" or "Devil's curse." Convulsions, muscle spasms, vomiting, hallucinations, and a gangrenous pain where the victim's limbs, fingers, toes, and nose were "eaten up by the holy fire that blackened like charcoal" characterize ergot poisoning. Victims often lost parts of their extremities or entire limbs due to blood vessel constriction associated with gangrenous ergotism.

Julius Caesar lost legions of soldiers to ergot poisoning during his campaigns in Gaul. Severe ergot epidemics in France between 900 AD and 1300 AD killed between

20,000 to 50,000 people, leaving the nation susceptible to invasions that eventually toppled this Holy Roman kingdom into what became two nations, France and Germany.

The ergot fungus contains a number of highly poisonous and psychoactive alkaloids, including lysergic acid (LSD), which was synthesized from the ergot fungus in 1938 by chemist, Albert Hoffmann. Ergot poisoning is a proposed explanation of bewitchment. Most historians today believe that the witchcraft trials that led to thousands of deaths and burnings at the stake in Europe during the Dark Ages were likely related to outbreaks of ergot poisonings. The unfortunate victims of the Salem witch trials of 1692 also exhibited symptoms of ergot poisonings. Ergotism is rare today due to careful screening of cereal grains.[1]

Ergot alkaloids is a general term used to describe a number of different chemical compounds produced by the fungus ergot (Claviceps purpurea). Over the centuries humans have learned to use these chemicals for their own benefit:

One of the compounds (Ergonovine) is used to hasten labor and prevent postpartum bleeding. This is still used today! It is given to women in the third stage of labor to prevent hemorrhaging by maintaining uterine contraction and tone. The blood vessels are also reduced and compressed so there is less blood flow. The interesting thing about this compound is that if it is ingested by a pregnant mammal before in labor, it increases the risk of female mortality and can cause spontaneous abortions. Ergonovine is only one of many compounds that ergot produces.

Ergotamine is another compound produced by ergot and is a powerful vasoconstrictor, which means it constricts the blood vessels and thus the blood flow. This is useful in migraine headaches because it reduces extra cranial blood flow and the amplitude of the pulsations in these arteries. Another aspect of ergot is that it is a serotonin agonist. This quality has also been proven to help with throbbing headaches.

Ergot is also known to be a dopamine agonist. This means that it increases the effects of dopamine (a neurotransmitter) in the brain. Between all the individual nerve cells in the brain (called neurons), there is a tiny gap called the synapse. To communicate across this gap, one neuron releases the neurotransmitters and the other reads them and they are eventually taken back up by the first neuron so they can be used again. To be a neurotransmitter agonist, like ergot, the re-uptake of the neurotransmitter is inhibited, so its effects are amplified. It is for this reason specifically that ergot derivatives are used to help treat patients with Parkinson's disease.

Other things that are either in use or in research for treatment with ergot or some of its derivatives is hyperprolactinemic disorders, muscle relaxer (hypertonia), circulatory diseases, angina pectoris, and possibly an anti-tumor drug that regulates the proliferation of the tumor cells.

The three most common things ergot derivatives are used for are treatment during labor, headaches and Parkinson's.[2]

During graduate school at Purdue University my NIH (National Institute of Health) grant was to study the effects of ergot toxicity on reproductive hormones. The primary toxicological effect of ergot alkaloid involves vasoconstriction and/or hypoprolactinaemia. Ingestion of ergot alkaloid by livestock can cause a range of effects, including poor weight gain, reduced fertility, hyperthermia, convulsions, gangrene of the extremities, and death. After taking account of impact on equines and on both small and large ruminants, it is estimated that the combined losses due to ergot alkaloid intoxication of animal feed in the USA are likely to exceed $1 billion annually (J of Animal Sci, 2011).

Prolactin is involved in several actions, such as lactation, ovarian luteal function, reproduction, appetite, suppression of fertility, homeostasis, osmotic balance, immunity, and coagulation. In addition, prolactin is also known as an important factor that mediates adaptive responses related to parental behaviors.

While there is no male equivalent of lactation, many of the other functions of prolactin in females can also be observed in males. For example, as in females, prolactin seems to be involved in parental behavior in males.[3]

Dopamine is a complex and key neurotransmitter responsible for many of our daily physical and mental functions. Changes in levels of this brain chemical can alter our behavior, movement, mood, memory, and many other reactions. Dopamine agonists (DA) are medications that work by imitating the actions of dopamine when levels are low. These medications improve condition-related symptoms by fooling the brain into thinking dopamine is available. They are useful in treatment of Parkinson's symptoms and restless legs syndrome.

Medications are mostly prescribed for their effects on movement related and hormone related disorders. They can improve other related troubles such as sleep disorders, pain, and emotional concerns that co-occur with certain dopamine-linked conditions. These medications are not as strong as medications used for Parkinson's disease.

There are two main categories of dopamine agonist medication, ergoline (derivative of ergot) and non-ergoline (derivative of morphine).[4]

In the 1930's, Stoll and Hofmann attempted to isolate ergot's toxic alkaloids in hopes of finding a cure for psychosis. Instead, they created a drug that made these symptoms worse in patients already suffering and caused those who were considered healthy, to essentially go mad.

LSD (Lysergic acid diethylamide) was first synthesized by the Swiss chemist, Albert Hofmann in 1938 when he was doing research on the fungus for medicinal purposes. He writes about his experiences in his book, *LSD: My Problem Child*, where he says: "Last Friday, April 16, 1943, I was forced to interrupt my work in the laboratory in the middle of the afternoon and proceed home, being affected by a remarkable restlessness, combined with a slight dizziness. At home I lay down and sank into a not unpleasant intoxicated-like condition, characterized by an extremely stimulated imagination. In a dreamlike state, with eyes closed (I found daylight to be unpleasantly glaring), I perceived an uninterrupted stream of fantastic pictures, extraordinary shapes with intense, kaleidoscope play of colors. After some two hours, this condition faded away." Later in 1948, LSD was introduced to the medical world as a psychiatric cure-all drug and it was prescribed extensively.[2]

In 1953, Sidney Gottlieb persuaded the CIA to spend $240,000 to buy the world's entire supply of LSD from its sole producer, the Swiss pharmaceutical firm Sandoz. Over the next decade, he used his unique stash for two purposes. Some of it went to prisons in the United Sates and to CIA "safe houses" in Europe and East Asia, where it was used in heinous experiments on unwitting or unwilling human subjects. In one of them, seven African American inmates at a prison in Kentucky were given what the prison doctor called "double, ripple and quadruple doses" of LSD every day for 77 days. Experiments abroad, in which LSD was used in concert with other drugs and with torments like electroshock, were even harsher, and caused an unknown number of deaths. These were the most extreme experiments on human subjects that have ever been conducted by an officer or agency of the US government.

The CIA used and experimented on LSD using a top-secret mission, MK-ULTRA, through which they were hoping to find a mind controlling agent. They were looking to use it as a form of psychological torture and they ran tests on members of the general public and CIA agents, often without their knowledge or consent. Many of the people that were involved in this experiment underwent such a severe trauma that many either committed suicide or wound up in a psychiatric ward. The researchers of this drug eventually realized that LSD was WAY too unpredictable to be used effectively.

There is also a theory that the CIA covertly advocated for the use of LSD in the American youth in the 60's as a way to undermine the growing anti-war movement and emerging counterculture. Production was halted in 1965, however, because it was growing too popular and there was a lack of positive long-term effects and they were actually finding a lot of adverse side effects, like flashbacks and terrors.

Even though the use of LSD in the medical community for medicinal purposes was declining, history tells us that LSD was still very popular in the 1960s. One man that you have probably already heard of is Dr. Timothy Leary. Dr. Leary was a professor at Harvard University and was pro-LSD. He was giving it to students and running experiments on prisoners, which he claimed resulted in a 90% success rate in preventing repeat criminal offenses. Then his students began to take it recreationally and Leary later told Playboy Magazine that LSD was a potent aphrodisiac, something that got him expelled from the university. Shortly after this, President Nixon claimed that he was the "most dangerous man in the U.S."

Leary did not stop there. In order to combat the extensive anti-LSD propaganda being issued by the government, he coined the phrase, "Turn on. Tune in. Drop out.", short for turn on your mind, tune in to what you believe, and drop out of the things you're not happy about.

Many believe that much of the great music produced by the Beatles was a result of taking some trips down LSD lane. In particular, the song "Lucy in the Sky with Diamonds" primarily written by John Lennon, is believed to be the offspring of LSD. Plus, the initials of the song are LSD, which I thought was a little ironic. Other bands, such as Grateful Dead helped give birth to the terms psychedelic or acid rock. LSD was very popular with the rebellious youth of the 60's and continues to be popular among college and high school age students. This is most likely because it only requires a small amount of LSD to send you on a trip and it is easy to make.

Side effects of LSD are mainly due to the fact that LSD is similar to serotonin, which regulates memory, anxiety, mood, aggression, learning and sleep. LSD is the most potent naturally occurring hallucinogen and is considered a "clean drug." This is because it only stays in the body for 30 hours and is not addictive. But what does it make you feel like? The mental side effects for LSD are pretty variable and dependent on one's personality, mood, expectations and surroundings. Many times, however, people report seeing, hearing and touching things that don't exist, which makes sense because LSD is a powerful hallucinogen. People also report an altered sense of time, mixing of senses, distortion of space, strange body sensations and changed and intensified thoughts. The physical effects include dilated pupils, higher body temperature, increased heart rate and blood pressure, sweating, loss of appetite, sleeplessness, dry mouth and tremors.[2]

Sidney Gottlieb's decade of MK-ULTRA mind controlling experiments led him to two conclusions: *He had proven conclusively that with the application of enough drug overdoses and other extreme techniques over extended periods, it is possible to destroy a human mind; the trail of ruined lives he left in his wake is horrific testimony to his success. Yet he was also forced to admit that he had failed to find a way to insert a new mind into the resulting void.* As MK-ULTRA ended in the 1960s, Gottlieb concluded that psychoactive drugs are "too unpredictable in their effect on individual human beings, under specific circumstances, to be operationally useful."

A current LSD review of the literature published in 2019 concludes that alcohol use disorder patients may benefit from LSD treatment. Other studies with a lower quality control group (patients did not receive a treatment comparable to the treatment group) also found significant differences in favor of LSD treatment in alcoholism. Likewise, according to a retrospective analysis of studies published in the late 1960s, LSD is a potential therapeutic agent for the treatment of chronic alcoholism. A recent meta-analysis of six of the clinical trials chosen for this review showed the superiority of LSD over placebo in the treatment of alcoholism. This study found that a single LSD dose was comparable in terms of effectiveness with the daily intake of naltrexone, acamprosate, or disulfiram in alcoholism treatment. Other studies in the review found promising results regarding LSD use for the treatment of heroin use disorder, anxiety, depression, psychosomatic illnesses, and anxiety in relation to life-threatening diseases.[5]

At the age of 22 when I began graduate school at Purdue University, it was probably a good thing that I was pursuing the effects of ergot alkaloids on the reproductive hormone prolactin. If I had of been brilliant enough to attend Harvard University, I may have worked under Dr. Timothy Leary and "turned on. tuned in. and dropped out" of life.

1– *Ergot: The Psychoactive Fungus that Changed History, USDA Forest Service.*

2– *History of LSD, Kaitlyn Miedema, Last Updated 04/15/2011.*

3– *Hypoprolactinemia, Fertilitypedia & John Hopkins Medical, 2012.*

4– *Understanding Dopamine Agonists, National Institute of Health (NIH).*

5– *NIH, Front Psychiatry. 2019; 10:943.*

CHAPTER 13

THOUGHTS ABOUT BARK

Euell Theophilus Gibbons (09/08/1911 – 12/29/1975) was an outdoorsman and early health food advocate, promoting eating wild foods during the 1960s. During one difficult interval of homesteading, Gibbons began foraging for local plants and berries to supplement the family diet. After leaving home at 15, he drifted throughout the Southwest, finding work as a dairyman, carpenter, trapper, gold panner, and cowboy. The early years of the Dust Bowl era found Gibbons in California, where he lived as a self-described "bindle stiff" (hobo).

The growing return-to-nature movement in 1962 and Gibbon's books on foraged foodstuffs brought him fame. He made guest appearances on The Tonight Show and The Sonny & Cher Comedy Hour, and received an honorary doctorate from Susquehanna University. A 1974 television commercial for Post Grape-Nuts cereal featured him asking viewers, "Ever eat a pine tree? Many parts are edible." While he recommended Grape Nuts over pine trees (including the oft-repeated quote that Grape Nuts› taste reminded him "of wild hickory nuts"), the commercials gained attention and fueled Gibbons' celebrity status. *Wikipedia*

I remember as a youth in the 60s many jokes about Gibbons and how he thought you could eat a tree. When he died of an aneurism, jokes were made that he died from eating pine trees. I don't know how much he knew about the nutritional value of trees or if it were just an "attention getter."

To humans, eating the bark of trees likely seems quite unpalatable. But for many animals with the proper digestive system, tree bark actually supplies an abundant source of nutrition, especially in the winter months when other food sources are scarce.

The cell walls of plants contain cellulose, hemicellulose, and lignins, with individual cells held together by pectins. Cellulose and hemicellulose are complex carbohydrates, but only some animals contain the required enzymes, cellulase and hemicellulase, to digest them. Certain colonies of microbes found in the gut of bark-eating animals produce cellulase and hemicellulase. The pectins and pectic acids that hold neighboring cells together provide sugars to bark-eating animals. Lignin, however, is by far the least digestible compound as most bark-eating animals do not contain microbes that produce the enzyme necessary, ligninase, to break lignin down.

The outer layer of bark consists mainly of layers of crushed, dead cells with a high lignin content. The inner layer of bark, however, is comprised of living cells packed with the complex carbohydrates, sugars, and minerals bark-eating animals can digest.[1]

Amylase is a digestive enzyme predominantly secreted by the pancreas and salivary glands and found in other tissues at very small levels. Amylase was first described in the early 1800s and is considered one of the first enzymes in history to be scientifically investigated. Amylases' main function is to hydrolyze the glycosidic bonds in starch molecules, converting complex carbohydrates into simple sugars.

Cellulose is an insoluble substance which is the main constituent of plant cell walls and of vegetable fibers including wood. It is known as a polysaccharide consisting of chains of glucose monomers. Cellulose has as much food value as starch, but only animals that maintain colonies of microorganisms in their gut that produce the enzyme cellulase are capable of digesting it.

To use bark and wood as food, organisms must possess specialized digestive systems and the necessary enzymes. The function of these adaptations is to break down huge macromolecules (proteins, fats, starch, cellulose, and hemicellulose) into smaller molecules (amino acids, fatty acids, and sugars) that can be absorbed into the circulatory system.

For carnivores and omnivores adapted to eating meat as well as fruits and nuts with their concentrated food value, the digestive system is relatively simple. Strict herbivores have a big challenge since the vegetation they consume is a far less concentrated food, more difficult to digest, and often protected by defensive compounds. In addition, the rigid cell walls of plant material must be broken down to gain access to proteins and carbohydrates inside living cells.

For animals, the breakdown of foodstuffs is accomplished through a combination of mechanical grinding and enzymatic processes beginning in the mouth. To further degrade ingested food, the digestion system of herbivores is uniquely modified. It varies considerably among species, but in all cases depends on microorganisms that inhabit special compartments of the stomach (rumen), intestines (cecum, an out pocketing of the terminal portion of the small intestine where it joins the large intestine), an exceptionally long intestine, or an enlarged colon. Protozoa and bacteria that function similarly to microorganisms that degrade woody debris in the outside environment by secreting digestive enzymes that are brought "indoors" to the protection of the gut. There they basically conduct the same fermentation processes. The cellulases, hemi-cellulases, and other enzymes that they produce, release sugars, organic acids, and amino acids from woody materials, nourishing both the host animal and the millions of microorganisms living in its digestive system.

The stomach of herbivorous animals can be a single saclike compartment (monogastric) or complexly subdivided into various chambers (digastric). In monogastric herbivores such as horses, rhinoceroses, rodents, and rabbits, protein is digested and absorbed in the single-chambered stomach. Cellulosic material is digested by microorganism-aided fermentation in the intestine, often modified to have either a cecum or enlarged colon. In these animals the intestine is very long, often 25 times the body length, to insure adequate time for digestion and absorption. Monogastric animals that have the ability to digest cellulosic materials are referred to as hindgut fermenters.

In digastric animals like deer, antelope, moose, camels, sheep, goats, and cattle, the stomach is divided into four chambers, the first being the rumen which contains the symbiotic microorganisms. Digastric animals only partially chew their food as they quickly gather it. Later when resting and watchful for predators, they regurgitate and re-chew it. This cycle is repeated until the mechanical and chemical breakdown of the food is adequate for it to pass to the next chamber of the stomach. Digastric animals are called foregut fermenters.

Several hindgut fermenters (rodents, rabbits, and others) increase the digestion of their food by eating 25 to 60 percent of their feces. This practice, known as coprophagy, is important for small mammalian species with relatively high metabolic rates and sustained caloric needs. The first pass of food through the digestive tract does not provide enough opportunity for microorganisms to digest the coarse food particles. Coprophagy is somewhat analogous to a ruminant animal chewing its cud, the difference being the point in the digestion process at which the food is rechewed. Animals that practice coprophagy usually consume their feces when resting.

Beavers are a good example of a hindgut fermenter. They are primarily bark-eaters, ingesting the bark of young twigs and sapwood of branches and small tree trunks. In the spring and fall, about half of the beaver's food is woody vegetation, but in winter it feeds on woody vegetation almost exclusively. They actively cut trees and shrubs in the summer, storing sections of the wood under water as a winter food supply beneath the ice. Beavers have many adaptations for their woody diet. Large jaw muscles power sharp incisors that slice through wood and flat molars grind the fibrous bark. Their large cecum contains bacteria and fungi that aid in digesting about 30 percent of the dietary cellulose. To improve the extraction of nourishment from wood and bark, beavers practice coprophagy, thereby running food through their digestive system several times.

Rabbits have a simple stomach, but an enlarged cecum and colon inhabited by symbiotic microorganisms allow digestion of their herbivorous diet. Particularly in winter when other sources of food are scarce, rabbits may gnaw the bark of trees, creating consternation for homeowners, foresters, nurseryman, and Christmas tree growers. Rabbits practice coprophagy, allowing them to meet their nutritional requirements in spite of the fast transit time of food through their digestive system. Coprophagy increases protein digestibility from 50 percent in one pass through their digestive system to 75 to 80 percent upon re-ingestion. Cellulose digestion is increased from 14 percent in one pass through their digestive system to two or three times that amount when the feces is re-ingested.

In summer, porcupines feed on ground vegetation, but in the winter, they spend most of their time in trees eating the inner bark and twigs from a great variety of species, making themselves a pest in the opinion of most tree and shrub owners. Much of the damage is due to girdling the base of seedlings and saplings, as well as from deforming the growth of young trees by randomly pruning branches as they feed. To digest the high percentage of fiber in their diet, porcupines are equipped with a cecum housing cellulase- and hemicellulase-producing microorganisms. In addition, porcupines have 20 teeth to reduce their food to dust-like consistency for efficient breakdown. The large intestine also is extremely long, resulting in a slow passage time and more absorption of the fermented products of the cecum. (Porcupines crave salt and are attracted to and consume axes, boat oars etc. that have human sweat on them).

Ruminants with chambered stomachs and foregut fermentation are represented by a large number of animals that dominate woodlands and prairies. Deer and moose are just a couple of examples. The herbaceous diet of deer frequently includes the foliage and twigs of woody plants that they chew just enough to swallow. After a deer fills its rumen, the first chamber of its stomach, it lies down in a secluded place to regurgitate and chew its cud, re-swallowing the food for further microbial fermentation and eventual passage to the second portion of the stomach, the reticulum. After about 16 hours, food passes to the third chamber, the omasum, where intensive digestion and absorption take place. The last compartment, the abomasum, produces acid to break down food pieces for easier absorption of nutrients in the intestines.

The diet of moose includes leaves of trees and shrubs and both terrestrial and aquatic plants when available. During the winter months their food becomes even more woody, consisting almost solely of 30 to 45 lbs of twigs and shrubs each day. As food becomes scarce in late winter, moose will strip bark from trees, especially poplars. Like deer, the ruminant digestive system of moose extracts sustenance from these woody tissues.[2]

The bacteria and protozoan present in the digestive tract of herbivores varies according to the plant material eaten. Sudden changes in diet can be fatal to the animal.

WALTER R. HOGE, DVM

Montana State University extension wildlife specialist, Jim Knight, discusses: The deer you plan to feed over the winter may need some "tough love" instead. Just as people have learned that sometimes well-meant help facilitates unhealthy behavior, so winter feeding of deer is unhealthy - or even deadly - for deer. Feeding seems like a generous answer to starving wildlife at first. However, most people don't know that some common feeds can harm deer or change their behavior to the point that it leads to their destruction.

Many people think that feeding deer in a hard winter can do nothing but help. But, that's not always the case. Knight relates the following scene he witnessed during the winter of 1996-97:

A tearful woman was talking to a central Montana wildlife biologist. "We can't afford any more food, and the poor things are dying," the woman complained. "Every day more and more come to the feeders, but we're already spending $100 a month. Isn't there something you can do?"

"I'm sorry, ma'am," the wildlife biologist said, "but you're drawing deer from all over the area. They aren't used to a diet of hay and corn, so I'm afraid you're going to have more of this," he said, pointing to two frozen carcasses of yearling deer only feet from hay-filled feeders.

This scene is repeated many times each winter in Montana, says Knight. Feeding deer hay or corn can kill them, because they cannot always digest it. Deer digestion involves protozoa and bacteria that help break down food. Different micro-organisms help digest different types of vegetation. If a deer has been feeding on aspen or willows, it has built up the micro-organisms that digest only this kind of vegetation. If this same deer suddenly fills its stomach with corn or hay, it may not have enough of the corn- and hay-digesting micro-organisms in its stomach to digest the food. A deer can starve to death with a full stomach…In truth, you may hurt more deer than you help if you feed them. There is a way to help, however. "Create and maintain a natural habitat and combine that with proper hunting. It's the only way to minimize starvation and work for both deer health and humane treatment," says Knight. "If deer populations aren't controlled by man or other predators, you will have starvation."[3]

Edible tree cutting or hinge cutting can be used to help prevent deer starvation during heavy winters. A hinge cut refers to the practice of partially cutting a tree then pushing it over where it continues to grow horizontally. This creates a natural habitat for wildlife and produces screen covers and natural fences to prevent some game animals from entering a certain area or escaping from it.

In general, hinge cutting serves three purposes:

- Food: A tree growing horizontally provides an easy-to-reach source of food for small animals that cannot reach the leaves and twigs of an upright tree.
- Cover: The natural screen cover that a hinge cut tree makes attracts wildlife to the newly formed landscape. This helps create a teeming ecosystem and transforms the area.
- Hunting: Hunters will benefit from the many game animals taking cover in the area. The movement of animals can be directed somewhat, which makes the hunting experience more successful.

Of all wildlife, deer, in particular, seem to like hinge-cut trees the most. For one thing, half-fallen trees allow small vegetation and saplings to grow and thrive. At the same time, the hinge-cut tree itself is very much alive and growing. Its leaves, fruits, and young shoots are conveniently handy for the deer to reach.

Additionally, the notoriously shy deer can find cover behind the trees and hide between the branches.

Most small wildlife would be attracted to an area where one or more hinge-cut trees dot the landscape. These trees are a good natural cover as well as a sustainable source of food. Rabbits also build their nests near these trees and hide whenever they sense danger. The same applies to squirrels and even quails and turkeys. The improved landscape offers better nesting opportunities for them.[4]

History is littered with hardship, but more often than not, we focus on human-caused disasters such as war, slavery, and religious conflict rather than focus on how nature might have shaped us and our habits. There are a few popular exceptions, of course, such as the Irish potato famine, but when it comes to how famine, in general, changed how and what we eat, many of us would be none the wiser.

Famine (a significant lack of food that leads to malnourishment and starvation) influences many, if not all, parts of society, but one of the things it forces people to go look for alternative food sources. You see, when hunger eats away at your body, you're willing to try anything. According to The Health Board, when traditional crops and livestock begin to fail, our ancestors looked to wild food resources that aren't normally farmed. Kelp was consumed in Ireland during the Great Famine (1845 – 1851), wild grass was eaten by the Russians when they went to war, and in Scandinavia, when times were tough, people turned to trees.

When we think of using trees as food, oftentimes we concern ourselves with the fruits and nuts they bare, the syrups they produce, or the lumber they supply for cooking. It is significantly less common to hear about people eating tree bark itself for a meal, but that's exactly what the Indigenous Sami people native to northern Scandinavia have been doing for centuries! Atlas Obscura tells us that the Sami have used the inner bark (aka the phloem) of pine and birch trees as a source of nutrition. It has long been one of their staple food items, and it is their knowledge that Nordic farmers and citizens used during times of famine to stay alive. People would strip the bark off of trees, dry and roast the wood, and grind it into flour to make bark break which, in Finland, they call pettuleipä.

According to Lund University's publication on "Famines in the Nordic Country," the tree bark wasn't the only natural foodstuff people would turn to during famine. Things like flower buds, nettles, leaves, and hay were all desperately devoured, though they offered little relief from hunger and unfortunately malnutrition killed an unfathomable amount of people throughout history. Researchers confirm that people throughout Sweden and Finland, not just the Sami people, took to eating bark by the mid-17th century due to persistent food scarcity; it was during this time that pettuleipä became popular.

The pine bark often used to make pettuleipä today may contain some potential health-benefiting properties such as antimicrobials and antioxidants. In JSTOR's abstract on "Sami Resource Utilization and Site Selection:

Historical Harvesting of Inner Bark in Northern Sweden," the harvesting of bark from native trees leaves a mark. The evidence of pettuleipä-making can still be found in the old forests of Scandinavia. Nature bears the scars of this once-necessary harvest and researchers can study the forest to discover how often and how much the inner bark was harvested over the centuries.[5]

During a 2016 BYU Women's Conference Elder Dale G. Renlund mentioned a literary work that his Finnish dad often quoted from the writings of the 19th-century Finnish author and poet Johan Ludvig Runeberg: "My father was born in northern Finland, outside the town of Jakobstad, which is also known as Pietasaari. My dad loved Finnish literature, especially the works of Runeberg. Like my father, Runeberg was born in Jakobstad. Dad would quote Finnish literature to us as bedtime stories. These stories were really rather somber. It seemed to us as children that the moral of these stories was "fight valiantly against impossible odds and then die." It was like listening to the book of Job without the happy ending.

One of Runeberg's poems that we heard over and over was the story of Farmer Paavo. Paavo was a poor peasant farmer who lived with his wife and children in Saarijärvi, in the lake region of central Finland. Several years in a row, some combination of the runoff from the spring snowmelt, summer hailstorms, or an early autumn frost killed most of his crop. Each time the meager harvest came in, his wife said, 'Paavo, Paavo, you unfortunate old man, God has forsaken us.' Paavo, in turn, said, 'Woman, mix bark with the rye flour to make bread so we won't go hungry. I will work harder to drain the marshy fields. God is testing us, but He will provide.'

Every time the crop was destroyed, Paavo directed his wife to double the amount of bark that she mixed into the bread to ward off starvation. Poor Paavo worked even harder. He dug ditches to drain the marsh, to decrease his fields' susceptibility to the spring snowmelt and to the exposure of an early autumn frost. Finally, Paavo harvested a rich crop. Overjoyed, his wife said, 'Paavo, Paavo, these are happy times! It is time to throw away the bark and bake bread made only with the rye.' But Paavo took his wife's hand and said, 'Woman, mix half the flour with bark, for our neighbor's fields have frosted over.' Left unstated in the poem was Paavo's intent to help his devastated, destitute neighbor…

It wasn't to try to get us to sleep. I think that my father was teaching us that charitable giving is something we do because of our humanity. It is something we do because we care about our fellow human beings. The poem invites us to ask ourselves, 'What would we do if we were in Paavo's shoes? Would we help this unfortunate neighbor? Would we, in the future, help others in need?'" *Joha Ludvig Runeberg (1804-1877),* Saarijarven Paavo, *is considered to be the national poet of Finland.*[6]

Scientists have figured out how to turn cellulose from wood, bushes and grasses into edible starch.

For Percival Zhang, growing up in China meant learning to appreciate just how critical a stable food supply is to avoiding social unrest and disasters like famine. When he became an associate professor of biological systems engineering at

Virginia Tech, he got to thinking just how risky growing food has become because of the finite resources it requires: land, water, seeds and fertilizer. Plenty of other plants on Earth, on the other hand, aren't so demanding.

Wood, bushes, grasses — they don›t need special attention, and in nature, there›s more than 100 times more of this nonfood biomass than the starch we currently grow as food. So, he got an idea: What if we could convert the cellulose in this plentiful biomass to edible starch, which makes up 50 to 60 percent of the human diet? Maybe a technology like that could feed people while reducing the environmental impact of agriculture.

In a study, colleagues in the Proceedings of the National Academy of Sciences, Zhang explains a process he developed to transform solid cellulose, which could come from wood, grass or crop residue (like corn husks), into a carbohydrate called amylose. The process is a form of synthetic biology and relies on enzymes to break down the cellulose into smaller units and then restitch the molecules into the edible product, starch. The completely synthetic powder tastes sweet and resembles other complex carbohydrates like corn starch.

Zhang is far from the only one to entertain this zany-sounding idea. Even astrobiologists at NASA are interested in transforming inedible parts of plants into food. They say astronauts may want to grow plants for food on long-term missions, and it would be handy if they could utilize the cellulose in the plants.

Cellulose also contains glucose, so why not just turn wood or corn husks into sugar? Zhang says he wants to create a healthier food product that wouldn't cause blood sugar levels to rise and fall. He would like to develop a slow-metabolized sugar like starch so that humans can keep blood glucose levels nearly constant. That's especially important these days, given that the modern diet, high in sugar, is contributing to the risk of developing diabetes and other chronic diseases.

One company, Ingredion, which has developed all kinds of products from corn, tapioca, wheat, potatoes and other raw materials, is already turning the cellulose in the husks of genetically modified corn into edible products. But Zhang says his process is unique because he can use any kind of biomass, and he can convert it efficiently.

He thinks his starch might be useful as a low-calorie, easily digestible coating to transform the texture of other food products. For example, Zhang says, his powder could be subbed in for bread crumbs to coat and fry chicken. But in the long term, he hopes that this kind of technology will allow humans to turn to cellulose as a food source if and when traditional agriculture is up against more severe resource limitations.

Currently the production of starch made from wood or corn husks is too costly. Enzymes, in particular, are expensive and unstable. But Zhang says he's confident that the cost will come down. If this technology does eventually make it to market, it wouldn't be the first time that many of us would have eaten products derived from cellulose. Turns out, the food industry has already figured out that you don't even need to convert cellulose into starch to eat it.

Cellulose products are commonly used as an additive in processed foods to improve consistency and mouthfeel and to add bulk in products such as salad dressings, Wendy's

Frosty milkshakes, KFC popcorn chicken and ice cream. But unlike Zhang's invention, this cellulose doesn't provide useful nutrients. It just passes through the body. Like fat, cellulose can also help keep food moist, making it a popular substitute for oil or butter in low-fat baked goods, according to the Mayo Clinic.[7]

Imagine being able to do something like a beaver, moose, rabbit, porcupine or even a termite - utilizing enzymes from other living organisms to make starch out of trees. If through the evolutionary eons of time or guidance from Mother Nature, who focuses on the life-giving and nurturing aspects of earth, can change trees into starch – why not man? This new technology could be a paradigm shift fundamentally changing famine to food in abundance for all mankind. World starvation might someday become one of the least problems we face in our society. I excitedly looked for more information on this 2013 report and found little.

Then I googled Percival Zhang and my enthusiasm for advances in this new technology was cooled: "U.S. Attorney's Office, Western District of Virginia, Roanoke, Virginia 09/09/2019 – Yiheng Percival Zhang, a former Virginia Tech professor studying artificial sweeteners, was sentenced last week in U.S. District Court to time served, which included incarceration for approximately three months, and home incarceration for approximately two years, First Assistant United States Attorney Daniel P. Bubar announced today. Zhang was convicted of committing federal grant fraud, making false statements and obstruction by falsification following a bench trial in September 2018. Zhang, 47, of Blacksburg, Va., was found guilty of one count of conspiracy to defraud the United States, three counts of making false statements, and one count of obstruction by falsification."

In MIT Technology Review dated 04/11/2022, Mark Harrisarchive wrote: "Sugar will be the new oil," Zhang's email signature at Virginia Tech once pronounced. But Zhang today isn't sitting proudly at the helm of Bonumose's research division, or formulating healthy chocolate, or racing a sugar-powered car. When MIT Technology Review spoke to him in January, he was sitting alone in an empty lab in Tianjin, China, after serving a two-year sentence of supervised release in Virginia for conspiracy to defraud the US government, making false statements, and obstruction of justice. He still seems dazed from his dealings with Rogers—his former business partner—and the US government. If you ask Zhang, he was guilty of nothing worse than poor judgment and ignorance of the rules; he sees himself as a man brought low by treachery. "They cheated the technology from me. They robbed me and took everything," he says.

Turn an ear to Bonumose, however, and it's about the triumph of American entrepreneurship over the Communist government of China. "We did not cheat anyone," Rogers told MIT Technology Review. "Even though we had this pretty bitter battle with Zhang, we don't wish him any ill will at this point. Maybe he wants to blame someone other than himself, but he should look in the mirror."

Whichever version hews closest to the truth, one thing seems clear. If sugar is the new oil, the global battle to control it has already begun.

I wonder if maybe more could be getting accomplished solving world hunger if the government and Bonumose hadn't taken another approach for handling Zhang's dilemma:

In the Renlund's story about Farmer Paavo they stated, "Finally, Paavo harvested a rich crop. Overjoyed, his wife said, 'Paavo, Paavo, these are happy times! It is time to throw away the bark and bake bread made only with the rye.' But Paavo took his wife's hand and said, 'Woman, mix half the flour with bark, for our neighbor's fields have frosted over.' Left unstated in the poem was Paavo's intent to help his devastated, destitute neighbor…

I don't think the poem ending being left out was to try to get us to sleep. I think that my father was teaching us that charitable giving is something we do because of our humanity. It is something we do because we care about our fellow human beings. The poem invites us to ask ourselves, 'What would we do if we were in Paavo's shoes? Would we help this unfortunate neighbor? Would we, in the future, help others in need?… What do you think the Apostle Paul means by 'a more excellent way'? I think 'a more excellent way' was charity. Paul says that rather than seeking specific spiritual gifts, even though that would be helpful, 'a more excellent way' was to develop a very specific characteristic or quality that is referred to as charity. The word charity derives from the Greek word agape. Agape has been used as a verb in Greek from Homeric times. It does not mean brotherly love, erotic love, or the kind of love I have for chocolate. It does not mean giving alms, although a desire to do so stems from it. In the Greek, agape means open, or a gape, tolerance, fairness, and kindness. The King James

Version of the Bible translates agape as charity. In other versions of the Bible it is translated as love."6 And love and charity never fails (1 Corinthians 13:4-5, 7-8).

Just maybe if Zhang was still employed at Bonumose's research division, working with his business partner Rogers, and making progress synthesizing starch from trees while he served his Forrest Gump "stupid is as stupid does" debt to society in the United States – I might have had better luck finding more recent research on producing starch from trees to help save the world. Maybe some tolerance, fairness and kindness (charity) from all sides may have been a much better approach for everyone involved.

For example think about Operation Paperclip the secret United States intelligence program in which more than 1,600 German scientists, engineers, and technicians were taken from former Nazi Germany to the U.S. for government employment after the end of World War II in Europe, between 1945–59. Some were former members and leaders of the Nazi Party.

The effort began in earnest in 1945, as the Allies advanced into Germany and discovered a wealth of scientific talent and advanced research that had contributed to Germany's wartime technological advancements. The U.S. Joint Chiefs of Staff officially established Operation Overcast on July 20, 1945, with the dual aim of leveraging German expertise to assist in the ongoing war effort against Japan, and to bolster U.S. postwar military research.

The operation was characterized by the recruitment of German specialists, along with their families, bringing the total to more than 6,000 relocated to the US for their expertise, valued at US$10 billion in patents and industrial processes. These recruits included notable figures such as Wernher von Braun, a leading scientist in rocket technology, and were instrumental in the development of the U.S. space program and military technology during the Cold War. *Wikipedia*

Also, that empty lab in Tianjin, China might eventually bustle with activity and produce a bundle of patents on producing starch from trees as well winning the "global war to control sugar." There was an expressed feeling that what was done to Zhang was a triumph of American entrepreneurship to control global sugar over the Communist government of China. It might turn out that we should have kept him in the US to continue his research. We just may have cheated ourselves out of winning the "global war to control sugar."

Despite Operation Paperclip in 1945-59 contributions to American scientific advances, it has been controversial due to the Nazi affiliations of many recruits, and the ethical implications of assimilating individuals associated with war crimes into American society. What a mistake it would have been if the US hadn't responded the way it did.

1– *Discover 5 Animals That Eat Tree Bark, AZ Animals, Cammi Morgan, 01/03/2024.*

2– *Why Do Animals Eat the Bark and Wood of Trees and Shrubs? William R. Chaney, Professor of Tree Physiology, Dept. Forestry & Natural Resources, Purdue University, FNR-203.*

3– *Deer Need a Little "Tough Love" in Winter, Jim Knight, Montana State University, Extension Wildlife Specialist.*

4– *Jamie, Categories Trees, WhyFarmIt.com.*

5– *The Bark Bread That Resulted From A Widespread Scandinavian Famine, Natasha Bailey, 02/07/2023.*

6– *Transcript: Elder and Sister Renlund at 2016 BYU Women's Conference, "One in Charity", BYU Women's Conference, 04/29/2016.*

7– *Let Them Eat Wood! (If It's Turned Into Starch), NPR-The Salt, Eliza Barclay, 06/05/2013.*

CHAPTER 14

COPPER THOUGHTS

Dr Douglus G. Adler writes about seeing a patient in the ED. The patient, Chad, was calmly sitting up on a stretcher, surrounded by a group of trendy-looking young adults. He was a 20-year-old man who had been brought to the hospital by some of his college classmates. Chad was dressed casually in jeans and a T-shirt, and he obviously needed a shave and a shower. His hair stuck out of at odd angles clearly not having been combed for some time. He presented a stark contrast to his well-dressed and groomed friends.

Chad himself did not have what physicians call a "chief complaint," or a specific reason for coming to the doctor. Rather, his friends convinced him to come with them to the ED because they were worried about his recent odd behavior. Chad, however, insisted to me that he felt fine.

Chad's roommate, reported that he was experiencing sudden behavioral changes. He used to be a straight-A student, but now he mostly skipped class. He had started siting still for long stretches of time without moving, while at other times he appeared to have boundless energy, staying up all night reading voraciously or listening to music- and then going out for a long run as soon as the sun came up.

Meanwhile, a tearful young woman in the group said that, until just a few weeks ago, she had been Chad's girlfriend. They used to be very close, almost inseparable, but a few weeks ago he started to become very irritable as if everything she said bothered him. She described how Chad abruptly became distant and appeared to lose all interest in dating – or anyone else. They ended up breaking up because of it.

The emergency physician had already ordered routine bloodwork by the time Dr Alder and Chad wanted to leave as soon as possible. He was convinced to stay until his tests came back. The physical exam was unremarkable; he looked like a healthy young man. What's more, his bloodwork showed that he was not under the influence of any drugs or alcohol. Most of his lab results were entirely normal except for his liver function tests (LFTs), which were all slightly elevated.

The ability to accurately analyze LFTs is a skill that most physicians acquire slowly, over years of practice. There are many different patterns of injury that this handful of blood test results can indicate. Is the source of the abnormal blood test the liver, the gallbladder (which sits underneath the liver), or the bile ducts? The pattern of LFT's can help diagnose all of these things.

The tests themselves measure whether certain types of liver cells are breaking open and leaking their contents into the blood stream, as well as the extent that the liver is failing to metabolize toxins in the body. These markers can inform physicians whether the liver is inflamed, infected, harboring a tumor or on the edge of organ failure. LFTs can also often distinguish between a healthy liver and a diseased one in a patient with cirrhosis, or if someone is suffering from inadequate blood flow, among other maladies.

Chad's LFTs did not fit any of the typical patterns normally seen in most patients with liver disease; he was not jaundiced, didn't appear to have an infection and didn't show obvious signs of cirrhosis. Dr Alder mentioned that the lab results stirred his memory when, but he couldn't quite put his finger on it.

After getting the blood test results back, the ER physician told Dr Alder he was going to let Chad be discharged. He could not think of a reason to keep him in the hospital. And people are allowed to be strange. Dr Alder went back into Chad's room to meet with him again. He was bent over and putting his shoes on, but as he started to speak, he looked up. Dr Alder caught a view of his eyes that he had not previously noticed, since he had been sitting up and looking towards the floor. That's when Dr Alder noticed Chad had a ring of dark, golden-brown coloring around the corneas in both eyes. Instantly, it hit him – Chad had Wilson's disease.

Fortunately, Chad's case had not progressed that far. A dietician educated him on how to avoid copper-rich foods, including nuts, certain meats and shellfish, among others. Chad was also started on a drug (d-penicillamine), to actively remove copper from his body.

During a follow-up visit a month later, blood tests showed that Chad's copper levels had started to normalize. Chad was clearly embarrassed about how unusually he had been acting; he said that it was difficult to think about all that he had said and done in the weeks leading up to his diagnosis. His then-former (and now-current) girlfriend accompanied him and told me that he was behaving more like his old self. She was keeping a close eye on him to make sure that he was compliant with his new diet and dedication regimen. After everything, he had taken a semester off from school to recover.

Chad would need to watch his diet and would likely stay on copper-lowering medications for life. It was fortunate that the correct diagnosis was made before things got to the point where he needed an emergency liver transplant – Chad was grateful to start feeling like himself again.[1]

Copper plays a key role in the development of healthy nerves, bones, collagen and the skin pigment melanin. It is an essential trace element that is used as a cofactor in many redox reactions, including mitochondrial oxidative phosphorylation, free radical detoxification, neurotransmitter formation, pigment synthesis, connective tissue synthesis, and iron metabolism. Normally, copper is absorbed from food, and excess amounts are excreted through a substance produced in your liver (bile). But in people with the rare inherited disorder of Wilson's disease, copper isn't eliminated properly and instead accumulates in the body, possibly to a life-threatening level. When diagnosed early, Wilson's disease is treatable, and many people with the disorder live normal lives. Most people are diagnosed between the ages of 5 and 35.

Wilson's disease is present at birth, but signs and symptoms don't appear until the copper builds up in the brain, liver or other organs. Signs and symptoms vary depending on the parts of your body affected by the disease. They can include fatigue, lack of appetite or abdominal pain, a yellowing of the skin and the whites of the eye (jaundice), golden-brown eye discoloration (Kayser-Fleischer rings), fluid buildup in the legs or abdomen, problems with speech, swallowing or physical coordination, and uncontrolled movements or muscle stiffness.

Wilson's disease is inherited as an autosomal recessive trait, which means that to develop the disease you must inherit one copy of the defective gene from each parent. If you receive only one abnormal gene, you won't become ill yourself, but you're a carrier and can pass the gene to your children. You can be at increased risk of Wilson's disease if your parents or siblings have the condition. Genetic testing can be used to detect Wilson's disease. Diagnosing the condition as early as possible dramatically increases the chances of successful treatment.

Untreated, Wilson's disease can be fatal. Serious complications include: Scarring of the liver (cirrhosis). As liver cells heal from the damage done by excess copper, scar tissue forms in the liver, making it more difficult for the liver to function.

Liver failure can occur suddenly (acute liver failure), or it can develop slowly over years. A liver transplant might be a treatment option. There also might be destruction of red blood cells (hemolysis) leading to anemia and jaundice.

Persistent neurological tremors, involuntary muscle movements, clumsy gait and speech difficulties usually improve with treatment for Wilson's disease. Despite treatment, some people have persistent neurological difficulties, including psychological problems such as personality changes, depression, irritability, bipolar disorders or psychosis.

Wilson's disease can also damage the kidneys, leading to problems such as kidney stones and an abnormal number of amino acids (proteins) excreted in the urine.

Diagnosing Wilson's disease can be challenging because its signs and symptoms are often hard to tell from those of other liver diseases, such as hepatitis. Also, symptoms can evolve over time. Behavioral changes that come on gradually can be especially hard to link to Wilson's. Doctors rely on a combination of symptoms and test results to make the diagnosis:

Blood tests can monitor liver function, check the level of a protein that binds copper in the blood (ceruloplasmin) and the level of copper in your blood. The amount of copper excreted in the urine can also be monitored.

Using a microscope with a high-intensity light source (slit lamp), an ophthalmologist checks for Kayser-Fleischer rings, which are caused by excess copper in the eyes. Wilson's disease also is associated with a type of cataract, called a sunflower cataract, that can be seen on an eye exam.

Removing a sample of liver tissue for testing (biopsy) is obtained by placing a needle into the liver and laboratory tests of the tissue looks for excess copper. Excess copper found in the liver and genetic testing for mutations that cause Wilson's disease are confirmative tests. Genetic screening is also valuable in identify siblings in order to begin treatment before symptoms arise. *Mayo Clinic Staff*

Low amounts of copper are found in foods such as animal liver, crustaceans, shellfish, green vegetables, dried fruit, nuts, and chocolate. High levels of copper can cause toxicity, often secondary to exposure to pesticides, fungicides, copper-contaminated pipe water and water treatment systems.

A 12-month-old female with no significant medical history presented to the ED with listlessness four days following one day of resolved gastrointestinal symptoms. Her symptoms began after ingestion of birthday cake with rose-gold frosting from a local bakery, the consumption of which led to copper toxicity.

Within 20 minutes of cake consumption, the patient experienced six episodes of non-bloody, non-bilious vomiting and several episodes of non-bloody diarrhea. Multiple other guests developed similar symptoms that resolved after several hours. The patient saw her pediatrician, who suspected a foodborne illness or other toxic exposure and called the regional poison control center, which in turn involved the Department of Health (DOH). The DOH found that only guests who ate frosted cake developed vomiting or diarrhea.

Guests who did not eat the cake or ate cake without frosting had no symptoms. The DOH did not report the discovery of bacteria or other infectious agents. The DOH conducted an investigation into the bakery. The cake had been frosted with a rose-gold luster dust labeled "non-edible non-toxic for decoration only" that was mixed into a butter extract and painted onto the cake. The results were released four days later confirming that the patient and guests were exposed to copper toxicity from the cake.

Prior studies on copper toxicity have focused on copper salt ingestions, such as copper sulfate. Elemental copper ingestions, such as in coin ingestions, usually do not cause toxicity unless in an acidic environment when elemental copper can transform into reactive copper ions. There have been prior copper toxicity cases in the setting of consuming beverages exposed to copper-contaminated bottle pourers, boilers, and cocktail shakers. At this time there were no published cases of copper powder ingestion causing toxicity. This patient case is therefore the first documented case of elemental copper powder ingestion causing toxicity in humans.[2]

A 2-year-old girl was presented to the ED after mother witnessed her swallowing a penny. Abdominal radiograph showed a round metallic 19 mm object at the left upper quadrant, confirming a penny in the stomach. Given no symptoms and normal physical examination, family was instructed to observe for abdominal signs, to strain stool and repeat an abdominal radiograph in 2 weeks.

Over the following 2 weeks, the patient developed intermittent abdominal pain with decreased appetite. Serial abdominal radiographs showed persistence of the object in the left upper quadrant. However, the last radiograph showed an irregular appearance of the object's periphery, more lucent than the prior studies. The decision was made to proceed with upper endoscopy with foreign body removal. A 1989-minted penny with scalloped edges and multiple small metallic pieces.

On the basis of a clinical report of the NASPGHAN Endoscopy Committee on management of ingested foreign body, gastric coins are managed expectantly unless overt gastrointestinal (GI) symptoms are noted, regardless of coin type. However, zinc toxicity from pennies in the stomach is reported. Concern is particularly focused on pennies minted after 1982; these have significantly increased composition of zinc from 5% pre-1982 to 97.6% post-1982, and are coated by only a thin layer of copper. After ingestion, the chemical reaction between gastric acid and post-1982 pennies starts within a few hours, with radiographic changes, such as scalloped edge and erosions visible within 24 hours.

After the copper shell is eroded, zinc reacts with gastric acid and forms zinc chloride, which is corrosive, highly absorbable and toxic. Locally, zinc chloride can cause corrosive injury resulting in nausea, vomiting, abdominal pain, ulcerations, and bleeding. Once absorbed, systemic symptoms can occur because of the high levels of zinc and associated copper deficiency. Systemic symptoms include anemia, leukopenia, pancreatitis, hepatic necrosis, liver and kidney dysfunction, or even death from multisystem organ failure.[3]

According to petMD 2008, copper storage hepatopathy (also called Wilson's disease because the disease is similar to that found in people) is a condition caused by an abnormal accumulation of copper in the animal's liver, which leads to progressive damage and scarring of the liver (cirrhosis). This condition may be secondary to a primary disease or the result of genetic-based abnormal copper metabolism. Bedlington terriers, Doberman pinschers, West Highland White terriers, Skye terriers, and Labrador retrievers are dog breeds known to be susceptible to this disease. Copper storage hepatopathy is more prevalent in females than in males. It also can be found in cats.

Acute and chronic liver disease may show symptoms of: Lethargy, vomiting, anorexia/weight loss, depression, vomiting, icterus or jaundice, anemia, dark urine due to the presence of bilirubin (bile), blood in the urine (hemoglobinuria), diarrhea, excessive thirst, abdominal distention from fluid buildup (ascites), bloody stool, and neurological symptoms.

Most research on Wilson's disease in dogs has been done with Bedlington Terriers. Camden Pet Hospital had a client, Mrs. Batt, who loved the breed. She insisted on "trying another one", even though facing the possibility of chronic liver disease treatment or death of her pets.

Selective breeding programs in the Netherlands has decreased the prevalence of Bedlington Terrier copper-associated liver disease from 46% (1976-1986) to 11% (1990-1997). DNA testing for Wilson's disease is now available. However, liver biopsy for quantitative copper and morphologic examination remains the best option for diagnosis in the individual dog.[4]

We all know good nutrition is critical for the health and longevity of our dogs, and most of us rely on commercial dog foods to help us achieve that. Now, what if we told you those complete-and-balanced diets — the quality food you've carefully chosen for your dog — may be slowly killing them?

It's true, says Dr. Sharon Center, the James Law Professor of Internal Medicine at Cornell University's College of Veterinary Medicine (CVM). Center is nationally renowned for her expertise in liver diseases of dogs and cats. She says the excess amount of the essential trace mineral copper in commercial dog food can cause a serious, potentially lethal illness called dietary-induced copper-associated hepatopathy (CAH). The incidence of CAH (also known as copper storage disease and Wilson's disease) is increasing at a rate that's causing alarm among veterinarians and dog owners, with one study showing that 30% of canine liver biopsies have evidence of CAH.

CAH is no longer considered just a disease of predisposed breeds like Bedlington Terriers, Labrador Retrievers, Dalmatians, Dobermans and Westies. First, it can happen to any dog, and it is expected to happen more and more if copper levels in dog foods remain too high. Second, it can be actively happening in the liver of a dog showing no outward signs of illness.

CAH occurs when the amount of dietary copper ingested exceeds a dog's tolerance level and accumulates in the liver. Once in the liver, it can cause acute, severe liver inflammation with immediate, disastrous consequences, or it can cause chronic, insidious damage over time, resulting in widespread scarring of the liver (cirrhosis) and liver failure. Symptoms of CAH are similar to Wilson's disease in humans: Abdominal swelling, decreased appetite, diarrhea, increased thirst, jaundice, lethargy, and vomiting.

Joseph J. Wakshlag, DVM, Ph.D, professor of clinical nutrition and of sports medicine and rehabilitation noted that CAH may very well be related to a lack of safe upper limits of consumption and higher than expected levels in dog foods. Right now, the recommendation for the amount of copper in a dog food is 7.3 mg/kg (milligrams per kilogram), but that means little to the average consumer because the copper level is rarely listed on your dog's food label. Currently, there is no maximum limit for copper in dog's food. At one point, there was, but that was eliminated when the recommended type of copper used in dog foods was changed to a more bioavailable form. Why the limit was eliminated is not clear, but the results most certainly are.

Like humans, treatment for CAH usually includes administration of an oral copper-chelating agent (a compound that binds to copper to help remove it) called d-penicillamine. Dogs with CAH are also fed a copper-restricted diet to prevent further copper accumulation in the liver. Antioxidants like vitamin E and SAMe (S-adenosyl-methionine) are recommended as supplements.

It can take many months of treatment for the liver damage to resolve. Repeat liver biopsies are the only definitive way to determine how the affected dog is doing. Because this is an expensive proposition — and most of us don't want our dogs undergoing multiple invasive surgical procedures — progress is usually monitored with sequential ALT liver function blood tests. All affected dogs should be fed copper-restricted diets for life, and some dogs will require chronic, low-dose chelation therapy.[5]

While gold and silver are irrefutably the most well-known of the 95 metals in the Periodic Table of Elements, to metallurgists and metal connoisseurs, they are nothing out of the ordinary. The real icon in the world of metals is copper, and for a number of good reasons. Copper is believed to be the first metal humans discovered, dating back to 10,000 years ago. Even before rulers of the first empires wore golden crowns and accessories, copper was already widely utilized for cookware, work tools, and fittings.

It has many properties that are useful for a vast array of structural and decorative applications. copper is prized for its many useful properties:

- Copper is a malleable and ductile metal. It can be hammered or rolled into thin sheets and drawn into small wires without breaking. It can be made less pliable and durable by combining it with zinc or lead.

– Copper has high electrical and heat conductivity. Silver is the only metal that is more electrically conductive than copper, but its heat resistance is not as good.

– Copper oxidizes by developing a protective layer on its surface, called patina. The longer the exposure, the tougher the patina gets. This green layer of protection can preserve the inside of copper for thousands of years.

– Copper is also one of the few metals that can produce the oligodynamic effect, a phenomenon in which ions of copper break down certain proteins that make up single-celled organisms, killing or resisting bacteria, mold or mildew.

– Over 80 percent of all the copper ever mined and manufactured are still in use today, and they are all recyclable.

Copper anniversaries are celebrated for the seventh or the twenty-second year of marriage. Copper is a traditional gift for these anniversaries because it symbolizes prosperity, good luck, and good fortune.

Copper is a durable and sturdy metal that has been used for thousands of years. It has a reddish orange color that corrodes to give it a patina.

Hopefully copper in your life will not be tarnished by:

– Marrying into a family that has defective DNA for Wilson's disease.

- Celebrating by eating a cake laced with toxic copper.
- Having the miss fortune of swallowing a post-1982 dated copper penny that doesn't pass out of the stomach.
- Have a dog that is genetically sensitive to copper or has been fed with excess laced copper from a "complete and balanced" commercially nutritious diet.

Makes me wonder is I should back off eating so many nuts that nutritionists promote – supposedly to help me live into my 100s maintaining good brain plasticity and eliminating brain fog. You Betcha!

Just because there's tarnish on the copper, doesn't mean there's not a shine beneath. Laurence Yep

1– *A Penny for Your Thoughts, Douglas G. Adler, Science Magazine, Nov/Dec 2023.*

2– *A Case Report of Cake Frosting as a Source of Copper Toxicity in a Pediatric Patient, Clin Pract Cases Emerg Med: 4(3): 384-388. 08/02/2020.*

3– *Penny Ingestion: Can We Really Manage Expectantly? Journal of Pediatric Gastroenterology & Nutrition, 09/2020.*

4– *In r, 2013*

5– *The looming concern about copper in dog food: Copper overload is quietly killing our dogs, Cornell University, College of Veterinary Medicine, 01/28/2022.*

CHAPTER 15

WE DON'T HAVE TO THINK TO HELP OTHERS; JUST LET YOUR ANIMAL SELVES EXPRESS THEMSELVES

The act of helping others out of empathy (feeling of awareness) and feelings of compassion (emotional response to empathy or sympathy and creates a desire to respond) has long been associated strictly with humans and other primates, but new research shows that rats exhibit this prosocial behavior as well. Laboratory rats have been shown repeatedly to freed their cage-mates from containers, even though there was no clear reward for doing so. The rodents didn't bother opening empty containers or those holding stuffed rats.

To the researchers' surprise, when presented with both a rat-holding container and a one containing chocolate — the rats' favorite snack — the rodents not only chose to open both containers, but also to share the treats with those they liberated.

Peggy Mason, a neuroscientist at the University of Chicago and lead author of the study, says the research shows that our empathy and impulse to help others are common across other mammals.

"Helping is our evolutionary inheritance," Mason told LiveScience. "Our study suggests that we don't have to cognitively decide to help an individual in distress; rather, we just have to let our animal selves express themselves."[1]

"If you want others to be happy, practice compassion. If you want to be happy, practice compassion." These words from the Dalai Lama are instructive because they refer to the emotional benefits of compassion to both the giver and recipient. In other words, the rewards of practicing compassion work both ways. But what exactly is meant by 'compassion?' Various definitions of compassion have been proposed by researchers and philosophers. For example, in his detailed review, Cassell (2009) reported the following three requirements for compassion:

1– "That the troubles that evoke our feelings are serious;"

2– "that the 'sufferers' troubles not be self-inflicted— that they be the result of an unjust fate;" and

3– "we must be able to picture ourselves in the same predicament."

As such, compassion is not an automatic response to another's plight; it is a response that occurs only when the situation is perceived as serious, unjust and relatable. It requires a certain level of awareness, concern and empathy.

Consistent with the above definition, seeing a homeless man on the sidewalk will register differently depending upon how this situation is uniquely perceived by passersby. The amount of compassion elicited by others will be dependent upon how serious his situation is deemed, as well as the perceived degree of fault attributed to him for his predicament.

This example is pertinent to a quote that is prevalent in studies of compassion: "Make no judgments where you have no compassion." Judging a person's predicament in the absence of compassion amounts to little more than judgment. Compassion can be painful to feel because it requires empathy for others, but it is also necessary because it evokes positive action.

Psychologists are also interested in the role of compassion towards oneself. When individuals view their own behaviors and shortcomings without compassion, they may ruminate about their faults and inadequacies in such a way that erodes self-esteem and happiness. Because of the importance of self-kindness and -forgiveness to mental health, the concept of 'self-compassion' is occurring more often in the psychological literature. Self-compassion has been defined as involving "self-kindness versus self-judgment; a sense of common humanity versus isolation, and mindfulness versus overidentification." It is a way of recognizing one's inability to be perfect and to see oneself from a comforting rather than critical perspective. Self-compassion is gaining popularity in psychology because of its reported relationships with reduced feelings of anxiety, depression, and rumination, as well as increased psychological wellbeing and connections with others. As research emerges suggesting that self-compassion represents an important protective mechanism, increased numbers of psychological interventions are including self-compassion as a key treatment component.

The field of positive psychology "is founded on the belief that people want to lead meaningful and fulfilling lives, to cultivate what is best within themselves, and to enhance their experiences of love, work, and play." It is a field that encompasses an array of positive experiences such as contentment, optimism, and happiness which cover past, present and future timepoints; as well as individual and group level traits. Considering positive psychology's focus on the promotion of positive emotions, traits, and behaviors that ultimately foster positive wellbeing; the study of compassion fits in well with the interests of positive psychologists. The role of compassion in positive psychology is being increasingly supported by science.[2]

In previous studies, researchers found that rodents show the simplest form of empathy, called emotional contagion — a phenomenon where one individual's emotions spread to others nearby. For example, a crying baby will trigger the other babies in a room to cry as well. Likewise, rats will become distressed when they see other rats in distress, or they will display pain behavior if they see other rats in pain.

For the new study, Mason and her colleagues wanted to see if rats could go beyond emotional contagion and actively help other rats in distress. To do so, the rats would have to suppress their natural responses to the "emotions" of other rats, the result of emotional contagion. They have to down-regulate their natural reaction to freeze in fear in order to actively help the other rat.

The researchers began their study by housing rats in pairs for two weeks, allowing the rodents to create a bond with one another. In each test session, they placed a rat pair into a walled arena; one rat was allowed to roam free while the other was locked in a closed, transparent tube that could only be opened from the outside.

The free rat was initially wary of the container in the middle of the arena, but once it got over the fear it picked up from its cage-mate, it slowly began to test out the cage. After an average seven days of daily experiments, the free rat learned it could release its friend by nudging the container door open. Over time, the rat began releasing its cage-mate almost immediately after being placed into the arena.

When the free rat opened the door, he knows exactly what he's doing. He knows that the trapped rat is going to get free. "It's deliberate, purposeful, helping behavior."

The researchers then conducted other tests to make sure empathy was the driving force in the rats' behavior. In one experiment, they rigged the container so that opening the door would release the captive rat into a separate arena. The free rat repeatedly set its cage-mate free, even though there was no reward of social interaction afterwards. This is selfless behavior like humans and chimps show.[1]

Police in Warwickshire, England, opened a garden shed and found a whimpering, cowering dog. The dog had been locked in the shed and abandoned. It was dirty and malnourished, and had quite clearly been abused. In an act of kindness, the police took the dog, which a female greyhound, to the Nuneaton Warwickshire Wildlife Sanctuary, which is run by a man named Geoff Grewcock, and known as a haven for animals abandoned, orphaned, or otherwise in need. Geoff and the other sanctuary staff went to work with two aims... to restore the dog to full health, and to win her trust. It took several weeks, but eventually both goals were achieved. They named her Jasmine, and they started to think about finding her an adoptive home.

Jasmine, however, had other ideas. No one quite remembers how it came about, but Jasmine started welcoming all animal arrivals at the sanctuary. It would not matter if it were a puppy, a fox cub, a rabbit or any other lost or hurting animal. Jasmine would just peer into the box or cage and, when and where possible, deliver a welcoming lick.

Geoff relates one of the early incidents. "We had two puppies that had been abandoned by a nearby railway line. One was a Lakeland Terrier cross and another was a Jack Russell Doberman cross. They were tiny when they arrived at the center, and Jasmine approached them and grabbed one by the scruff of the neck in her mouth and put him on the settee. Then she fetched the other one and sat down with them, cuddling them."

"But she is like that with all of our animals, even the rabbits. She takes all the stress out of them, and it helps them to not only feel close to her, but to settle into their new surroundings. She has done the same with the fox and badger cubs, she licks the rabbits and guinea pigs, and even lets the birds perch on the bridge of her nose."

Jasmine, the timid, abused, deserted waif, became the animal sanctuary's resident surrogate mother... a role for which she might have been born. The list of orphaned and abandoned youngsters she has cared for comprises five fox cubs, four badger cubs, fifteen chicks, eight guinea pigs, two stray puppies and fifteen rabbits... and one roe deer fawn. Tiny Bramble, eleven weeks old, was found semi-conscious in a field. Upon arrival at the sanctuary, Jasmine cuddled up to her to keep her warm, and then went into the full foster-mum role. Jasmine, the greyhound, showers Bramble, the roe deer, with affection and makes sure nothing is matted.

"They are inseparable," says Geoff. "Bramble walks between her legs, and they keep kissing each other. They walk together round the sanctuary. It's a real treat to see them." Jasmine will continue to care for Bramble until she is old enough to be returned to woodland life. When that happens, Jasmine will not be lonely. She will be too busy showering love, affection and showing compassion for the next orphan or victim of abuse.

Pictured from the left are: "Toby," a stray Lakeland dog; "Bramble," orphaned roe deer; "Buster," a stray Jack Russell; a dumped rabbit; "Sky," an injured barn owl; and "Jasmine," with a mother's heart doing best what a caring mother would do... and such is the order of God's Creation...[3]

Each of us in our own way can try to spread compassion into people's hearts. Western civilizations these days place great importance on filling the human 'brain' with knowledge, but no one seems to care about filling the human 'heart' with compassion. This is what the real role of religion is. Dalai Lama

    1– *Empathetic Rats Help Each Other Out, LiveScience, by Joseph Castro, 12/08/2011.*

    2– *Positive Psychology, The Concept of Compassion in Psychology, Heather S. Lonczak, Ph.D., 06/06/2019.*

    3– *A Love Story, this greyhound could teach mankind a huge lesson, Blanche, received Oct 22, 2014.*

CHAPTER 16

FRESH WATER

During the summers of 1963 through 1965 I worked with my future father-in-law, Ivan Gardner, on his farm. Some of his crops were watered by flood irrigation from canals fed by the Snake River near Blackfoot Idaho, and the rest came from wells sunk deep enough to tap water from the Snake River Plain Aquifer. When standing near one of his shut off wells on his Rising River Farm you could hear water rushing sounds. Ivan told me that the well was tapping an area deep in the ground that had a continuous water supply like a river. He also told me not to turn on the well to get a drink of water because it cost, as I remember, about $50 to start up the pump.

At the time I didn't know what the term aquifer or how large or deep the Snake River Plain Aquifer was lying beneath that well. The most productive part of this aquifer is the upper 300-500 feet, where ground water flows the most rapidly (the total thickness of the aquifer is estimated to be more than 5,000 feet). Ivan's son Lance recently told me that when Ivan bought the Rising River Farm he had the depth of the well increased. From the early 60s until this day every time the well is started it still produces water.

The Snake River Plain Aquifer covers a significant portion of southern Idaho. It is about the size of Lake Erie, covering about 10,000 square miles of Idaho, starting near the Wyoming border. It's fed by streams coming out of mountain ranges. The water and snowmelt seeps underground into a network of cracks and crannies of rock. It is a saturated network of fractures, mainly within basalt, in these lava flows. The best way to think of it is an interconnected series of pores (like a sponge) created by the Yellowstone Hotspot.

The water can take 200 to 300 years to move through this 150 milelong sponge. But it's not a uniform process. Water flows in some areas, stops in others, pooling in the cracks.

Some of the spring water coming out of the rocks in a canyon at the western end of the aquifer yield as much as 180,000 gallons of water a minute. Thousand Springs water empties into the Snake River just south of Hagerman Idaho on US30 after first passing through a power plant or a fish hatchery. If a single drop of water starting at the northeastern edge of the aquifer made it all the way here, it would be in the neighborhood of 150 to 200 years.

No one knows how much water is in the aquifer -- it's hard to measure a sponge. But the Department of Water Resources does know that about 7.5 million-acre feet of water is moving through the aquifer every year. And they know that amount is dropping. There's been a moratorium on the issuance of new water rights across the eastern Snake River Plain since 1992. Growing cities, if they run out of water, have to buy an old right. Buying an old right means some farm or company goes out of business. That has put the brakes on growth. As farmers switched from flood irrigation to sprinklers in the 1950s, less water seeped back into the aquifer. That, along with the drilling of new wells, power generation needs and climate change has all contributed to a shrinking aquifer.

Currently, an agreement for groundwater users on the Snake River Plain collectively are to reduce their groundwater use by 240,000 acre feet a year. That will stop the decline of the aquifer but it won't stop the growing demand for water. The state will recharge 250,000 acre feet a year.[1]

"Water wars" describes conflicts between countries, states, or groups over the right to access water resources, usually freshwater. Freshwater is necessary for drinking, irrigation, and electricity generation, and conflicts occur when the demand for potable water exceeds the supply, or when allocation or control of water is disputed.

The first known war over water took place between the Sumerian states of Lagash and Umma around 2500 BCE. A dispute over the Gu'edena (edge of paradise) region of Mesopotamia led Urlama, King of Lagash, to divert water, thus depriving Umma. Urlama's son II followed in his father's footsteps and he cut off the water supply to Girsu, a city in Umma. Today, the world's exploding population and climate change are the two main factors that are igniting water wars.

According to the Centers for Disease Control and Prevention (CDC), an estimated 790 million people, or 11 percent of the world's population, don't have access to clean drinking water. Ninety-six percent of the Earth's freshwater is contained in underground aquifers, while the remaining four percent is in streams, lakes, rivers, and wetlands. Satellite images have shown that groundwater depletion is occurring in arid and semi-arid portions of the world. Flashpoints can develop if those upstream take water from their downstream neighbors, or, since aquifers cross boundaries, if neighbors pump more than their fair share of groundwater.

Water laws in the U.S. conform to four major legal principles: "First in time, first in right" - this "prior appropriation" doctrine is used in most U.S. states, and it says that the first one to claim and begin using water is guaranteed as much of it as he or she needs for as long as it's needed; a related doctrine is called "Use it or lose it." In her 2019 book *Downriver: Into the Future of Water in the West*, Heather Hansman stated that between 2000 and 2014, inflow into the Colorado River decreased by almost 20 percent, with around one-third of that due to global warming. Hansman wrote, "Between evaporation, reduced inflow, and increased use, the West is sucking itself dry." When burgeoning cities in the Southwest want more water, they use their large municipal coffers to purchase water from agricultural users, in a process known as "buy and dry." Water that once nourished crops now pours out of shower and sprinkler heads, and this has led to concerns over the food supply.[2]

On an early-December morning in California's Mojave Desert, the Geoscience Support Services geohydrologist Logan Wicks squats in the sand and fiddles with a broken white pipe. Here on a sandy road off Route 66, past miles of scrubby creosote and spiny mesquite, Wicks monitors the pumps and pipes of a promising desert extraction project. But he's not looking for oil or gas. Crouching under the shade of a 10-foot lemon tree, at the edge of a citrus orchard that spans hundreds of acres, Wicks is here for water.

In fact, there might be as much as 34 million acre-feet, or enough to flood 34 million acres one foot deep. Wicks and his colleagues drilled 300 feet below the desert's surface to reach the massive Fenner aquifer. Today, the nine water wells on Cadiz Ranch support a 3,500-acre oasis of lemons, hemp, and other crops. But the company's ranch taps only a tiny fraction of the aquifer, which extends 700 square miles between two of California's mountain ranges, the New York Mountains and the Old Woman Mountains.

If it seems improbable that so much water lies under the desert, it is. Just 20 miles from Cadiz Ranch, the ghost town of Bagdad still holds the record for the driest spell in American history: Between 1912 and 1914, this town went 767 consecutive days without rain. The wetter climate that filled the Fenner aquifer ended about 10,000 years ago. Cadiz Inc., is drilling for what some call "fossil water"— water that has been buried deep in the Earth for millennia. According to new radiocarbon and other isotopic age-dating tools, the water in this aquifer hit the surface as rain during the last Ice Age, when mammoths still lived here. In the current desert climate, this groundwater will never replenish itself, at least not on a human time scale. Once we use it, it's never coming back. And unless the aquifer is actively refilled, its depletion could have serious consequences for ecosystems aboveground.

Fossil water, also called paleowater, is the largest nonfrozen freshwater resource on the planet. But for most of human history, few knew it existed. In the 1950s, oil prospectors began turning up vast, untouched supplies of water, often hidden under deserts. Like oil deposits, the buried water inspired opportunists: In Libya, the dictator Muammar Qaddafi tapped the Nubian sandstone aquifer to power his Great Man-Made River, one of the world's largest irrigation projects. In India, desert aquifers fed the Green Revolution, transforming the country into the world's second-largest producer of wheat. In California in 1983, NASA imagery revealing the size of the Fenner aquifer attracted the British entrepreneur Keith Brackpool, who bought the land, co-founded Cadiz, Inc., and started digging wells.

The company's plan for the aquifer goes far beyond lemons and hemp: Cadiz intends to channel ancient water through two pipelines that would cross hundreds of miles of desert to deliver water to Southern California water districts. The plan has persisted through a decade of political and legal challenges.

That doesn't mean the Cadiz project and others like it are justified, argue a coalition of anthropologists, philosophers, lawyers, and hydrologists. They say existing laws and regulations don't address the ethics of water use, and that water management in the age of climate change requires not just new pipes, but also new paradigms. The Fenner aquifer is "an emergency supply," the University of New Mexico anthropologist David Groenfeldt says. "How can we possibly justify using it now?"

In studies of aquifer management in her home country of Costa Rica, the University of Southern California anthropologist Andrea Ballestero has seen how detailed conversations about the geology—and vulnerability—of local aquifers can anchor otherwise abstract decisions in a unique and familiar place. Add age data, she says, and decisions begin to be anchored in time as well.

Traveling to Bonanza Spring, Chris Clarke - a member of the National Parks Conservation Association staff, pointed out a group of brown, spiky-crowned yucca stalks. They were 40 feet across with a dozen lolling heads. He mentioned it was probably around 4,000 years old and that Yucca grow in clonal clusters. The bigger the cluster, the older the plant roots. When that yucca germinated, he thinks, humans were still hunting big game across the desert, but Ice Age rainfall flowing below the ground had barely completed half its journey through the Fenner aquifer.

Reaching Bonanza Spring, we tramp downward through slick grasses and mud, skirting coyote scat and bighorn-sheep tracks. Pushing through a stand of cattails, we reach a split rock spilling water like an open mouth. The water is surprisingly warm. This spring is the largest natural water source for 1,000 square miles. "In the equation of Southern California water, Cadiz is really a drop in the bucket," Clarke says. "But for the desert, this water is everything."

In the Chemehuevi tradition, the Salt Songs were a storytelling device, a ritualized memory. People traveled hundreds of miles across the desert to this place, where they drew pictographs, held funerals, and otherwise honored the water they knew was ancient. That tradition might keep the water here. In December 2021, in part due to the lawsuit filed by the Native American Land Conservancy and other plaintiffs, the Biden administration petitioned a federal judge to invalidate a key permit for Cadiz's planned 220-mile pipeline, which would cross parts of the protected Mojave Trails National Monument. On September 13, 2022, the same judge agreed to send the project back to the Bureau of Land Management for environmental review. If blocked, the company will likely bide its time, as it has for more than 30 years, until the political winds change again. Some believe that it won't be long before construction begins on the remaining infrastructure: It is said that the company, is "shovel ready."[3]

Back in the 1960s the U.S. Geological Survey drilled a series of vertical boreholes off the New Jersey coast, looking for sand deposits and other resources. They unexpectedly struck fresh water, which was baffling. Years later researchers obtained water samples from the same location and analyzed the chemistry, finding to their surprise that the liquid was a mix of recent rainwater and seawater.

Only about 2.5 percent of all the surface water on this ocean planet is fresh. As the global population grows toward an estimated 10 billion people by 2100, the stresses on our water supply will increase -especially in coastal regions, where 30 percent of the U.S. population now lives. Climate change is also altering rainfall patterns, pollution is compromising extant bodies of water, and agriculture and development are sucking underground reservoirs dry. Could large, hidden reservoirs only a few dozen kilometers out to sea save lives and help irrigate dry crops?

Records of fresh water being found offshore go as far back as the 1800s. Fishers off Florida have occasionally reported "boils" of water on the ocean's surface, which they assume leaked upward from below. In some cases, they sampled the water and it did not taste salty; fresh water is less dense than seawater, so it rises.

A continent does not stop at its shoreline; it extends well offshore as a rocky underwater shelf. The shelf ends at a steep slope that transitions sharply to deep oceanic seafloor. The rock and sediments that make up the world's continental shelves are not dry. Some rocks crack, allowing seawater to penetrate. And most shelves are covered by layers of sedimentary rock, which are like hard sponges with small, interconnected, water-filled pores.

Sediments at or just below the seafloor are typically 40 to 50 percent porous. The weight of the ocean above pushes water down into the sediment as far as it can go. Geoscientists still debate the maximum depth, but it can be at least several kilometers, although the seepage decreases rapidly with depth as the increased pressure closes up cracks and pore spaces. The rock's permeability—the ease with which water can flow through it—depends on how extensively its various pores are interconnected.

Because the shelf is a continuation of the continent, models of groundwater flow in land along the northeastern U.S. coast suggest there could be substantial amounts of fresh water hidden within the rocks and sediments below the continental slope's seafloor. But there are competing hypotheses about how such water might get there—and remain there.

On land, subsurface water is stored in geologic layers of water-bearing rock called aquifers. Some aquifers are shallow and can be replenished by rainfall. Others are much deeper and hold water that has been in place for thousands of years, perhaps left there by glaciers during the last ice age. The composition of aquifers varies across regions, from limestone layers below Florida to more sedimentary layers in the Northeast. Groundwater—the fresh water contained in aquifers—makes up roughly 90 percent of the total available fresh water in the U.S., even when we factor in rivers and lakes. About 25 percent of the water consumed in the U.S. is pumped from aquifers through private or municipal wells.

Off the U.S. East Coast the continental shelf extends anywhere from close to shore to more than 300 kilometers out to sea. Perhaps not surprisingly, the geologic layers that form aquifers under land do not stop at the shoreline; they often extend outward as part of the shelf.

When rain falls on coastal land, it can percolate down into an aquifer and through highly permeable rocks, traveling under and across the shoreline and eventually out to the seabed. For this long-distance flow to occur and for the water to remain fresh, there needs to be a cap over the marine aquifer—a layer that is not permeable, usually of compacted clay-rich sediment. Clay is paradoxical: it can hold a lot of water when loose, but when it is compacted it becomes almost impervious. This cap prevents the less dense fresh water from rising up to the seafloor.

An entirely different mechanism could also leave fresh water under the seafloor. During past ice ages, giant ice sheets and glaciers grew, soaking up large volumes of ocean water. Sea level was much lower, and long sections of continental shelves were exposed as land open to the elements. During the last ice age, roughly between 12,000 and 20,000 years ago, rain falling on these areas could have percolated down into the subsurface, just as it does onshore today. If that water flowed underneath a cap, it could have remained trapped as the ice sheets later melted and sea levels rose again. Yet another model posits that the great weight of the ice sheets pushed fresh water deep into the subsurface and below caps.[4]

The drenching storms that hit California in 2023 represented a long-sought opportunity for Helen Dahlke, a groundwater hydrologist at the University of California, Davis. Dahlke had been studying ways to recharge the state's severely depleted groundwater by diverting swollen rivers into orchards and fields and letting the water seep deep into aquifers. But carrying out such plans requires heavy precipitation—which had been scarce.

This week, water managers began to turn theory into practice. In the Tulare Irrigation District, which supplies water to more than 200 farms south of Fresno, officials started diverting water from the San Joaquin River into 70 fields as well as specially constructed ponds. Each day, some 1.5 million cubic meters of water—roughly equivalent to 600 Olympic-size swimming pools—had been pouring onto the landscape. "We are in full [groundwater] recharge mode," Aaron Fukuda, the district's general manager, wrote in an email. Similar flooding is underway in the Madera Irrigation District north of Fresno.

Over the past decade, experiments with submerging small plots have suggested intentional flooding can replenish aquifers without damaging either groundwater quality or crops. But bureaucratic hurdles and organizational inertia had blocked widespread use of the practice—despite state laws and policies designed to encourage it.

Dahlke stated that her frustrations were growing! This always looks so easy when you write these scientific papers, and give presentations, but to really implement [flooding] on a widespread scale is very hard. She and others are in hopes this winter's floods will encourage more of the state's water managers to embrace the practice.

California's farmers and others often extract far more water from aquifers than normally seeps in from the surface. The idea of using working farms to slow or reverse the trend was born in 2010, when independent hydrologist Philip Bachand and farmer Don Cameron flooded some of Cameron's vineyards. The vines thrived, and the water replenished the aquifers beneath Cameron's land.

Four years later, California adopted a landmark law, the Sustainable Groundwater Management Act (SGMA), that promotes the practice. It requires farmers to treat aquifers like bank accounts, clamping down on overdrafts but also allowing those who deposit water into them to make bigger withdrawals later.

The most catastrophically depleted aquifers lie in the San Joaquin Valley, the nation's largest single source of tree nuts, fruit, and vegetables. In places, groundwater extraction has caused the land to sink by several meters, and declining runoff from the Sierra Nevada means growers can no longer depend on a steady supply of river water. In this region, Dahlke says, capturing water during wet years and storing it underground for later use will be a matter of survival.

But several obstacles have stood in the way of recharge projects, experts say. Some districts need state permits and getting them is time-consuming. The SGMA's limits on extraction are only kicking in now, so farmers haven't had much incentive to spend the money required to flood their fields. Also, many farmers, aren't inclined to drown their fields when it's time to plant or pollinate their crops. Only certain crops are compatible with flooding during different times of year.[5]

Several years ago, while cruising up the United States western coast, we passed through the area of Portland Oregon and the Columbia River delta. The ship announcer related a short history of the area and the many ships that were lost and the massive amounts of fresh water entering the Pacific Ocean.

The Columbia River has a long history of shipwrecks. Its bar, where freshwater and saltwater meet, is one of the most difficult crossings of any river in the world, especially in the spring when the river's volume is so great that the freshwater plume extends 100 miles to sea, and in the winter when storms lash the jumble of waves to 50 feet and higher. The average flow at the mouth is 265,000 ft3/s (7,500 m3/s). It is the largest river by volume flowing from the Americas into the Pacific Ocean, and is the fourth largest by volume in the United States.

Historically, the crossing was particularly difficult for ships under sail because the two natural channels across the bar forced them to turn sideways to the current and the wind. To this day it is not uncommon for ships to wait a week or longer for the bar to calm enough to allow a safe crossing. The mouth of the Columbia and the near-shore areas to the north and south are littered with shipwrecks.

More than 200 (some say 330) are known to have occurred. Some which ran aground on the Oregon shore south of the river in 1906, are visible to this day.[6]

The observed "jumble of waves" and currents at the delta of the Columbia River on my family cruise has caused me to ponder the drought frequency we experience in California and the thousands of cubic feet of fresh water discarded by the Columbia River into the Pacific Ocean.

Kenneth Hahn, Los Angeles Board of Supervisors for 40 Years, advocated diverting a portion of the Columbia River to water-scarce Southern California at a time when the city faced withering drought, as it does today. Several times he unsuccessfully introduced resolutions calling for investigation of his diversion idea.

In May 1990, he wrote to then-Oregon Governor Neil Goldschmidt imploring him to "act like a good neighbor" and support diverting the Columbia. Talk about walking into a running Oregon chainsaw. "I have the distinct impression that you are trying to steal my water," Goldschmidt responded in a letter to Hahn. "I don't have enough water in the Columbia to raise the fish we need to rear, move the barges we are trying to move, generate the electricity that we all so badly need, irrigate the crops that need it, keep the native American tribes happy and then send some south to you." Goldschmidt ended with a curt, "hoping you're not serious."

None of those constraints has changed today. In fact, there are more constraints on Columbia River water today than in 1990—protecting threatened and endangered species of salmon and steelhead, for example—including in the estuary downstream of Bonneville Dam (40 miles east or Portland) where Hahn's pipeline would have started.[7]

I envisioned a pipeline being filled by the Columbia River water near its delta and flowing south in Oregon, being used in areas of need in that state, coursing into northern California and ending at the beginning of the 444-mile California Aqueduct. Established as part of a $1.75 billion bond passed by voters in 1960, it begins at the Harvey O. Banks Pumping Plant and parallels Interstate 5 south to the Tehachapi Mountains. The California Aqueduct maximum capacity is 13,100 ft/3s and the Columbia River's average flow at its delta is 265,000 ft/3s. Even if you tripled the CA Aqueduct flow from the river, that would be 4.94% of the average Columbia River flow. If the state of California increased aqueduct capacity to supply its southern water hungry state and paid Oregon for the water I see it as a win-win situation.

The basic needs for most living animals are food, water, air, and shelter to survive. If any one of these basic needs is not met, even humans cannot survive. Before past explorers set off to find new lands and conquer new worlds, they had to make sure that their basic needs were met. Water from the Columbia River would help provide California residents with the second and third (water and food) most essential ingredients for survival. You can't live longer than minutes without oxygen in the air, days without water and months (2-3) without food. Why would anyone in their right mind not prioritize the basic essentials of life first before adding other conveniences in our lives?

When Gov. Gavin Newsom unveiled his scaled down blueprint for the California bullet train four years ago, he proposed building a 171-mile starter segment in the Central Valley that would begin operating in 2030 and cost $22.8 billion.

Today, the blueprint is fraying — costs now exceed future funding, an official estimate of future ridership has dropped by 25%, and the schedule to start to carry people is slipping. That's raising fresh concerns about the future of the nation's largest infrastructure project.

New cost figures issued in an update report from the California High-Speed Rail Authority show that the plan to build the 171-mile initial segment has shot up to a high of $35 billion, exceeding secured funding by $10 billion. The cost of that partial system is now higher than the $33 billion estimate for the entire 500-mile Los Angeles to San Francisco system when voters approved a bond in 2008.

What's worse, that full system cost is set at up to $128 billion in the update, leaving a total funding gap of more than $100 billion for politicians to ponder. Also, it appears that there are no plans for the federal government to allocate another dollar to California for a highspeed rail.[8]

Spending some of the High-Speed Rail money on water projects, saving the Fenner Aquifer for emergencies, encouraging flooding crop lands with spring runoff water to help maintain existing aquifers, exploring the possibilities of tapping undersea fresh water, developing cost affective desalination of water projects etcetera makes a lot of sense to me.

I moved to California with my family in 1973. My wife was pleased because she would be closer to her relatives in southern CA, the climate, and her beloved Disneyland (opened July 17, 1955), where she was a nine-year-old when she started bonding with the amusement park during family visits most winters as her father's farms were resting under Idaho's cold, snow and ice.

My interests in California were the job opportunities for veterinarians, weather and anticipation of plenty of energy and water. Having studied nuclear isotopes some during my graduate studies, I envisioned nuclear power plants sprinkled up and down the coast of California. These would provide a reliable electrical grid and desalinate sea water used to provide a continuous fresh water supply for municipalities.

Many years later, a close friend Ronald Budd Simons (02/14/1936-06/22/2022), discussed his involvement as an engineer with GE and the building of the Fukushima Daiichi nuclear plant in Japan. He told me that the accident on 11 March 2011 would have been much less severe if the protocols for emergencies were followed. His take on it was that no one in the plant would make a decision until the "higher ups" told them what to do. He also mentioned that one of the projects GE was planning up until the stoppage of further nuclear development was small home and neighborhood nuclear power plants.

The 1970s proved to be a pivotal period for the anti-nuclear movement in California. Opposition to nuclear power in coincided with the growth the country's environmental movement. Opposition to nuclear power increased when President Richard Nixon called for the construction of 1000 nuclear plants by the year 2000.

The movement succeeded in blocking plans to build a large number of facilities in the state as well as closing operating power plants. The confrontation between nuclear power advocates and environmentalists grew to include the use of non-violent civil disobedience.

In 1976 the state of California placed a moratorium on new reactors until a solution to radioactive waste disposal was in place, and two years later state politicians canceled the proposed Sun desert Nuclear Power Plant. In September 1981, over 1,900 arrests took place during a ten-day blockade at Diablo Canyon Power Plant. As part of a national anti-nuclear weapons movement Californians passed a 1982 statewide initiative calling for the end of nuclear weapons. In 1984, the Davis City Council declared the city to be a nuclear free zone. Wikipedia

In 2013, San Onofre Nuclear Generating Station Units 2 and 3 were permanently closed, ending nuclear power in Southern California. The state's final two operating reactors at Diablo Canyon are scheduled to close no later than 2025. As of 2021, three nuclear power plants supplied about 10% of California's electricity. California has two operating nuclear power reactors at one plant, three nuclear facilities at various stages of decommissioning, and multiple research reactors that are operational or undergoing decommissioning. *CA.GOV*

Tapping aquifers, rivers dumping vast amounts of fresh water into the ocean, processing waste water, nuclear driven desalination plants, drilling for fresh water under sea beds, whatever: UNESCO has reported that the freshwater shortfall worldwide will rise to 500 trillion gallons/yr by 2025. They expect water wars to break out in the near-future. The World Economic Forum says that shortage of fresh water may be the primary global threat in the next decade.

But 500 trillion gallons/year only requires about 1,500 seawater desalination plants like the ones being built in California and Saudi Arabia. At a billion dollars a pop, that's a lot cheaper than war and starvation. Unfortunately, we presently desalinate only 10 trillion gallons/year worldwide.

The two main types of desalination are:

– thermal desalination by using heat energy to separate the distillate from high salinity water. Most desalination plants in the world use fossil fuels to power them, but it's even better to power them with nuclear energy. The new fleet of Small Modular Nuclear Reactors (SMRs) are ideal as they produce both thermal energy and electrical energy without producing greenhouse gases.

– reverse osmosis (RO) membrane separation, which uses a membrane barrier and pumping energy to separate salts from the water. These are common in homes and businesses.

Electrical energy is used for membrane-based systems and thermal energy is used for distillation systems. Some hybrid plants combine both membrane and distillation.

But only 15 out of the thousands of desalination plants operating today worldwide are powered by nuclear. A small one is at the Canyon Diablo Nuclear Plant in California, slated to be closed soon. The plant could power several huge desalination plants for decades that could desalinate its own cooling water, removing the most commonly stated problem with the plant.

California (and the rest of the world) better get moving. It's been a reasonable two years, but more Mega Droughts are on the way.[9]

However, I just might live long enough to partially see my youth's dream of California becoming a place where there is a reliable electric grid and enough clean fresh water:

According to the government's Department of Energy: Advanced Small Modular Reactors (SMRs) are a key part of the Department's goal to develop safe, clean, and affordable nuclear power options. The advanced SMRs currently under development in the United States represent a variety of sizes, technology options, capabilities, and deployment scenarios. These advanced reactors, envisioned to vary in size from tens of megawatts up to hundreds of megawatts, can be used for power generation, process heat, desalination, or other industrial uses. SMR designs may employ light water (H_2O) as a coolant or other non-light water coolants such as a gas, liquid metal, or molten salt. *Department of Energy (.gov)*

1– *Watering Idaho: The Snake River Plain Aquifer, Boise State Public Radio News, Samantha Wright, 09/19/2016.*

2– *Population growth and global warming are increasingly causing fights over water between U.S. states and among the countries of the world. Science, Marcia Wendorf, 02/24/2021.*

3– *It's legal to drink 10,000-year-old water. But is it right, Atlantic Planet Series, Brett Simpson, 01/23/2023.*

4– *Researchers are discovering freshwater reservoirs below the coastal seafloor that might someday save dry regions from drought, Rob L. Evans, Scientific American, 07/02/2023.*

5– *Can California's floods help recharge depleted groundwater supplies? Plans to drown orchards and farm fields to boost aquifers get off to a slow start, Bydan Charles, Science Insider, 01/23/2023.*

6– *Northwest Power and Conservation Council.*

7– *For drought-plagued California diverting Columbia River water is a pipe dream … for now, John Harrison, Oct 13, 2022.*

8– *CalMatters, Ralph Vartabedian, 03/09/2023.*

9– *How 1,500 Nuclear-Powered Water Desalination Plants Could Save The World From Desertification, Forbes, James Conca, 07/14/2019.*

CHAPTER 17

GANGRENE

On Wednesday morning, September 26, 2007, I received a call at work from my sister Bobbie. She told me that my mother was in the emergency room, where she was lifeless. I was shocked in unbelief. About a week before my wife, Shauna, and I had visited her in the Extended Care facility next to Bingham Memorial Hospital (BMH) in her home town. We were showing her pictures on her bed from our annual September wedding anniversary cruise and were about 2/3rds of the way through the slide show. She mentioned that we must be about through the slides. I told her there were a couple more slides, showed them and then put away the projector. She was hungry and couldn't wait to go visit with her friends in the cafeteria. She walked us down the hallway, seated herself down at the table and waved us goodbye with a big smile.

Bobbie asked me if we should take her off life support and let her go. She told me that the CAT scan showed no brain damage, her kidney and heart functions were low, and her white blood count was "sky-high." Her body was shutting down. We agreed that if it were God's will we shouldn't get in the way. She passed at 10:40 AM.

Shauna and I got our affairs in order and flew home. Our family met at the mortuary to make funeral arrangements and the mortician asked us if we would like to see her leg that had been casted for a small "crack" of her tibia and fibula sustained from a fall in August. During her care the doctor had only seen her once and the cast had not been removed or evaluated during her stay. Only Bobbie, some of her family and my brother, John, had been told at the time of her death that there was an open abscess found under her thigh above the cast. What the mortician showed was a clear plastic bag near full of purulent whitish debris (puss) covering her leg from gangrene. It was suspected that she had a Staphylococcal infection under the cast.

Our family was stunned and full of the what if' and why not' questions. Here we were planning to celebrate the life of our wonderful mother and the clouds of suspicion, anger, bitterness etcetera began creeping into our family. How could we prepare and participate in the proper frame of mind when a funeral may not have been necessary? Especially, how could have this occurred in the hospital our father worked in so many years as an MD and with people that our family knew and trusted with mom's care?

Fortunately, my sister Pat's husband an MD ophthalmologist, Jay counselled us that no matter what we did our mother would not come back and if we made an issue of the event there were many wonderful, dedicated staff members at BMH that may have their lives and careers interrupted or terminated from the neglect of a few. Also, we should think about what this event could do to our family if we dwelled on it too long. We dropped the issue and have all been able to put this event behind us and our relationships have always remained good.

According to Sigell Bell, MD: The safety movement has focused most of its efforts on preventing errors and adverse events while patients receive medical care. But when harm occurs, the extent of the emotional impact on patients and families — and how to support them in the immediate and long-term aftermath — is not well understood.

Patients and families can be overwhelmed by the emotional toll of serious harmful medical events. Some describe post-traumatic distress related to the event, guilt about not being able to prevent it, fear of retribution if they raise concerns, fractured trust, and isolation. Bell notes that, although there is a growing emphasis on transparency, some health care organizations may withhold information, leaving patients and families struggling to piece together the truth about a harmful event. "This can lead patients to experience additional emotional or psychological harm, such as depression, self-blame, or trauma-related anxiety."

There's a lack of longitudinal research that delves into the experiences of patients and families after an error. Based on the work done so far, however, Bell theorizes that Communication and Resolution Programs (CRPs) can play a role in preventing the long-term emotional impact of medical harm.

CRPs have been designed using data about what patients and families want after a medical error. These include open communication, acknowledgment of the error, and an apology. "Patients and families also want assurance that the organization has a plan to prevent what happened to them from happening to others," Bell remarks. "Organizations should also discuss compensation when appropriate."

These elements inform disclosure guidelines across the country. Bell suggests that recent and ongoing research also offers clues about what organizations may need to do to prevent emotional harm to patients.[1]

What has affected me these many years was why didn't someone sit down and discuss the series of events that resulted in the death of my mother? I know that if they just had "open communication, acknowledgment of the error, and an apology" I would have had a much better acceptance and less grief if I had known. On May 25, 2023 I requested a copy of the death certificate from the State of Idaho to see if I could resolve in my mind the events that led to my mother's death. The cause of death stated, "myocardial infarction" and the manner of death "natural." These statements made me think that more of a stink by our family may have encouraged more honesty. We did ask the mortician to let the hospital know that we saw and knew what had happened. Who knows? I really appreciated the mortician sharing what he found and I have to believe that he did not forget our conversation. Being a veterinarian and involved with some unfortunate treatment results – I am disappointed the MD, who placed his name on the Certificate of Death, dated October 15, 2007, took the easy out and probably did not use this event to help make BMH a little better in their patient care.

Gangrene refers to dead or dying tissues in the body. It occurs mainly due to the lack of blood supply for the survival of the tissues. Dry gangrene is the less harmful form of gangrene. It occurs due to local tissue death and is eventually removed from the body. However, if the dry gangrene develops into an infection and progresses to become wet gangrene, the severity is more harmful. In a biological scenario, the development of dry gangrene takes a longer time and is a slower process.

During dry gangrene formation, there is no formation of pus, wetness or crackly-feeling skin. It is mainly due to the fact that there is no gas production, owing to the absence of an infectious condition.

However, symptoms such as cool dry and discolored appendages can be observed in dry gangrene formation. Disease conditions such as atherosclerosis and diabetes may lead to the formation of dry gangrene. Furthermore, smoking enhances dry gangrene formation.

Wet gangrene is the most harmful form of gangrene. If this form of gangrene does not receive proper treatment, the patient develops sepsis and may die within a few days. Wet gangrene refers to the gangrene that forms during infection, resulting in the lack of blood supply leading to tissue swelling. In addition to infections, physical injuries such as wounds, cuts, and burns, etc. can also cause wet gangrene.[2]

Docking a sheep's tail is the common practice of shortening the length of the tail. For practical reasons it is done to avoid the long tail getting fly strike from urine and moist debris accumulation, and to reduce fecal soiling. When the tail is docked, it is recommended to leave a minimum length that covers the anal and vulva area of the animals.

Fly strike occurs mostly around the rear end of sheep when blow flies lay their eggs in soiled, wet wool and infected areas. The emerging larvae (maggots) can cause gangrene and death. At my work as a veterinarian, we fairly commonly see fly strike on animals during the summer months. They usually have been injured or are older and unable to take care for themselves from such things as cuts, bite wounds, abscesses, urine or fecal contamination – those that need nursing care.

The Blow fly is any member in a family of insects in the fly order, Diptera, that are metallic blue, green, or black in color and are noisy in flight. They are slightly larger than houseflies but resemble them in habits. Among the important members of this group are the screwworm, bluebottle fly, greenbottle fly, and cluster fly.

Adult blow flies feed on a variety of materials, but the larvae of most species are scavengers that live on carrion or dung. The adults lay their eggs on the carcasses of dead animals or fecal material, and the larvae (maggots) feed on the decaying material. The larvae of some species also infest open wounds of living animals. Although these larvae may assist in preventing infection by cleaning away dead flesh, some species may also destroy healthy tissue.

When modern medicine fails, it is often useful to draw ideas from ancient treatments. The therapeutic use of fly larvae to debride necrotic tissue, also known as larval therapy, maggot debridement therapy or biosurgery, dates back to the beginnings of civilization. Despite repeatedly falling out of favor largely because of patient intolerance to the treatment, the practice of larval therapy is increasing around the world because of its efficacy, safety and simplicity.

The most common way of docking tails and castrating sheep is by using an elastic and expandable latex ring. The rubber ring is being expanded with an elastrator and put over the tail, where it is released. The ring will then cut off the blood supply to the tail and it will fall off, from dry gangrene, after a number of days.

Fitting the latex ring over the neck of the scrotum or using an emasculator that clamps down in the same area and crushes the blood vessels around the testes will cut off the blood supply causing tissue death, dry gangrene of the testes and they will eventually drop off. A major problem with using rings or emasculators on older lambs is the increasing size of the scrotum and associated structures. This can give rise to chronic inflammation, pain and infection until the scrotum falls off and healing occurs. For this reason, lambs should ideally be castrated as soon as possible after they have formed a secure maternal bond but not before they are 24 hours of age. *Several sources*

During high school I took vocational agriculture classes. During a farm visit at a sheep farm the instructor told us that we would get an "A" for this section of the class if we would castrate a lamb like the famous Basque sheep herders. The procedure was to cut off a portion the skin covering the tip of the scrotum. Then exposing each testicle through the opening, biting each testicle firmly with your teeth and pulling it away from the lamb. I had to secure a firm bite, pull hard and the feeling of living tissue giving way in my teeth, I will always remember. I also got my "A!"

At the call to arms during the Civil War, communities throughout the North and South began assembling troops. It was evident that insects also were amassing with the soldiers. Flies are an important group of insects medically because of the role they play in disease transmission. House flies, Blow flies & Bottle flies (that breed in dead or dying animals, feces and garbage) and Screwworm flies (lay eggs in wounds as well as body orifices and feed on living tissue in the area of any warm-blooded animal, including humans). These are all examples of some non-biting flies that can be extremely problematic and probably confronted the soldiers throughout the war.

The number of animals required to support both armies dwarfs anything by today's standards. In 1864, the Army of the Potomac was followed by more than 4,000 six-mule team wagons as it entered the Wilderness Campaign.

The total number of horses and mules that began that campaign was 56,499. Armies from the western theater also maintained a large animal entourage. General Sherman's army of 60,000 was accompanied by 2,500 wagons and 600 ambulances. It is probable that those wagons also were pulled by six-mule teams.

This, too, was an era before modern MREs (Meals Ready to Eat). Meat rations commonly were supplied as fresh beef, although this was often a luxury for many Confederate soldiers. To supply meat for the soldiers, large cattle trains had to be moved with the army.

Few recruits bothered to use the slit-trench latrines (and those who did usually forgot to shovel dirt over the feces) and most urinated just outside the tent--and after sundown, in the street. Garbage was everywhere, rats abounded, and dead cats and dogs turned up in the strangest places. The emanations of slaughtered cattle and kitchen offal together with the noxious effluvia from the seething latrines and infested tents produced an olfactory sensation which has yet to be duplicated in the Western Hemisphere.

As for water--and seldom was there enough--any source would do in the early camps. Frequently, it was so muddy and fetid the men held their noses when they drank the stuff. In many instances, the heavy rains washed fecal material directly into the supply with disastrous consequences.

The extensive untidiness made excellent breeding habitats for filth flies, especially during the warmer months. The flies' presence represented more than just a nuisance. The habit of crawling on refuse and excrement and then on humans and their food was a serious problem, one not fully realized at the time. Flies are potential vectors of pathogens that cause cholera, diarrhea, dysentery, and typhoid. By the end of the war, diseases would take the lives of more soldiers than would hostile fire.

Fly problems were bad enough during periods of noncombat, but they were even worse after battle and added to the horrors of war. Although modern warfare has provided mechanized equipment to dig mass graves, produced various residual chemical sprays to inhibit fly development, and even supplied large quantities of petroleum fuels for burning the corpses, such technology was not present or utilized during the Civil War. Bodies often were buried hastily or, in many cases, never buried. The carnage of the battlefield made a prime breeding and feeding ground for flies, but humans were not the only casualties of these battles. Fearful tolls also were exacted on the military animals.

If an exposed wound was not infested and gangrene set in on the field, there was a good chance it would become so at the hospital. One Union private described a hospital scene: "Near the hospital was a pile of arms, legs, hands, and feet that had been cut from the wounded. These had not been buried, just thrown in a pile and worms [maggots] had begun to work on them." Union surgeons got rid of maggots in wounds with chloroform. Because of shortages in medical supplies, Confederate doctors did not always have access to such supplies. They discovered accidentally that the maggots were actually more efficient at digesting necrotic tissue than a scalpel or nitric acid. J. F. Zacharias, a surgeon in the Confederate army wrote: During my service in the hospital at Danville, Virginia, I first used maggots to remove the decayed tissue in hospital gangrene and with eminent satisfaction. In a single day, they would clean a wound much better than any agents we had at our command. I used them afterwards at various places. I am sure I saved many lives by their use, escaped septicemia, and had rapid recoveries.[3]

In maggot therapy, large numbers of small maggots consume necrotic tissue far more precisely than is possible in a normal surgical operation, and can debride a wound in a day or two. The area of a wound's surface is typically increased with the use of maggots due to the undebrided surface not revealing the actual underlying size of the wound. They derive nutrients through a process known as "extracorporeal digestion" by secreting a broad spectrum of proteolytic enzymes that liquefy necrotic tissue, and absorb the semi-liquid result within a few days. In an optimum wound environment maggots molt twice, increasing in length from about 2 mm to about 10 mm, and in girth, within a period of 48–72 hours by ingesting necrotic tissue, leaving a clean wound free of gangrenous tissue when they are removed.

Secretions from maggots are believed to have broad-spectrum antimicrobial activity including allantoin, urea, phenylacetic acid, phenylacetaldehyde, calcium carbonate, proteolytic enzymes, and others. In vitro studies have shown that maggots inhibit and destroy a wide range of pathogenic bacteria including methicillin-resistant Staphylococcus aureus (MRSA), group A and B streptococci, and Gram-positive aerobic and anaerobic strains. Other bacteria like Pseudomonas aeruginosa, E. coli or Proteus spp. are not attacked by maggots, and in case of Pseudomonas even the maggots are in danger.

Written records have documented that maggots have been used since antiquity as a wound treatment. There are reports of the use of maggots for wound healing by Maya, Native Americans, and Aboriginal tribes in Australia. Maggot treatment was reported in Renaissance times. Military physicians observed that soldiers whose wounds had become colonized with maggots experienced significantly less morbidity and mortality than soldiers whose wounds had not become colonized. These physicians included Napoleon's general surgeon's reports during the French campaign in Egypt and Syria (1798–1801) that certain species of fly consumed only dead tissue and helped wounds to heal.

The use of maggots to clean dead tissue from animal wounds is part of folk medicine in many parts of the world. It is particularly helpful with chronic osteomyelitis, chronic ulcers, and other pus-producing infections that are frequently caused by chafing due to work equipment.

Maggot therapy for horses in the United States was re-introduced after a study published in 2003 by veterinarian Dr. Scott Morrison. This therapy is used in horses for conditions such as osteomyelitis secondary to laminitis, sub-solar abscesses leading to osteomyelitis, post-surgical treatment of street-nail procedure for puncture wounds infecting the navicular bursa, canker, non-healing ulcers on the frog, and post-surgical site cleaning for keratoma removal.

There have not been many case studies done with maggot debridement therapy on other animals, and as such it can be difficult to accurately assess how successful it is. *Wikipedia*

Grieving is an essential part of living. It helps us move forward with our lives after we experience deep loss. Grieving means we feel sorrow, and because we do, we are able to free ourselves from bad feelings, like anger and regret. When a loved one dies, when a child wanders, when poor health debilitates, or when a dream dissolves before our eyes, we are faced with a choice. We can deny the loss and get stuck in a state of nonfeeling, protecting ourselves from pain. Or we can grieve. We can feel the loss and open our souls to new vistas of hope and possibility.

Grieving helps us to redefine our outlook, to pick up the pieces, so to speak, after heartache and start living again. If we don't confront our losses or if we hold on to them for too long, we suffer; we deny the power of God to heal our broken hearts and give us new life.

In the Bible we read about Lot's wife, who, in a sense, refused to grieve. She was warned to leave Sodom and Gomorrah but stopped to look back because she could not accept the losses she faced. The reality of leaving family members, friends, and possessions behind overwhelmed her. She tried to stop the pain instead of passing through it. Not trusting that God would lead her through the valley of sorrow, she gave in to her fears and perished.

A physician who has counseled chronically and terminally ill patients and their families compares the fate of Lot's wife with the failure to grieve. She believes that grieving is essential to joyful living. "Grieving is not about forgetting," she writes. "Grieving allows us to heal, to remember with love rather than pain. It is a sorting process. One by one you let go of the things that are gone and you mourn for them. One by one you take hold of the things that have become a part of who you are and build again."

Remembering with love rather than pain lifts the burden of loss and helps us to feel joy again. Somewhere between shutting out memories and desperately holding on to them is a healing place called grieving. There we find the untapped strength we need to go on living—not just existing, but really living. The Lord, in His loving mercy, makes it all possible. He promises: "I am come that they might have life, and that they might have it more abundantly."[4]

December 20, 2007
Dear Friends of Barbara Hoge (my mother),

Christmas cards are coming to mother's home this month, and I know she would want us to let her friends know that she is no longer with us. Losing Mother is definitely the hardest thing we've ever experienced. This was so sudden, totally unexpected. She fractured her leg, just above the ankle, about August 10. She had just gone to answer the phone and rolled inward on her foot. The x-ray showed the fibula and tibia each had a small, straight, horizontal-line 'crack'. Since her family reunion was I Paris, Idaho, on Saturday, she opted not to have it set until Monday. We took her to the reunion, she in a wheelchair, and then stayed with her at her home both Friday and Saturday nights. When the Medicare hospital time ran out, they moved her to the back of the hospital to the BMH Extended Care facility.

The 'purple' cast went up to her knee, and they claimed it was necessary to remain there for therapy. That consisted of walking in a walker once a day. She only saw her doctor once after the leg was set. That was about three weeks before she died, when they wheeled her across the street (Dad's old office) to have it x-rayed. On September 26th, the hospital called to tell us she was going downhill really fast. We went to the emergency room, where she was lifeless. She was given oxygen and straight sugar (her blood level was low). They began to insert a ventilator, but she woke up so they didn't. she had an oxygen mask on she looked tired, but she recognized us (Mel & I, John, two of my daughters and their children). She was able to respond when they asked her to lift her arms, etc. she spoke a little through her mask. A CAT scan showed no bleeding in the brain. Kidney and heart functions were low and her white blood cell count was 'sky-high.

Anyway, she had an infection (probably staph), and her body was shutting down. later, a large, open abscess (the size of a half of a soccer ball) was found under her thigh, above the cast, and fluids were draining. We don't know why no one noticed, or why she didn't complain. We always went to see her at least once or twice a day, and she seemed fine the day before. She was extremely alert mentally, totally normal, and couldn't wait to go home. she still had a driver's license & drome her car before she fell. She had been planning to go home that weekend.

She loved adventure and we included her in trips to Utah, Jr. Olympics in Virginia, a California wedding, family reunions, programs, rodeos, etc. Barbara loved her friends and always enjoyed the cards, phone calls & letters. SHE WILL TRULY MISS EACH OF YOU! We were really blessed to have been able to enjoy her these last few years. Besides being our mother, she was also our 'best friend'. And, although she would have been 92 on Dec. 18, she 'never really grew OLD'.

Love, Melvin & Barbara Ann Lilya

1– *Addressing the Long-Term Impact of Patient Harm, Sigall Bell, MD, 03/07/2019.*

2– *Difference Between Dry and Wet Gangrene, Dr. Smanthi, 07/25/2019.*

3– *Insects and the Civil War, Historical Natural History + G.L. Miller (1997).*

4– *A Healing Place Called Grieving, Music & the Spoken Word, Program #3873, 11/09/2003.*

CHAPTER 18

TAIL DOCKING AND EAR CROPPING

In Roman times, dogs had their tails docked as a means to decrease the spread of rabies, while ear cropping was practiced to prevent ear damage during fighting and hunting. Today the reasons given for these surgical alterations include prevention of tail injury, decreased ear infections, breed conformity and a breeder's right to choose. However, there is very little research assessing the validity of these assertions. Despite this lack of evidence, ear cropping and tail docking have become defining features of many dog breeds. Historically, approximately one third of recognized dog breeds have their tails docked, but to our knowledge there are no reliable estimates of the extent to which both of these procedures are performed today.[1]

In 2009 Fred Lanting, AKC, International All Breed Judge & SAAB Member, commented: "In today's show ring, there is a danger that judges and writers of breed standards will be too hasty in defining what is "proper" tail carriage for breeds that have been exhibited for over a century with very little attention paid to tail stumps from docking. The same would hold for natural ears, although from what I've seen so far, there is less difference in natural ear carriage from one dog to the next within any breed. Perhaps it's because I saw so many natural ears in Boxers, etc. back in the 1960s as a handler in Canada.

As was included in a position paper by the Utah VMA (Resolution 4, reported in JAVMA News, June 15, 2009), "Cosmetic ear cropping and tail docking of dogs has little or no therapeutic basis." The truth of that statement will sooner or later be universally accepted, whether reluctantly or not, but until it is, I will oppose forced adherence to someone else's time schedule; compliance should be voluntary.

Other fires keep popping up, for an example a recently past law by Ohio states: "No person shall... dock a dog's tail, crop a dog's ear, remove a dog's claws, or debark a dog. [These] shall only be conducted by a licensed veterinarian. No person shall... permit a dog to have more than one litter per calendar year..."

Things haven't changed much over the debate what should be done with ear crops and tail docking in dogs. Eight years later Barbara J. Andrew, Editor-In-Chief of *The Dog in Place*, noted a comment from a reader, "What is your club doing - or not doing today? When this article ran in 2009 we received a lot of feedback from people in breeds that have cropped ears and/or docked tails as in breeds such as Rottweilers and Cockers which only dock the tail.

Breeders (and owners) are struggling in the battle against the purely political agenda of animal rights. Some national parent club members are reporting the club has been "infiltrated" by those who seek to change the club policy, its stance on cropping and docking, and even to change the Breed Standard.

Where does your parent club stand today? Does your current board still support cropped ears and docked tails? Do your breed leaders suggest the club shouldn't require people to mutilate their dogs? Has your national breed club membership dropped? Is cropping and/or docking an issue in your breed today? Has the public moved on to another breed?"[2]

The adult Doberman Pinscher stands 26 to 28 inches at the shoulder and weighs about 60 to 100 pounds. The Doberman has a wedge-shaped head and the ears may or may not be cropped. Uncropped ears naturally hang and the tail is docked. To learn more about this type of dog, check out our Doberman Pinscher Breed Guide.

When the ear cropping first began, it was done for functional reasons. The Doberman was a guard dog. Having ears stand upright allowed for increased hearing capabilities. This was an important feature for a watchdog. Today, ear cropping in Dobermans is usually done to comply with show standards or simply for the owner's personal preference.

A Doberman whose ears are not cropped takes on a very different appearance. In Dobermans, ear cropping contributes to the breed's identity and character. It is customary to identify a Doberman Pinscher by their cropped ears. Many feel it adds to the breed's striking appearance. The ear crop style can vary in shape or length. For instance, ear cropping styles include the short crop, the medium crop, and the longer crop that is known as the standard show crop.

Ear cropping is a surgical procedure in which a portion of the dog's ear is removed, producing ears that stand erect. The procedure is most often performed on Doberman puppies at around 8 to 12 weeks of age. The ears are trimmed and the edges are stitched. The ears are then taped to a hard surface for several weeks while they heal. This is done so that the ears will stay upright. The ear cropping should be done by a veterinarian with experience in ear cropping.

When I joined Camden Pet Hospital in 1976, the owner, Dr. Hylton, was known for cropping the ears free hand with the longer crop and he had a special style liked by breeders in the area. Some ears would not stand and he would burn off a length of plastic rod, place a large syringe needle into the length of the edge of the ear and thread the rode through the needle. The area around the rode would heal over and the ear stay erect.

Ear cropping surgery is done under anesthesia and takes about 30 minutes to complete. The ears will usually stand upright after being taped for 5 or 6 months, although some Dobermans may take up to one year before the ears will fully stand erect.

After ear cropping surgery, proper aftercare is essential to prevent infection and to ensure that the ears stand upright. If the owner is unwilling to commit to such a lengthy aftercare period, they should not engage in the ear cropping procedure. The ears are taped upright on racks and given a tranquilizer, called acepromazine, to sedate the puppy enough to prevent injury to the ears and dislodging the racks. Scheduled rechecks were made to follow the healing process and adjust the racks.

The most common uses of acepromazine in animals are as an oral sedative before stressful events (such as fireworks and thunderstorms), an injectable tranquilizer for particularly aggressive or fractious animals, and in combination with analgesics, sedatives and anesthetics. It is also labeled for use in preventing motion sickness. Its effects as a CNS depressant means that less opiates are required to reach the same amount of sedation, and it prevents the arrhythmia and vomiting that many opiates induce.

Acepromazine is a phenothiazine derivative that was introduced in the 1950s for the treatment of schizophrenia. Its use in humans was quickly abandoned due to side effects and lack of efficacy; however, it remains popular in veterinary medicine.

Literature from the 1950s raised concerns about phenothiazine-induced seizures in human patients. For this reason, caution has typically been advised when contemplating acepromazine use in epileptic canine patients, as it was widely believed to lower the seizure's threshold. More current studies, however, have failed to show a positive association between use of acepromazine and seizure activity and show a possible role for acepromazine in seizure control.

A 54-year-old woman intentionally ingested 950 mg of her dog's acepromazine. Within 3 h of ingestion, she developed central nervous system and respiratory depression along with hypotension requiring non-invasive ventilation and vasopressors. Clinical toxicity resolved over the following 8 h. Human acepromazine toxicity is rarely reported but results in clinical toxicity (central nervous system depression, respiratory depression, hypotension) that are similar to other phenothiazines.[3]

In 2015 a study was made on how tail docking and ear cropping effects the dog and those living around it. Their specific aims were to: 1) assess public awareness that a dog has had a tail docking and ear cropping, 2) determine whether physical alteration of a dog's appearance makes inferences about personality traits of the dog, and 3) to test whether owners of modified and natural dogs are perceived differently.

Dogs are a large and important part of society today. The current studies suggest that specific dogs with cropped ears and docked tails can be negatively perceived by the public and in turn this negative perception is reflected in their owners. In 2012, it was estimated that 70 million dogs are kept as pets in the United States alone. This is a large number of individuals and while to our knowledge the number of ear cropped and tail docked dogs is unknown, they are among the most popular dog breeds.

With regards to animal welfare the question arises as to whether these negative perceptions affect adoptability and relinquishment of these dogs? As an example, approximately 3.9 million dogs enter shelters every year in the United States, with aggression cited as one of the top reasons for owners to relinquish their pets. However, while relinquishment may not be a matter of 'perceived' personality traits, adoption is. When looking to adopt a new dog, potential owners are first drawn to appearance. However, if the adoptable dog in question has cropped ears and a docked tail it can be assumed from the results of these studies that the potential owner will perceive this dog more negatively and this dog may be overlooked. Appearance based stereotypes are common in our society and with pets it is no different.

Wright et al. (2007) determined that viewing one individual dog behaving badly or aggressively affected a person's perception of the entire breed. Many advocates for ear cropping and tail docking argue that the pain of the procedure has a very small impact on the individual. However, the results of this research show that by doing these procedures the perception and arguably treatment of these individuals is affected for their entire life.

Most interesting is that our findings indicate that by simply eliminating the procedures from these specific dog breeds we can shift the negative perception. Considering the lack of awareness of these procedures it appears that at least for those respondents that were unaware, the negative perception of short ears and short tail is unconsciously recognized. These three studies collectively provide evidence that human induced changes to a dogs' appearance can dramatically affect how the dogs and their owners are perceived, which has the potential to negatively impact the dog as well as the owner. To our knowledge this is the first study that addresses the question of whether members of the public are aware that tail length and ear conformation of some breeds are a consequence of surgery and subsequently how these surgeries affect perception of dogs and their owners.[1]

During a routine follow up exam of a puppy ear cropped by Dr. Hylton, I asked the young owner how things were going and if medications were working as expected. He told me that things were going great with his dog but when he gave his dog an acepromazine tablet he popped one also into his mouth. He said this resulted in a weird trip that he would never forget.

I told him that probably wasn't a wise choice. The medication is not recommended for humans and it may cause paraphimosis and priapism of the penis in stallions and some gildings. He asked me what those words meant.

I told him that the muscle that holds the penis up into the prepuce under the animal loses its strength and the horse's exposed 20 inch penis gets dry, bloody and swollen from the exposure to the environment, and it's really hard to get it back where it belongs. "Need I say more?" The look on his face made me comfortable that this young man did not pop another pill for another weird trip.

No man was ever so completely skilled in the conduct of life, as not to receive new information from age and experience. Terence (190-150 BC)

1– *Tail Docking and Ear Cropping Dogs: Public Awareness and Perceptions, Edna Hillmann, Editor, NIH-National Library of Medicine, National Center of Biotechnology, 2016.*

2– *The Dog in Place, Fred Lanting, AKC, International All Breed Judge & SAAB Member, 2009.*

3– *Acute Acepromazine Overdose: Clinical Effects and Toxicokinetic Evaluation, J Med Toxicol, 2015.*

CHAPTER 19

WHAT'S A PURR

We think we know what a cat's purr means. It is arguably the most recognizable sign of animal contentment: a pleasurable rasp that erupts whenever a cat is tickled or petted, the soundtrack to countless sessions sprawled on an owner's lap. But that's not quite the full story. There is a lot more going on with the cat's purr than you might reasonably expect.

Even the 'how' was long a subject of debate. Some thought it was linked to blood flowing to the inferior vena cava, a vein that carries deoxygenated blood to the right side of the heart. But with more research it seemed likelier that the noise came from the muscles within the cat's larynx. As they move, they dilate and constrict the glottis – the part of the larynx that surrounds the vocal cords – and the air vibrates every time the cat breathes in or out. The result? A purr.

Even though science is now fairly sure this is the process, there's no definitive answer as to what triggers the response. The biggest clue is a neural oscillator deep within the cat's brain, one that otherwise has no clear purpose.

Marjan Debevere, London cat shelter photographer and studying for a degree in feline psychology, states: People assume cats are happy when they're purring. That's just not always the case. Part of the mystery around the purr is that we often only notice cats purring when we tickle them in places that they like to be tickled. Yet they also purr when we're not around, and the extent of that purring varies between individuals. All cats are different, some never purr and some will purr constantly.

She has witnessed a lot of cats purring when they're dying, and when they're being put to sleep. The vet will say something like "They were purring right up until the end", and people assume they're happy when they're purring. That's just not always the case.

Gary Weitzman, a veterinarian and CEO of the San Diego Humane Society, says that while the purr does generally represent contentment for cats, it can also express nervousness, fear and stress. It's been speculated for decades that purring was a form of communication. In the early 2000s it was hypothesized that purring has other purposes besides this. It's likely that purring has communication, appeasement, and healing properties.

Cats begin purring when they are a few days old, which helps their mothers locate them for feeding time. This may persist with some adult cats who purr as they feed – or who purr beforehand as they try and convince a human it's dinner time. Some will purr loudly when they are cautiously investigating new environments. Cats may also purr after they've been startled, or after stressful episodes like being chased by a dog.[1]

Purring is mostly exclusive to cats, although certain other species can produce purr-like sounds, including raccoons, mongooses, kangaroos, badgers, rabbits, and guinea pigs. And cats are usually divided into those that purr (Felinae) and those that roar (Pantherinae); no cat species can do both. The latter category includes lions, tigers, jaguars, and leopards, and scientists have suggested that the roaring capability is due to an incompletely ossified hyoid bone in the larynx. "Purrers," by contrast, have a completely ossified hyoid, although the purring snow leopard is a rare exception.

We know the fundamental frequency at which cats purr—between 20 to 30 vibrations per second, although purrs can go up to about 150 Hz—but that is lower than expected based on vocal cord anatomy. As a general rule, larger animals have longer vocal cords and thus create lower-frequency sounds. But cats are relatively small, typically weighing on the order of a few kilograms, and their vocal cords are also relatively short. Hence the curiosity about how they produce such low-frequency purrs.

One theory, since discarded, suggested that blood surging through a large vein connected to the right side of the heart caused the purring sounds—the so-called "turbulent blood theory." More recent studies pointed to a different mechanism: cats constrict the muscles in the part of the larynx that touches the vocal cords, producing soft low-frequency rumblings as the cat inhales and exhales. Basically, the glottis opens and closes, building up and releasing pressure, resulting in purrs. It could be that a specific neural oscillator activates those laryngeal contractions, but what triggers the brain signals remains unclear.

In other words, purring is believed to be entirely reliant on neural driven muscle contractions, i.e., the "active muscle contraction" (AMC) hypothesis. This is contrary to how most mammals produce vocal sounds via self-sustaining oscillation of the tissues in the larynx, i.e., the myoelastic-aerodynamic (MEAD) principle. And there isn't much direct empirical evidence for AMC, so the authors of this latest paper set out to test the hypothesis further.

First, the researchers excised the larynxes of eight newly deceased domestic cats, all of which had contracted terminal diseases, resulting in their euthanizing. With the owner's approval, the larynxes were promptly flash-frozen in liquid nitrogen and stored at -20° Celsius. They were slowly thawed at room temperature the night before the experiments. Each larynx was cleaned, photographed, and mounted on a vertical tube, which was used to supply heated air with 100 percent humidity to the larynx.

The larynxes were stabilized using LEGO blocks and 3D-printed plastic mounts, and mini-electrodes were attached to the thyroid cartilage, on each side, to record the electroglottographic (EGG) signal. Gradually opening and closing a magnetic valve in the air supply chain controlled the subglottal pressure by pumping in air, which drove the oscillation in the mounted larynxes.

The authors successfully produced purring sounds in all eight of the excised larynxes when air was pumped through them, with no need for muscle contractions—given that all the adjacent muscles had been removed when excising the larynxes. So, what was driving the purrs? They concluded that it was the presence of connective tissue embedded in the vocal cords, which also served to lower the frequency of the purring sounds. In other words, cats rely on the same MEAD-based mechanisms to purr as other mammals do for their vocalizations.

This doesn't mean that the AMC hypothesis has been entirely debunked, per the authors, merely that it needs to be revised. It's possible that some combination of the two produces the low-frequency purrs. While further research, as always, is needed, "Our data unequivocally demonstrate that MEAD-driven vocal fold vibrations at purr frequencies are possible, without neural input of active muscle contraction," the authors concluded.

Why cats purr remains a matter of considerable debate. We associate purring with a happy, contented cat, but studies have shown that cats purr for any number of reasons. Mama cats typically purr when nursing, for example, perhaps to reassure their tiny offspring, and while in labor. This has led to the suggestion that purring might release a hormone in kitty brains to help them relax, relieve pain, or promote healing. And a cat's purr is subtly different when said feline is angling its human for food. According to a 2009 study, so-called "solicitation purrs" contain a high-frequency component that is absent from a typical purr, and human subjects consistently rated those solicitation purrs as less pleasant and more urgent. But you already knew your cat was manipulating you into those early morning feedings, right?[2]

During veterinary school at Purdue University, I was taught that the sound of a purr came from vibrations created in the respiratory system. I also raised Siamese cats in our very old rented poorly insulted upstairs apartment. My queen cat produced her loudest persistent purrs just before and during her delivery of kittens. My most treasured memory was during a very cold winter night when she brought her kittens under the covers of our bed and placed them between my sleeping wife and me. Her purrs as she was nursing her kittens made for me a special moment.

In my veterinary practice owners usually want to be with their companion pet during euthanasia. An IV fluid line is placed in a vein to deliver the anesthetic and often the owner will hold their cat in a blanket on their lap during the procedure. My experience during the euthanasia of cats is that they are less stressed and more relaxed when purring.

"But there was a kitten on my pillow, and it was purring in my face and vibrating gently with every purr, and, very soon, I slept." Neil Gaiman, The Ocean at the End of the Lane

1– *The complicated truth about a cat's purr, BBC, Stephen Dowling, 07/25/2018.*

2– *We now know how cats purr—why they purr is still up for debate, Jennifer Ouellette, 10/5/2023.*

CHAPTER 20

FOLLOWING AS SHEEPLES THE UNINFORMED CONFIDENT

Sheeple is a blended word that encompasses the words 'sheep' and 'people'. Sheeples are commonly docile, compliant, easily persuaded, and inclined to follow the crowd. Through a comparison with the herding behavior of animals, it has been observed how large numbers of people may act at the same time and in a similar fashion. It suggests that Homo sapiens are hardwired to imitate others, and, in stressful situations, do not independently seek out the information required to determine the correct course of action; with their fight or flight mechanism in overdrive, these sheeple simply follows the crowd.

It appears that sheeple behavior is triggered by a variety of neurological processes in the brain on detecting danger. In this context, it is pointed out that the catalysts signaling the need for action can take many forms, and that any perceived threatening situation, be it real or imaginary, can cause sheeple behavior. Consequently, it is suggested that apart from facing physical danger, situations such as social disapproval can provoke the brain's danger circuits.

Moreover, it is suspected that sheeple behavior is not only neurological processes, but that child development also plays a role. References are made to Homo sapiens' search for protective figures and other feelings that originate from childhood. Research highlights that sheeple behavior is ubiquitous, found everywhere from the financial sector to outbursts of mob violence, political movements, religious gatherings, sporting events, riots, strikes, and even in the context of consumer preferences such as fashion trends. In each of these instances, the individual adopts an opinion based on what other people say and do without bothering to consider the evidence for themselves... It is suggested that it is all too easy to regress into sheeple-like behavior without even being aware of it. The suggestion is made, however, that fostering independent thought will reduce the risk of the destructive elements of sheeple behavior, but it will remain a challenge distinguishing between the wisdom and the madness of crowds.[1]

We humans are far more likely to accept and believe information delivered confidently by a confident person, or by a source using confident language etc. And as the modern world has shown us repeatedly, this regularly leads to undesirable outcomes. Humans trusting confident people over unconfident ones is an established phenomenon. The 'Confidence heuristic' states that when two (or more) people are involved in a decision making process where they know different things, confidently expressed arguments are perceived as conveying better information, which determines the decision.

Why would this tendency come about? Humans are ultrasocial, and during our evolutionary development, most of our information about the world came from our tribe, i.e. other people. So, if ancient humans heard someone confidently declare "There's a predator coming!", instinctively believing them was a valuable survival trait. Humans are also hierarchical. We have social status, and our communities often have leaders, who tend to be confident sorts. In the wild, where there's danger everywhere, a tendency to unthinkingly believe the confident leader and quickly do what they say, is another useful survival trait.

On a more personal level, much of our thinking about, and perception of, others tends towards the egocentric; we relate what they do and say to our own experiences, because that's typically what our brain has to work with. If when we're confident it's for good reason, logically someone else being confident must have good reason to be too.

There are caveats, like credibility; a megaphone-wielding street preacher, bellowing that the world's about to end, may seem more confident than a friend recommending a restaurant is, but the latter will carry much more weight. Similarly, the manner of communication affects confidence assessments. Someone may be very confident in their claims/ideas, but if they deliver them hurriedly, or quietly, we're less likely to recognize this confidence. Slow, clear speech is associated with confidence.

So, there are many reasons why we trust confident people. Now, here are some why we shouldn't.

Confidently delivered information may be more persuasive, but that doesn't mean it's correct, even if the confident person genuinely believes it is. Even that's not certain; humans have long been able to deceive. It's extremely possible for certain people to feign confidence convincingly, even if conveying the most meaningless guff.

But 'wrong confidence' need not mean deceit. For one, confidence is linked to intelligence. We've all met someone who confidently lectures others on how the world works, despite being wrong about literally everything. It's the Dunning-Kruger effect, where people with low ability/experience/knowledge about something often significantly overestimate their abilities/expertise regarding it. This is because the ability to recognize your intellectual limits requires sufficient intelligence. Lacking that, you won't question your (limited) understanding, so can spout laughable nonsense with utmost confidence.

Meanwhile, higher intelligence makes you more aware of what you don't know, leading to imposter syndrome, diminishing confidence. Suddenly, mistrust of experts and rejections of their conclusions makes more sense.

However, someone with perfectly normal intelligence may still end up excessively confident, if they have a particularly privileged existence. An affluent, pampered life, particularly during childhood, can mean never suffering the consequences of being wrong. So, you could end up believing you aren't wrong. Ever. Your brain never had the opportunity to recognize this occurrence. So, you'll deliver every utterance with unshakeable confidence, purely because it's you saying it.

This happens later in life too. As stated, much of what we understand about the world, and ourselves, comes via information from other people. So, if you achieve success in your field legitimately, and your confidence is therefore 'valid', you can still end up surrounded by those who agree with and support you, i.e. people who validate everything you say or think. Big celebrities, surrounded by whole networks of people dedicated to serving them and keeping them happy, regularly develop massive egos, which often leads to them confidently, and publicly, stating the most ridiculous things.[2]

At 6:40 AM on 11/06/2023 I was lying in bed typing on my computer (CPU). Suddenly an alert and warning sign began flashing stating that my CPU had been infected by a virus. I could not exit the screen. It told me not to turn off the computer and instructed me to call a number next to the Micro Soft logo. Panic struck in and I dutifully called the number on the screen.

The voice on the phone instructed my wife that she should not hang up my phone or use it to make any other calls, they were investigating what had occurred and they would give me instructions as to what I should do on my CPU. They helped me get into a blackened screen that reminded me of the DOS screen used when my CPU had 5 1/4" floppy disk drives in the 80s. These disks always seemed to need to be rebooted every time I was doing something important like - calculating payroll or figuring state and federal withholding taxes for Camden Pet Hospital.

My wife was told that there had been two money wire transfers to Russia out of her banking accounts: $10,000 for gambling and $2,800 for a porn site. Shauna argued that she had not made these money transfers and was very offended that anyone would accuse her of "such a thing." He told her not to hang up, they would inform our banks for us and it would take some time to change my CPU ID number and not to turn it off.

After we informed them that we were going to dress and go directly to the bank, the man told her to not disconnect my phone or use her phone, because it would give up important private information to the hackers, and leave my CPU on. He also instructed her to withdraw $12,800 in cash from the bank and wait in her car at the bank parking lot. They were arranging for the hackers to be caught when they approached the car.

About this time, reality HIT US! I told Shauna to shut off the cell phone and we were going directly into the bank to check out her deposit balances – all this occurred as she was listening to the caller telling her, "DO NOT GO INTO THE BANK."

Fortunate for us, our finances were untouched in all our accounts. My wife and I, couldn't believe we had been fooled. Her career was a bank manager and mine owning a business - we should not have taken the bait. Dutifully we demonstrated at least one of Charles Darwin's theories to be true: "Ignorance more frequently begets confidence than does knowledge." Our sheeple trust in a stranger, who confidently delivered information about the internal workings of banks and computers we know little about in a knowledgeable way, could have easily blindly led us like sheep into the wolf's lair. Potentially leading to undesirable outcomes in our personal and financial wellbeing.

With all our experiences in life, we seem to be less aware than that 10-year-old Sasha Smith who coined the term combining the two words 'sheep' and 'people': 'sheeple'.

We live in a highly interconnected, increasingly complex society, where innumerable people and worldviews end up overlapping constantly. So, someone who is objectively, unquestionably wrong, but still unshakably confident can end up convincing many others that they're right.

Often by providing easy answers for complex modern issues, particularly ones that 'confirm' pre-existing worldviews or prejudices. This makes them more high-profile, thus more legitimate and convincing, so they gain more support and followers, and the cycle continues.

Left unchecked, it can end up with individuals with no abilities or redeeming traits beyond unshakeable confidence being put in charge of entire countries. And that won't end well for anyone. You can be confident in that conclusion.[2]

1– *Are You a Sheeple? Entrepreneurship and Family Enterprise, 10/19/2022.*

2– *Human evolution has led to us naturally believe statements delivered in a more assured manner, BBC Science Focus Magazine, Dean Burnett, 06/23/223.*

CHAPTER 21

RACCOON DOG MYSTICAL FAIRY TALE

Have you ever heard about the Tanuki? With its atypical look and its comical air, this Yokai (a catchall Japanese word for ghosts, demons, monsters, shapeshifters, tricksters, and other kinds of supernatural beings and mysterious phenomena). Yokai interacts with the human world and spark common notions of frightful things and is very popular in Japan. Funny face, bouncy belly, straw hat and a bottle of sake; who on earth is this strange creature?

The term tanuki refers to the Japanese raccoon dog, a subspecies of the Asian raccoon dog. In Japanese folklore, the Tanuki is considered a yōkai, a forest spirit with disproportionate attributes and magical powers. The raccoon dog is a canid species native to Asia that lives in mountains and forests. Of omnivorous nature, this animal mainly goes out at night in search of food. It can be recognized by its long hair and characteristic facial mask. The Tanuki has the particularity to hibernate. Besides, it is regularly mistaken for a raccoon or a badger.

In Japanese mythology, the raccoon dog has magical powers. This forest spirit has the ability to transform itself at will in order to fool men, is known for its large scrotum and its love for sake. The Tanuki is a source of jokes for Japanese people.

Like most Japanese mythical creatures, the Tanuki has celestial powers. As a shape-shifting creature, it can transform and take on any appearance desired, such as that of an object or a human. Moreover, he has mastered the art of disguise. His paunchy belly serves him as a drum.

The Tanuki is known to be a symbol of prosperity and good fortune, that's why it is often found in Japanese stores or at the entrance of bars and restaurants. Considered as a lucky charm, Tanuki sculptures are also found in front of houses or stores. Note that in Japan, testicles are symbolic of luck and wealth. He is best known for its large size balls used for multiple functions. He uses them as a weapon, a tool, an umbrella or even as a fishing net depending on the situation. In fact, the flexible skin of the tanuki's testicles was used to wrap gold inside when making gold leaf. This particularity inspired the famous myth of the family jewels that could be stretched up to 8 tatami mats if not 1000! For good reason, this prankster spirit is the source of many legends and humorous representations.[1]

When health emergencies arise, scientists seek to discover the cause — such as how a pathogen emerged and spread — because this knowledge can enhance our understanding of risks and strategies for prevention, preparedness, and mitigation. Yet well into the fourth year of the Covid-19 pandemic, intense political and scientific debates about its origins continue. The two major hypotheses are a natural zoonotic spillover, most likely occurring at the Huanan Seafood Wholesale Market, and a laboratory leak from the Wuhan Institute of Virology (WIV).

China withheld the data from public domain for 3 years, their scientists uploaded the data but then removed it and in response to pressure from WHO – China restored those data to GISAID (the Global Initiative on Sharing All Influenza Data).

Of the three possibilities — natural, accidental, or deliberate — the most scientific evidence yet identified supports natural emergence. More than half of the earliest Covid-19 cases were connected to the Huanan market, and epidemiologic mapping revealed that the concentration of cases was centered there.

Proponents of the accidental laboratory leak theory stress the geographic location of the WIV in the city where the pandemic began. They point to the presence of the bat coronavirus RaTG13 strain at the laboratory, arguing that genetic manipulations such as gain-of-function (GOF) research may have produced SARS-CoV-2. Most scientists refute this theory because there is considerable evolutionary distance between the two viruses. However, the possibility that the laboratory held a different progenitor strain to SARS-CoV-2 that led to a laboratory leak cannot be unequivocally ruled out. China's obfuscation may mean that we will never have certainty about the origins of the greatest pandemic in more than a century.[2]

Now, an international team of virologists, genomicists, and evolutionary biologists may have finally found crucial data to help fill that knowledge gap. A new analysis of genetic sequences collected from the market shows that raccoon dogs being illegally sold at the venue could have been carrying and possibly shedding the virus at the end of 2019. It's some of the strongest support yet that the pandemic began when SARS-CoV-2 hopped from animals into humans, rather than in an accident among scientists experimenting with viruses.

The samples were already known to be positive for the coronavirus, and had been scrutinized before by the same group of Chinese researchers who uploaded the data. But that prior analysis, released as a preprint publication in February 2022, asserted that "no animal host of SARS-CoV-2 can be deduced." Any motes of coronavirus at the market, the study suggested, had most likely been chauffeured in by infected humans, rather than wild creatures for sale.

The new analysis, led by three prominent researchers who have been looking into the virus's roots—shows that that may not be the case. Within about half a day of downloading the data, the trio and their collaborators discovered that several market samples that tested positive for SARS-CoV-2 were also coming back chock-full of animal genetic material—much of which was a match for the common raccoon dog, a small animal related to foxes that has a raccoon-like face. Because of how the samples were gathered, and because viruses can't persist by themselves in the environment, the scientists think that their findings could indicate the presence of a coronavirus-infected raccoon dog in the spots where the swabs were taken.[3]

The raccoon dog, also known as mangut or tanuki, is an East Asian animal native to China, Korea, Japan and the far eastern regions of Russia. The raccoon dog is a very old species, but until recently there has been no interest in taming and keeping it as a pet. In Eastern Europe it's considered an invasive species, and in Spain, among other countries, it is forbidden to trade or bring it to the wild; keeping it as a pet is out of the question.

Even if it were legal to own a raccoon dog, AnimalWised does not advise anyone to adopt a tanuki or mangut as a pet. The raccoon dog is a basal species of canid, that is, an ancestral species. The habits of the raccoon dog are more like those of a badger or a fox than any breed of dog. They are crepuscular and nocturnal, meaning that their active periods are at dusk and throughout the night, while during the day they sleep hidden in their underground burrows. During the spring and summer, raccoon dogs gain fat in order to face the winter; they are the only canid species that hibernates.

The appearance of the raccoon dog largely resembles a raccoon - hence their name - especially its face; however, the two species are not related at all. Like the vast majority of canines, the raccoon dog benefits from a double coat. The first woolly layer is matte gray in color, while the top layer is very colorful. In fact, tanukis were brought over from the Far East to Europe to make use of their fur.

This second layer is very long and dense, with a mottled red and grey coloring. If you look closely at a raccoon dog's fur, you will clearly see that it has several perfectly segmented colors. The roots are gray, the same shade as the inner coat. Next, you will usually see a pastel orange color, which is the dominant color of the strand of hair. The top of the hairs are shiny black, except for the ivory white tip.

The raccoon dog is native to Japan, and it's not uncommon to find the suburbs of Japanese cities teeming with them in search of rubbish. The tanuki lives in social groups and is an omnivorous animal. This is one of the reasons why it is not in danger of extinction.

From the late 1920s onward, the raccoon dog started to be imported to Europe from Asia with the intention of setting up farms intended for the sale of its fur. Many animals escaped from farms in the former Soviet Union, Scandinavia, Poland, Germany and other Central European countries.

The raccoon dog has become an invasive species in all of these places, with the additional problem that European tanukis have been bred to be almost twice as large as the original ones.

Much like foxes, the prospects of having a raccoon dog as a pet are very weak. They are very fearful, elusive animals and are nocturnal. They remain frozen with fear when caught in the headlights of cars, and in Japan many of them die on roads every year. The tanuki plays a prominent role in Japanese mythology, where it is considered good luck.

On a practical level, keeping raccoon dogs as pets is not advisable. Since they are not domesticated animals, they will not adapt well to home environments, especially in apartments and small homes. They can be destructive and many people abandon them as pets because they are unable to provide the serious amounts of attention they require.

Additionally, raccoon dogs have anal glands which are used for marking territory, similar to their cousin the fox. The smell these glands produce is unpleasant and will not likely be well tolerated in the home. Their nocturnal habits mean it is unlikely they would adapt well to human families.

The raccoon dog is monogamous. It is not a violent animal in any circumstance. It likes to live as part of a small group in warm burrows in wooded areas, where females give birth to 5-7 pups during the spring. These are cared for by males while the females go away to hunt. Being omnivores, raccoon dogs will eat anything: Birds, rodents, reptiles, berries, fruit or vegetables, even carrion or rubbish.[4]

A new paper by a prominent American virologist, Jesse Bloom, has called into question a string of high-profile news reports about the role that raccoon dogs may have played in the emergence of the Covid-19 pandemic. The data has since sparked a firestorm of discussion, including numerous stories in mainstream news outlets that have relied on the data to report a link between raccoon dogs and Covid's origin. Bloom's new paper helps clarify what has become something of a confused, and confusing, media spectacle.

Before the report was ready to be released publicly, the press got wind of the team's work. What followed was a bumper crop of bold headlines. "The Strongest Evidence Yet That an Animal Started the Pandemic," declared The Atlantic in a March 16 headline. "New Data Links Pandemic's Origins to Raccoon Dogs at Wuhan Market," announced the New York Times that same day. "New Evidence Supports Animal Origin of Covid Virus through Raccoon Dogs," wrote the Scientific American a day later. The news of a link between raccoon dogs and Covid's origins spread like a conflagration.

What was this strong evidence? The Atlantic's March 16 story described the international team's work like this: "A new analysis of genetic sequences collected from the market shows that raccoon dogs being illegally sold at the venue could have been carrying and possibly shedding the virus at the end of 2019," wrote The Atlantic's Katherine Wu. "It's some of the strongest support yet, experts told me, that the pandemic began when SARS-CoV-2 hopped from animals into humans, rather than in an accident among scientists experimenting with viruses."

Wu reported, among other things, that the international team of researchers had "discovered that several market samples that tested positive for SARS-CoV-2 were also coming back chock-full of animal genetic material — much of which was a match for the common raccoon dog, a small animal related to foxes that has a raccoon-like face." At the time The Atlantic published its article on March 16, the international team's report was not yet publicly available; it wouldn't be released until the following week.

In the end, based on these and other findings, the international team stated the following in their report: "Although we cannot identify the intermediate animal host species from these data, a plausible explanation for the co-occurrence of the genetic material of SARS-CoV-2 and susceptible animals is that a subset of these animals were infected. Combined with the previously published observation of the strong association of the earliest reported Covid-19 cases with the west side of the market, and the clustering of SARS-CoV-2-containing environmental samples near the wildlife stalls, this provides further support for the hypothesis that wildlife were the source of the first human SARS-CoV-2 infections."

Elsewhere in the report, the authors wrote that their findings identify "these species, particularly the common raccoon dog, as the most likely conduits for the emergence of SARS-CoV-2 in late 2019."

Blooms response: "It just sort of suggests that by the time these samples were collected, SARS-CoV-2 was all over the place, probably unrelated to the distribution of the animals and animal products [at the market]."

Bloom notes that his preprint confirms many of the international team's findings, including the presence of raccoon dogs and other susceptible mammals at Huanan market in the run-up to January 1, 2020. But the bottom line, Bloom said, is that "when looked at carefully these data are not sufficient to conclude anything either way about whether there were infected animals." He also had pointed words (at least in the context of a staid scientific paper) for the media coverage of this matter. The findings from his preprint, Bloom writes, "are somewhat inconsistent with related media articles that emphasized co-mingling of raccoon dog and viral material — in fact, raccoon dogs are one of the species with the least co-mingling of their genetic material and SARS-CoV-2." Instead, Bloom found that the greatest co-mingling of viral and animal material involved species that were "almost certainly not infected with SARS-CoV-2," such as fish and livestock.

In terms of the broader picture — the overall debate about the origin of Covid-19 and whether it spilled over from nature or emerged out of a lab — Bloom said he remains agnostic: "I mean it is obviously hard when you are interpreting what is all circumstantial evidence. All publicly available evidence right now about how SARS-CoV-2 entered humans, it is all circumstantial. I think it is very unclear how SARS-CoV-2 first entered humans."[5]

There are three possibilities how Covid-19 infections began — natural, accidental, or deliberate — the most scientific evidence yet identified supports natural emergence. More than half of the earliest Covid-19 cases were connected to the Huanan market, and epidemiologic mapping revealed that the concentration of cases was centered there. Proponents of the accidental laboratory leak theory stress the geographic location of the Wuhan Institute of Virology (WIV) in the city where the pandemic began. They point to the presence of bat coronavirus strain at the laboratory and possibility other progenitor strains that led to a laboratory leak.

Could blaming the Raccoon Dog for the worst pandemic experienced by this planet in over a century amount to one of these well-known sayings: "A lie is halfway round the world before the truth has got its boots on." If so, in this case a more accurate version might be: "A confidently told lie is halfway round the world before the truth has got its boots on?" *Author Unknown*

My theory is that all three possibilities were involved with the most disruptive and costly pandemic that has affected mankind in many a moon. Even from the information reported and questionable research – I think the culprit was the Raccoon Dog better known as Tanuki in Japan. These Raccoon Dogs were all over the market place near the WIV laboratory waiting to be brutely killed by slamming their heads against the ground and pulling off their hide for the clothing industry to provide fur for insensitive humans.

With their magical and celestial powers, these small creatures can "transform themselves in ways to fool, they can take any appearance desired and are a master of disguise." I'm sure several Tanukis, knowing bats are resistant to a lot of different viral diseases (including rabies which can make them sick but rarely kills them) transformed themselves into bats. They allowed themselves to be trapped and placed into the WIV laboratory where they mutated virus' into Covid-19. Changing themselves into hummingbirds, the WIV staff let the "poor trapped" beautiful birds out through an open door, where they proceeded to share the virus with the venders selling the Raccoon Dogs for slaughter. WA HA – a pandemic caused from natural, accidental, and deliberate means!

One thing that really caught my attention is that in Japan, testicles are symbolic of luck and wealth. Tanukis are best known for their large size balls used for multiple functions. He uses them as a weapon, a tool, an umbrella or even as a fishing net depending on the situation. In fact, the flexible skin of the tanuki's testicles can be used to wrap gold inside when making gold leaf. Statues of Tanukis are often found displayed at restaurants, bars and homes as a symbol of luck and wealth. I have ordered a small Tanuki tea mug to display for "luck and wealth" in my "Museum of Shame."

I have a kangaroo scrotum that I've used as a coin purse for years. I would be most grateful if a Tanuki would send me his scrotum full of fine gold for my honoring the Raccoon Dog and helping them be given full credit for the intelligent creatures they are. I would stretch the organ wide enough so I could keep all my favorite coins in one place.

"Since incorporating the comments he received, Bloom has submitted his preprint for peer review at a scientific journal. According to Débarre, the international team is working on new analyses that it hopes to submit for peer review at a future date." If they can tie in hummingbirds – who knows – but the great mystery may be solved…

1– *Tanuki, a Curious Yōkai, Japan Avenue, 06/23/2021.*
2– *Origins of Covid-19 – Why it Matters (or Doesn't), N Engl J Med; 388:2305-2308, 06/22/2023.*
3– *The Strongest Evidence Yet That an Animal Started the Pandemic, Atlantic, Katherine J. Wu, 03/16/2023.*
4– *Raccoon Dogs as Pets: Guidelines and General Tips, Josie F. Turner – Animal Welfare, 02/19/2020.*
5– *The Rise and Fall of The Raccoon Dog Theory of Covid-19, Jimmy Tobias, 05/10/2023.*

CHAPTER 22

BEN FRANKLIN AND
THE JERSEY DEVIL

In *Wikipedia's popular folklore*, the Jersey Devil originated with a Pine Barrens resident named Jane Leeds, known as "Mother Leeds." The legend states that Mother Leeds had twelve children and, after discovering she was pregnant for the thirteenth time, cursed the child in frustration, declaring that the child would be the "devil." In 1735, Mother Leeds was in labor on a stormy night while her friends gathered around her. Unfortunately for her, the thirteenth child was born normally. However, it screaming, the child beat everyone with its tail before flying up the chimney and heading into the pines.

Mother Leeds was supposedly a witch and the child's father was the devil himself. Legend has it that local clergymen attempted to exorcise the creature from the Pine Barrens.

During 1859, the Atlantic Monthly published an article detailing the Leeds (Jersey) Devil folk tales popular among Pine Barren residents (or "pine rats"). A newspaper from

1887 describes sightings of a winged creature, referred to as "the Devil of Leeds", allegedly spotted near the Pine Barrens and well known among the local populace of Burlington County, New Jersey:

Whenever he went near it, it would give a most unearthly yell that frightened the dogs. It whipped at every dog on the place. "That thing," said the colonel, "is not a bird nor an animal, but it is the Leeds devil, according to the description, and it was born over in Evesham, Burlington County, a hundred years ago. There is no mistake about it. I never saw the horrible critter myself, but I can remember well when it was roaming around in Evesham woods fifty years ago, and when it was hunted by men and dogs and shot at by the best marksmen there were in all South Jersey but could not be killed. There isn't a family in Burlington or any of the adjoining counties that does not know of the Leeds devil, and it was the bugaboo to frighten children with when I was a boy.

While visiting the Hanover Mill Works to inspect his cannonballs being forged, Commodore Stephen Decatur sighted a flying creature and fired a cannonball directly upon it, to no effect. Joseph Bonaparte, elder brother of Napoleon, is also claimed to have seen the Jersey Devil while hunting on his Bordentown estate about 1820. Earlier accounts of the Jersey Devil were recorded:

During 1840, the Jersey Devil was blamed for several livestock killings. Similar attacks were reported during 1841, accompanied by tracks and screams. During the week of January 16–23, 1909, newspapers published hundreds of claimed encounters with the Jersey Devil from all over South Jersey and the Philadelphia area. Among these alleged encounters were claims the creature "attacked" a trolley car in Haddon Heights and a social club in Camden. Police in Camden and Bristol, Pennsylvania supposedly fired on the creature to no effect. Other reports initially concerned unidentified footprints in the snow, but soon sightings of creatures resembling the Jersey Devil were being reported throughout South Jersey and as far away as Delaware and Western Maryland. The widespread newspaper coverage created fear throughout the Delaware Valley prompting a number of schools to close and workers to stay home. Vigilante groups and groups of hunters roamed the pines and country sides in search of the devil.

In Greenwich Township, in December 1925, a local farmer shot an unidentified animal as it attempted to steal his chickens, and then photographed the corpse. Afterward, he claimed that none of 100 people he showed it to could identify it. On July 27, 1937, an unknown animal "with red eyes" seen by residents of Downingtown, Pennsylvania was compared to the Jersey Devil by a reporter for the Pennsylvania Bulletin of July 28, 1937. In 1951, a group of Gibbstown, New Jersey boys claimed to have seen a ‹monster› matching the Devil›s description and claims of a corpse matching the Jersey Devil›s description arose in 1957. During 1960, tracks and noises heard near Mays Landing were claimed to be from the Jersey Devil. During the same year the merchants around Camden offered a $10,000 reward for the capture of the Jersey Devil, even offering to build a private zoo to house the creature if it was captured.

The recent prevalence of 'fake news' may make it seem like misinformation is a relatively modern invention. But wild claims, falsehoods and conspiracy theories have been part of human culture for about as long as it's existed. This is because misinformation originates with, and is spread by, other people; and the people factor has a really strong influence.

According to Dr. Dean Burnett: If you've ever had to communicate an important, but complex, issue to a general audience, you'll be well aware of just how frustrating the people factor can be. You may have terabytes of the most reliable data, meticulously worked-out rebuttals to any possible argument, the most elegant PowerPoint slides and the full backing of every renowned expert in the relevant field. And yet, you can still be less persuasive than someone whose entire argument is: "A guy I met…told me something different."

The source of this revered information isn't always some random stranger you met, obviously. Sometimes it's a friend, or a friend of a friend, or a distant cousin. It may even come from a series of people with ever-more tenuous connections ("My mother's neighbor's stepson's boss's barber said…") In fairness, the individual source of the information will (supposedly) have some relevant experience or insight. Say you're discussing the safety of vaccines and end up arguing with someone whose cousin's roommate "works for a pharmacist."

In a perfectly sensible, logical world, someone who knows someone that's loosely affiliated with a vaguely connected field or industry wouldn't carry the same clout as actual data, or the leading experts in the field. But humans aren't perfectly sensible, logical creatures and neither is the world we live in. For all our impressive cognitive powers, how we see the world, and the information we latch onto and retain, are heavily shaped by the instinctive, subconscious and emotional processes that make up much of our brain. And if there's one thing that engages these subconscious, emotional processes, it's our fellow humans.[1]

Conspiracy theories are everywhere, and they can involve just about anything. People believe false conspiracy theories for a wide range of reasons – including the fact that there are real conspiracies, like efforts by the Sackler family to profit by concealing the addictiveness of oxycontin at the cost of countless American lives. Or the extreme consequences of unfounded conspiratorial beliefs could be seen on the staircases of the U.S. Capitol on Jan. 6, 2021, and in the self-immolation of a protestor outside the courthouse holding the latest Trump trial.

But if hidden forces really are at work in the world, how is someone to know what's really going on?

H. Colleen Sinclair states: That's where my research comes in; I'm a social psychologist who studies misleading narratives. Here are some ways to vet a claim you've seen or heard. Sometimes there's nothing but the maze itself:

Step 1: Seek out the evidence: Real conspiracies have been confirmed because there was evidence. For instance, in the allegations dating back to the 1990s that tobacco companies knew cigarettes were dangerous and kept that information secret to make money, scientific studies showed problematic links between tobacco and cancer. Court cases unearthed corporate documents with internal memos showing what executives knew and when. Investigative journalists revealed efforts to hide that information. Doctors explained the effects on their patients. Internal whistleblowers sounded the alarm.

But unfounded conspiracy theories reveal their lack of evidence and substitute instead several elements that should be red flags for skeptics:

- Dismissing traditional sources of evidence, claiming they are in on the plot.
- Claiming that missing information is because someone is hiding it, even though it's common that not all facts are known completely for some time after an event.
- Attacking apparent inconsistencies as evidence of lies.
- Overinterpreting ambiguity as evidence: A flying object may be unidentified – but that's different from identifying it as an alien spaceship.
- Using anecdotes – especially vaguely attributed ones – in place of evidence, such as "people are saying" such-and-such or "my cousin's friend experienced" something.
- Attributing knowledge to secret messages that only a select few can grasp – rather than evidence that's plain and clear to all.

Step 2: Test the allegation: Often, a conspiracy theorist presents only evidence that confirms their idea. Rarely do they put their idea to the tests of logic, reasoning and critical thinking.

- While they may say they do research, they typically do not apply the scientific method. Specifically, they don't actually try to prove themselves wrong.
- So a skeptic can follow the method scientists use when they do research: Think about what evidence would contradict the explanation – and then go

looking for that evidence. Sometimes that effort will yield confirmation that the explanation is correct. And sometimes not. Like a scientist, ask yourself: What would it take for you to believe your perception was wrong?

– Look closely at allegations of massive conspiracies.

Step 3: Watch out for tangled webs: When theories claim large groups of people are perpetrating wide-ranging activities over a long period of time, that's another red flag.

– Confirmed conspiracies typically involve small, isolated groups, like the top echelon of a company or a single terrorist cell. Even the alliance among tobacco companies to hide their products' danger was confined to those at the top, who made decisions and enlisted paid scientists and ad agencies to spread their messages.

– False conspiracies tend to implicate wide swaths of people, such as world leaders, mainstream media outlets, the global scientific community, the Hollywood entertainment industry and interconnected government agencies.

The online manifesto of Max Azzarello – the man who self-immolated on the steps of a New York courthouse in April 2024– railed against a conspiracy allegedly including every president since Bill Clinton, sex offender Jeffrey Epstein, even the writers of "The Simpsons."

– Remember that the more people who supposedly know a secret, the harder it is to keep.

Step 4: Look for a motive:

- Confirmed conspiracies tell stories about why a group of people acted as they did and what they hoped to gain. Dubious conspiracies involve a lot of accusations or just questions without examining what real benefit the conspiracy nets the conspirators, especially when factoring in the costs. For instance, what purpose would NASA have to lie about the existence of Finland?

- Be particularly suspicious when conspiracies allege an "agenda" being perpetrated by an entire sociodemographic, which is often a marginalized group, such as a "gay agenda" or "Muslim agenda." Also look to see whether those spreading the conspiracy theories have something to gain. For example, scholarly research has identified the 12 people who are the primary sources of false claims about vaccinations. The researchers also found that those people profit from making those claims.

Step 5: Seek the source of the allegations:

- If you can't figure out who is at the root of a conspiracy allegation and thus how they came to know what they claim, that is another red flag. Some people say they have to remain anonymous because the conspiracists will take revenge for revealing information. But even so, a conspiracy can usually be tracked back to its source – maybe a social media account, even an anonymous one.

- Over time, anonymous sources either come forward or are revealed. For instance, years after the Watergate scandal took down Richard Nixon's presidency, a key inside source known as "Deep

Throat" was revealed to be Mark Felt, who had been a high-level FBI official in the early 1970s.

Even the notorious "Q" at the heart of the QAnon conspiracy cult has been identified, and not by government investigators chasing leaks of national secrets. Surprise! Q is not the high-level official some people believed.

Step 6: Beware the supernatural: Some conspiracy theories – though none that have been proven – involve paranormal, alien, demonic or other supernatural forces. People alive in the 1980s and 1990s might remember the public fear that satanic cults were abusing and sacrificing children. That idea never disappeared entirely.

– And around the same time, perhaps inspired by the TV series "V," some Americans began to believe in lizard people. It may seem harmless to keep hoping for evidence of Bigfoot, but the person who detonated a bomb in downtown Nashville on Dec. 25, 2020, apparently believed lizard people ran the Earth.

– The closer the conspiracy is to science fiction, the closer it is to just being fiction.

Step 7: Look for other warning signs:

– There are other red flags too, like the use of prejudicial tropes about the group allegedly behind the conspiracy, particularly antisemitic allegations.

– But rather than doing the work to really examine their conspiratorial beliefs, believers often choose to write off the skeptics as fools or as also being in on it – whatever "it" may be.

Ultimately, that's part of the allure of conspiracy theories. It is easier to dismiss criticism than to admit you might be wrong.[2]

Dr. Burnett continues: While our brains can and will take in and retain abstract information and raw data, they don't really like to. The ability to think rationally and analytically is a relatively recent addition to our suite of mental abilities (in the evolutionary sense). And it costs our brains a lot of energy and effort.

The more established, fundamental systems in our brain, which shape memory and learning, are heavily reliant on emotion. The more emotionally stimulating something is, the easier it is to retain and remember, particularly compared to objective data and facts. That's why we can spend months revising the material for a crucial exam, but struggle to remember any of it once we've passed. Meanwhile, the humiliating time we slipped and landed on our backside in the school cafeteria… that memory endures until our dying day.

Logically, the emotions of guilt or embarrassment can't occur if nobody else is involved in the events. And we've evolved very sophisticated neurological systems for recognizing and sharing the emotions of others, such as empathy.

It goes beyond just the emotional connection, though, because so much of our brains are dedicated to gleaning information from other people. We have dedicated regions for processing faces, language, speech and more. Indeed, some experts argue that the reason we evolved language at all is so we could gossip.

The importance of other people when it comes to the information we absorb is visible everywhere you look. For instance, it would be much easier, cheaper and more practical to share important information, such as the latest news bulletins, with simple words on a screen – especially in the earlier days of television. But even so, every culture you can think of used – and continues to use – newsreaders. Why? Because they give a human face, a human connection, to otherwise abstract, intangible information. It's also (partly) why so many of us react with, "At last, a human being!" after spending long periods dealing with an automated calling system.

Ultimately, we've evolved to accept information more readily when it's provided by another person. They help us process, contextualize and relate to the abstract, the intangible. Whether the information we get from others is reliable or even plausible doesn't seem to matter, the more hardcore sceptic type will often say, "facts don't care about your feelings," which is correct. But feelings don't necessarily care about facts either. And ultimately, feelings have more of a say in what we think and do. and that's why the person cutting your hair can seem more believable than a whole archive of published research.[1]

Brian Regal, a historian of science at Kean University, theorizes that the story of Mother Leeds, rather than being based on a single historical person alone, originated from the reputation of the local prominent Leeds family in the southern portion of the colonial-era Province of New Jersey, where religious-political disputes became the subject of folklore and gossip among the local population. The folk legends most likely originated from disputes evolving through the years and ultimately resulted in the modern popular legend of the Jersey Devil during the early 20th century. Regal contends that "colonial-era political intrigue" involving early New Jersey politicians, Benjamin Franklin, and Franklin's rival almanac publisher Daniel Leeds (1651–1720) resulted in the Leeds family being described as "monsters", and it was Daniel Leeds' negative description as the "Leeds Devil", rather than any actual creature, that created the later legend of the Jersey Devil.

Much like the Mother Leeds of the Jersey Devil myth, Daniel Leeds' third wife had given birth to nine children, a large number of children even for the time. Leeds' second wife and first daughter had both died during childbirth. Leeds and his family were prominent in the South Jersey and Pine Barrens area.

As a royal surveyor with strong allegiance to the British crown, Leeds had surveyed and acquired land in the Egg Harbor area, located within the Pine Barrens. The land was inherited by Leeds' sons and family and is now known as Leeds Point, one of the areas in the Pine Barrens currently most associated with the Jersey Devil legend and alleged Jersey Devil sightings.

Starting in the 17th century, English Quakers established settlements in Southern Jersey, the region in which the Pine Barrens are located. Daniel Leeds, a Quaker and a prominent person of pre-Revolution colonial southern New Jersey, became ostracized by his Quaker congregation after his 1687 publication of almanacs containing astrological symbols and writings. Leeds' fellow Quakers deemed the astrology in these almanacs as too "pagan" or blasphemous, and the almanacs were censored and destroyed by the local Quaker community.

In response to and in spite of this censorship, Leeds continued to publish even more esoteric astrological Christian writings and became increasingly fascinated with Christian occultism, Christian mysticism, cosmology, demonology and angelology, and natural magic. In the 1690s, after his almanacs and writings were further censored as blasphemous or heretical by the Philadelphia Quaker Meeting, Leeds continued to dispute with the Quaker community, converting to Anglicanism and publishing anti-Quaker tracts criticizing Quaker theology and accusing Quakers of being anti-monarchists. In 1700, the local South Jersey Quaker community retaliated against Leeds' anti-Quaker tracts with their own tract, Satan's Harbinger Encountered ... Being Something by Way of Answer to Daniel Leeds, which publicly accused Leeds of working for the devil.

During 1716, Daniel Leeds' son, Titan Leeds, inherited his father's almanac business, which continued to use astrological content and eventually competed with Benjamin Franklin's popular Poor Richard's Almanack. The competition between the two men intensified when, during 1733, Franklin satirically used astrology in his almanac to predict Titan Leeds' death on October of that same year. Though Franklin's prediction was intended as a joke at his competitor's expense and a means to boost almanac sales, Titan Leeds was apparently offended at the death prediction, publishing a public admonition of Franklin as a "fool" and a "liar". In a published response, Franklin mocked Titan Leeds' outrage and humorously suggested that, in fact, Titan Leeds had died in accordance with the earlier prediction and was thus writing his almanacs as a ghost, resurrected from the grave to haunt and torment Franklin. Franklin continued to jokingly refer to Titan Leeds as a "ghost" even after Titan Leeds' actual death in 1738. Daniel Leeds' blasphemous and occultist reputation and his pro-monarchy stance in the largely anti-monarchist colonial south of New Jersey, combined with Benjamin Franklin's later continuous depiction of his son Titan Leeds as a ghost, may have originated or contributed to the local folk legend of a so-called "Leeds Devil" lurking in the Pine Barrens.

During 1728, Titan Leeds began to include the Leeds family crest on the masthead of his almanacs. The Leeds family crest depicted a wyvern, a bat-winged dragon-like legendary creature that stands upright on two clawed feet. Regal notes that the wyvern on the Leeds family crest is reminiscent of the popular descriptions of the Jersey Devil. The inclusion of this family crest on Leeds' almanacs may have further contributed to the Leeds family's poor reputation among locals and possibly influenced the popular descriptions of the Leeds Devil or Jersey Devil. The fearsome appearance of the crest's wyvern and the increasing animosity among local South Jersey residents towards royalty, aristocracy, and nobility (with whom family crests were associated) may have helped facilitate the legend of the Leeds Devil and the association of the Leeds family with "devils" and "monsters".

Although the "Leeds Devil" legend has existed since the 18th century, Regal states that the more modern depiction of the Jersey Devil, as well as the now pervasive "Jersey

Devil" name, first became truly standardized in current form during the early 20th century. *Wikipedia popular folklore*

So…During the pre-Revolutionary period, the Daniel Leeds family soured its relationship with the Quaker majority … The Quakers saw no hurry to give their former fellow religionist an easy time in circles of gossip. His wives had all died, as had several children … as a joke and to boost his almanac sales, Franklin satirically uses astrology in his almanack to predict Titan Leeds' death (Daniel's son) … Titan publicly calls Franklin a "fool" and a "liar"… In a published response, Franklin mocked Titan Leeds as being dead, writes his almanack as a ghost, resurrected from the grave to haunt and torment Franklin…he continued the "joke" even after Titan Leeds' actual death (1738)…

Benjamin Franklin (January 17, 1706 – April 17, 1790), was an American polymath: a leading writer, scientist, inventor, statesman, diplomat, printer, publisher, and political philosopher. Among the most influential intellectuals of his time, Franklin was one of the Founding Fathers of the United States; a drafter and signer of the Declaration of Independence; and the first postmaster general.

Franklin became a successful newspaper editor and printer in Philadelphia, the leading city in the colonies, publishing the Pennsylvania Gazette at age 23 (1729). He became wealthy publishing this and Poor Richard's Almanack, which he wrote under the pseudonym "Richard Saunders". After 1767, he was associated with the Pennsylvania Chronicle, a newspaper known for its revolutionary sentiments and criticisms of the policies of the British Parliament and the Crown.

Franklin was already pursuing a successful career as a newspaper editor when Poor Richard's Almanack was first published in 1732. During 1716, Daniel Leeds' son Titan, inherited his father's almanack business and in 1733 the competition between the two men intensified when Franklin used astrology in his almanack to predict Titan's death.

In his 20s was Benjamin Franklin that aggressive and heartless to use such distasteful thoughts against the Leeds family, who had endured many personal tragedies, to promote an almanack in search of the almighty buck? I think there was much more to it that deeply touched Franklin and the future of America:

— As a royal surveyor with strong allegiance to the British crown, Leeds had surveyed and acquired land in the Egg Harbor area, located within the Pine Barrens. The land was inherited by Leeds' sons and family and is now known as Leeds Point, one of the areas in the Pine Barrens.

In the 1690s Leeds was endorsed by the much-maligned British royal governor of New Jersey, Lord Cornbury, despised among the Quaker communities. Leeds also worked as a councilor to Lord Cornbury about this time. Considering Leeds as a traitor for aiding the Crown and rejecting Quaker beliefs, the Quaker Burlington Meeting of southern New Jersey subsequently dismissed Leeds as "evil".

- Franklin was one of the founding fathers of the constitution of the United States. This brought together, in one remarkable document, ideas from many people and several existing documents, including the Articles of Confederation and Declaration of Independence. Those who made significant intellectual contributions to the Constitution are called the "Founding Fathers" of our country.

The signers' mutual pledge to themselves to sacrifice their lives, fortunes, and sacred honor for the cause of independence shows that these men took seriously their duties to the people of the new nation.

Benjamin Franklin was the oldest of the signers of the declaration. Prior to setting sail for France in late 1776 to ask the French for assistance in the war, Franklin gave his entire fortune to Congress to help fund the war.

His life and legacy of scientific and political achievement, and his status as one of America's most influential Founding Fathers, have seen Franklin honored for more than two centuries after his death on the $100 bill and in the names of warships, many towns and counties, educational institutions, and corporations, as well as in numerous cultural references and a portrait in the Oval Office.

Dr. Burnett's final comments: Ultimately, we've evolved to accept information more readily when it's provided by another person. They help us process, contextualize and relate to the abstract, the intangible. Whether the information we get from others is reliable or even plausible doesn't seem to matter. The more hardcore sceptic type will often say, "Facts don't care about your feelings," which is correct. But feelings don't necessarily care about facts either. And ultimately, feelings have more of a say in what we think and do. And that's why the person cutting your hair can seem more believable than a whole archive of published research.[1]

So why would someone revered as much as Benjamin Franklin play a role in promoting the conspiracies and folklore surrounding the "Jersey Devil." I don't think the "Devil made him do it." I suspect it had a lot to do with the Leeds' strong allegiance to the British crown.

1– *Why your misguided mate in the pub trumps experts and evidence, Dr. Dean Burnett, BBC Science Focus, 04/16/2024.*

2– *How to tell if a conspiracy theory is probably false, The Conversation, H. Colleen Sinclair, 05/07/2024.*

CHAPTER 23

JUST A SPAY

We all want to feel positive emotions—contentment, safety, peace, joy, happiness. And that universal demand for good feels matched by an endless line of purveyors of emotions—via tech, chemicals, entertainment, educational achievement, workplace promotions, travel. And yet, as rates of depression and anxiety increase throughout society, happiness has never been so elusive.

It may be that we're just doing it wrong. Indeed, BYU experts in psychology and experience management say that chasing happiness is almost always futile. They tout a better approach: build a meaningful life and let happiness find you.

Here these experts share how to create conditions that make enduring happiness more likely, from understanding brain chemistry to adopting daily practices that put you in the sweet spot for happiness to catch up with you.

Thomas Jefferson had it all wrong, according to BYU psychology professor Jared S. Warren: "The Declaration of Independence talks about the pursuit of happiness as if (happiness is) something we've got to chase down, tackle, tie up - then we've got it. We don't chase happiness. It's something we cultivate, and then it can emerge as a natural consequence of living well."

Research shows that obsessing over happiness tends to leave people feeling more depressed and less happy, notes Brian J. Hill, an experience design and management professor who purposefully named his BYU course Creating a Good Life - not Pursuing Happiness. "Chasing happiness is actually a pretty negative path. People who are that self-focused are not usually happy."

Part of the problem may be where people tend to look for happiness - in money, power, fame, pleasure, and comfort. While such attainments can give temporary satisfaction, they have less power as an "ultimate good."

Warren agrees: "(The) excitement doesn't last nearly as long as we expect it to, and we don't get all the value out of it that we predicted. We fall back to a set point where our mood usually is. This tendency, called the hedonic treadmill, keeps us constantly looking for the next thing. When we notice ourselves having thoughts of, 'I'll be happy when . . . ' We're usually setting ourselves up for disappointment.

A better pursuit, is of what the Greeks called eudaimonia, meaning 'flourishing' or 'the life well lived.'"

Flourishing is at the heart of the positive-psychology movement, founded by Martin Seligman in the late 1990s. Seligman believed psychological principles could be applied to help people live well, not just address problems.

Hill's Creating a Good Life course (like other popular positive-psychology courses on campuses around the country) is a go-to for students wanting tools to build a foundation for lasting happiness.

First, it's helpful to understand how our brains, both in their physical processes and thought patterns, can contribute to - or hinder - feelings of well-being. Chemicals in our brains (serotonin, dopamine, oxytocin, and endorphins) are increased by our behaviors, by what we do and what we think. Dopamine, the brain's feel-good chemical, increases when we have a sense of notable achievement and victory, while serotonin increases when we make contributions and add value through our life's endeavors.

Endorphins, which make us feel relaxed and secure, significantly reduce pain. They come from exercise, crying, and laughing. Oxytocin is released in response to connection with others and touch, like a hug. When oxytocin is released, it increases feelings of love and emotional closeness.

Daley notes that "happiness is more likely when people do the things that support healthy brain chemistry. Foundational are adequate sleep, eating healthy, and exercising regularly. People want the secret to happiness without recognizing the importance of laying the foundation that provides the biochemistries you need in your brain to be happy. It's hard to think positively and function if you don't take care of your body."

Just as important is to pursue healthy thought patterns. The brain is naturally on the lookout for potential threats and negative possibilities, which can cause undue stress and unhappiness. The brain is wired for surviving, not for thriving."

Jenny Cook Thueson, a BYU alumna and certified life coach, notes that brains are designed to find evidence for whatever we believe—good or bad. "My brain is on the lookout everywhere I go to back up whatever my belief is. If I believe that I'm inadequate or incapable, my brain's on the job, searching for proof."[1]

I will have been doing surgery as a veterinarian for fifty years in June of 2023. The old proverb I learned in school for anesthetic risk is: "the longer time one is under an anesthetic the greater the risk of hypotension; hypotension leads to shock and shock can lead to death."

Removing the ovaries and uterus (called a spay) of dogs has routinely been done by me on a weekly basis. The ovariohysterectomy procedure is not without potential complications. The pancreas, ureters, fat, urinary bladder, spleen and other vital structures are in the area, and there is always the risk that blood vessels may not be tied off properly leading to an abdomen full of blood. When there's been complications that result in blood loss &/or extended anesthetic time during the procedure, there occurs an increased flow of adrenalin in my body, closer monitoring is needed for the patient, and often an extra pair of gloved hands in the abdomen. Following a difficult spay the comment is often made: "It was just a spay!"

This last two years Camden Pet Hospital employed two young veterinarians that I mentored during surgery. One had been trying to improve her surgery skills by volunteering in a county spay and neuter clinic, and the other had been in practice several years struggling during the spaying of large dogs.

The problems they were having included: not being able to find the uterus or ovaries in the abdomen, unable to release the ligament that holds the ovaries firm near the kidneys, traumatizing the tissue covering the organs or the organs themselves resulting in bleeding or potential scaring of tissue after surgery, and providing a closure that would heal without complications.

I've mentored colleagues over the years in surgery on as simple a task of removing a toe to the more complicated surgery performed on a knee and experienced the satisfaction of veterinarians becoming good competent surgeons. However, there was no success helping these two doctors. I watched how hard they made the surgery and that they were mentally prepared to fail before they started.

The experience psychologically made my brain begin to lookout for failures, like the two veterinarians were having. I began to wonder if I was becoming inadequate or incapable of surgically spaying a large dog and my brain began "searching for proof."

The experience mentoring these two veterinarians are now memories from the past. However, I still sweat some and fret with concern until I find the uterus with my index finger inside the dog's abdomen. My brain's job, seems to be "searching for proof" that I may fail especially at my age when failures in all kinds of stuff is expected.

Adapting olden-day instincts to modern-day realities takes conscious effort. And, when something goes wrong, thought patterns can influence how long and deep the drop in happiness will be. "Our minds are set up so that one bad experience reminds us of other bad experiences, says Dianne M. Tice, a BYU psychology professor. Some people are more optimistic and quickly return to seeing the bright side, while others—because of brain chemistry, reinforcement history, all kinds of things . . . —have a tendency to wallow.

It's a more difficult and conscious strategy to get out of the bad mood. You can consciously override the automatic wallowing and tell yourself, 'I've learned a lesson, and now I'm going to focus on positive things.'"

The experts recommend trying to get comfortable with some discomfort. We're wired to seek out positive emotions and experiences and also to avoid discomfort and distress and difficult emotions. But that's not reasonable because a life well lived is going to include the full range of human experience.

Below are some thoughts listed by Jared Warren that may help us be more comfortable with discomfort:

- Acknowledge difficult emotions using words like frustration, impatience, and discouragement. It's a way of turning toward (the emotion) instead of resisting.

- Allow the emotion to exist. We can make room for it. . . . Say, yes, this is difficult, but can I allow this to be here just as it is? Bring a gentle curiosity to the experience, noticing the physical response in your body, like a tight chest or a hot face.

- Exercise self-compassion. Offer the same kindness to ourselves and our difficult experiences that we would naturally offer to a friend or loved one who is going through something similar. Avoiding negative emotions doesn't work long-term. When you push down difficult emotions, they come back even stronger. Because we're not actually dealing with the challenges.

When we approach periods of challenge or grief in a healthy way, it actually sets us up for more depth of experiences, including the capacity for more joy.

Having worked in therapeutic recreation since 1988, Widmer has seen many people thrive in the great outdoors. "Nature uniquely helps people who are struggling with behavioral and emotional problems. We underestimate its benefits; it's where people can peel away layers of issues and become more in touch with themselves." With this in mind us humans might consider trying:

- Eating lunch outside.
- Planting a garden or buy an indoor plant.
- Planning a couple of hours in nature every week.

Most of history humans saw themselves as part of nature - not separate from it - and modern society has lost track of that. Nature is a great teacher. It teaches about patience; cause and effect; and seasons of life. Even a small dose of fresh air can be beneficial. Time outside resets our mental capacities and makes us more effective, productive, and creative.[1]

Could it be that simple - that happiness finds us as we stop looking for it? It takes faith to exchange pursuing happiness for cultivating it day by day, little by little. But then, faith has always preceded miracles, including the miracle of happiness.[2]

Could it be that simple for me - I'm in hopes that little by little I'll get back into my game of spay, spay, spay one day of the week at a time with a song in my heart and making small talk with my surgical assistants. After all, "It's just a spay!"

1– *Let Joy Find You, Happiness isn't a destination; it's something that finds you along the way, by Emily Smurthwaite Edmonds, Article Podcast, Y Magazine, 2023.*

2– *Cultivating Happiness, Music & the Spoken Word, #4880 03-26-2023*

CHAPTER 24

CHOKING UNDER PRESSURE

Choking under pressure—it happens to the best of us. We tank an interview and don't get the job. We freeze while giving an important presentation. Or blank during a critical exam. And choking at a crucial moment of the game? That's an athlete's worst nightmare. To be clear, choking has nothing to do with having an off-day, performance-wise. When you choke, you perform much worse than your skill level indicates. Or, worse than you have in the past because you now find the situation stressful, cognitive scientist Sian Beilock, who has written two books on choking, tells New Scientist.

According to Beilock, the prefrontal cortex is the epicenter of our cognitive horsepower. Typically, we're not paying attention to all of the little steps that make up everyday tasks. "But in times of intense stress, like a playoff game, major presentation, or a job interview, your prefrontal cortex can go into overdrive. When the pressure is on, we often start focusing on the step-by-step details of our performance to try and ensure an optimal outcome and, as a result, we disrupt what would have otherwise been fluid and natural." This pressure leads to panic. We start overthinking, and suddenly, we face "paralysis by analysis."[1]

Sitting alone in a dim room in Pittsburgh, Pennsylvania, Earl flung his arm to the left. He slowed his movement down, examining the position of a cursor on the computer screen in front of him. Where his hand went, so did the cursor. Earl gestured the dot closer to a colorful target zone, just as he had done thousands of times before. This time, he expected a big reward, but instead—time's up. Earl, a rhesus monkey, choked under the pressure. He didn't move the dot into the target before the timer ran out.

Choking is when high stakes cause you to fail when you otherwise would have succeeded. In basketball, it's missing free throws late in a game; during a dance recital, or spelling bee, or job interview, it's the paradox of overanalyzing and amnesia that leaves you feeling like an alien in your own body. "You overthink it, you get too much in your head," says Steven Chase, a biomedical engineer at Carnegie Mellon who specializes in motor learning.

And yet, while choking is a common experience, its basis in the brain remains a mystery. What are the patterns of electrical signals and brain chemicals that explain choking—and where do they occur? Researchers have proposed theories based on human behavior and brain imaging. But to eventually perform neurological tests, the kind that involve implanted electrodes, they've needed to first observe the phenomenon in a lab animal.

For now, they've got Earl—plus Nelson and Ford, two other rhesus monkeys—and a simpler test that only involves observing their motion with a camera. Chase's team of researchers have shown for the first time that people are not the only primates that choke under pressure.

The researchers show that what triggers this behavior is the shot at an extraordinary prize—and their analysis offers clues as to why that might be. In the cursor-based game, the monkeys were tested on how quickly and accurately they moved a target into a box. The monkeys performed better as the reward offered to them improved: nothing for failure, and increasingly large sips of water for success. Until the jackpot—a really big swig of water. Monkeys who expected that rare and more valuable prize failed at tasks they'd normally ace.

Demonstrating choking in other species is interesting, and valuable for the field, says Sian Beilock, a cognitive scientist not involved in the study. "What I think it does is open up another opportunity to study it, If you can get a better sense of the underlying systems, you can start thinking about different ways to mitigate it."

Until this, it was just a weird thing human's did. But now a proposed model of choking could help researchers decode the neural signals of movement in high-stakes scenarios—for athletes using their limbs when the game is on the line or, perhaps one day, for humans using prosthetics they control with their brains.

Historically, researchers have held one of two perspectives on what causes choking. One is that it's a uniquely human fault, emerging from "superpowered minds." But if other animals choke, too, it may be a more fundamental issue in the wiring of the brain. Brains—animal and human—may fire cognitive or motor signals differently while chasing rare rewards.

The team designed their cursor game to be challenging for the monkeys but still simple to analyze. Motion-capture cameras tracked the monkeys' arm motion, which controlled the dot on the screen. The game itself was the same each time. Any differences in speed, position, and accuracy, the researchers figured, could only stem from the one variable they tested: the reward.

The monkeys learned to anticipate particular rewards with visual cues on the computer screen—different colored targets corresponded to each reward. Earl and the others excelled during the training period, when they earned nothing for failing or tiny sips for succeeding. They performed a little better when the reward they thought they would get doubled or tripled. If that trend held, a rare jackpot—a drink 10 times bigger than the average reward—should have motivated even better performance. But the jackpot did the opposite. The monkeys put up far more unsuccessful runs when the huge prize was up for grabs. Earl choked on 11 of his 11 jackpot opportunities.

To find a cause the research team scrutinized what was going on with the monkeys' arm motions during thousands of trials. Their reaction times and maximum speeds showed no clear trend. The Really only consistency seen was increase in caution.

Imagine the monkeys' arm gestures as a composite of two phases—a fast, initial "ballistic reach" motion to send the cursor closer to the target, followed by a slower, more precise "homing" step to land on-target. Earl, Ford, and Nelson repeatedly undershot in jackpot trials. Instead of starting as they normally would, with a fast ballistic reach that covered a lot of ground, their reach would stop short; the homing step dragged on until time ran out.

The monkeys were choking by being overcautious. Investigators linked choking to paying too close attention to their movements, a behavior called explicit monitoring. Thinking about your movements makes them slower. And they think that's what's going on; the monkeys are psyching themselves out and undershooting.[2]

Fortunately, Beilock has come up with several science-backed strategies to help us avoid choking under pressure:

- Distract yourself. First, accept that no amount of distraction will help if you haven't adequately prepped for whatever high-stress situation in which you'll soon find yourself. This trick assumes you have amply rehearsed, practiced, studied, etc., and in optimal conditions, would perform like a rock star.

  Five minutes before the Big Event, resist the urge to review every detail of what you're about to do, Beilock advises. Instead, take a few moments to focus on something else. Play a game on your phone. Scroll through Instagram. Plan your menu for dinner that night. It doesn't matter how you distract yourself. The point is to refocus your cognitive horsepower away from the thing you're about to do.

  By occupying your prefrontal cortex beforehand with unrelated activities you're less likely to overthink in the moment and more likely to communicate or perform effectively.

- Jot down worries: Researchers have found that writing down your concerns before a stressful event helps to download them from your mind—making them less likely to pop up in the moment. Expressive writing—where you write about your deepest thoughts and feelings—helps anxious people perform better on tests. There not sure exactly why this is, but one leading theory is that writing about test anxiety "offloads' worrisome thoughts, thereby freeing up mental resources to concentrate on the test."

- Learn your resume backward and forwards. Recruit a friend to conduct a mock interview with you. Practice giving your speech to colleagues or friends. For interviews or public speaking, it helps to record yourself in the process so you can suss out any verbal or physical tics that might distract your audience.

If you're studying for an important test, try to replicate the testing environment you'll encounter on the actual day. Close the book, practice retrieving the answer from memory under timed situations. The goal: make whatever the task is feel as fluid and natural as possible—like you're on autopilot.

To quote former pro basketball player Tim Duncan, "When you have to stop and think, that's when you mess up." But what if you still choke? It's not the end of the world. You might be disappointed and even embarrassed, but like most things in life, it's a learning experience. Take the opportunity to learn how to better handle the stress next time.[1]

Do we choke because we just can't see ourselves worthy of succeeding? Zig Ziglar, in *See You At The Top* (pg. 68), comments: "As individuals, we will consistently act according to the way we see ourselves. This is why you often see people do some incredibly ridiculous things and take unnecessary risks when they are on the brink of achieving a life-long dream. For example, a high percentage of athletes who have spent years preparing for the Olympics often have "accidents" in training, or in a preliminary event before the competition starts. They cannot "see themselves" as deserving a gold medal and subconsciously take the necessary steps to make certain they deny themselves the reward the world might confer upon them."

I'm doubtful a monkey ever thought he wasn't worthy of a "jackpot" reward. Maybe, Beilock should add one more suggestion to his science-backed strategies to help us avoid choking under pressure:

"-Lastly, ack like a monkey a few moments before the stressful event – they see themselves worthy of receiving the prize."

Saint Augustine once wrote that we are to "pray as though everything depended on God and work as if everything depended on you." That seems to me like a great philosophy to live by. When we have done everything in our power to prepare not to mess up or choke our "superpowered human minds" have another source of help not available to the rest of the animal kingdom.

Elder Richard G. Scott (1928–2015) of the Quorum of the Twelve Apostles explained: "The feeling of peace is the most common confirming witness that I personally experience. When I have been very concerned about an

WALTER R. HOGE, DVM

important matter, struggling to resolve it without success, I continued those efforts in faith. Later, an all-pervading peace has come, settling my concerns, as He has promised… the answer comes as a feeling with an accompanying conviction."[3]

Five minutes before a Big Event, resist the urge to review every detail of what you're about to do. Instead, take a few moments to focus on something else. If we are still continually focusing our "superpowered human minds"- think about Elder Scott's continual efforts in faith and Saint Augustine's thoughts on prayer and work; asking for all-pervading peace, settling of our concerns, having a calming of our minds and not fearing that we might choke.

We will have adequately prepped for the event, we will thoroughly have evaluated our deepest thoughts and feelings, we will know our material backwards and forewords, we will know the environment expected during the event and we will have exercised faith and prayed – knowing that God will be with us if we have done our part.

Lastly, act like a monkey a few moments before the stressful event – they see themselves worthy of receiving the prize.

1– *Choking Under Pressure, Dr. Srini Pillay, Harvard Business Review, Harvard Medical School, New Scientist, Performance Anxiety, Prefrontal Cortex, Sian Beilock, by Yvonne Milosevic, 09/19/2019.*

2– *You're Not Alone: Monkeys Choke Under Pressure Too, Science, Max G. Levy, 09/02/2021.*

3– *Richard G. Scott, "Using the Supernal Gift of Prayer," May 2007.*

CHAPTER 25

YOU CAN'T FOOL MOTHER NATURE

The Great Chinese Famine occurred between 1958 and 1962 in the People's Republic of China (PRC). It is widely regarded as the deadliest famine and one of the greatest man-made disasters in human history, with an estimated death toll due to starvation that ranges in the tens of millions (15 to 55 million). The major contributing factors in the famine were the policies of the Great Leap Forward (1958 to 1962) and people's communes, launched by Chairman of the Chinese Communist Party Mao Zedong. Such things as inefficient distribution of food within the nation's planned economy; requiring the use of poor agricultural techniques; the Four Pests (evils) campaign that reduced sparrow populations (which disrupted the ecosystem); over-reporting of grain production; and ordering millions of farmers to switch to iron and steel production.

For the Four Pests Campaign, ridding the country of rats (plague), mosquitos (malaria), flies (disease), and sparrows (famine – eat grain, fruit, and seeds) required mass mobilization of the Chinese population in order to change the natural world. Mao's slogan, ren ding sheng tian, meaning *"man must conquer nature"*, became the rallying cry for the campaign. A firsthand account from a former Sichuan schoolchild at the time of the campaign recounted, "It was fun to 'Wipe out the Four Pests'. The whole school went to kill sparrows. We made ladders to knock down their nests, and beat gongs in the evenings, when they were coming home to roost."

On a particular poster it reads, "Eradicate pests and diseases and build happiness for ten thousand generations". Therefore, the potential result of this campaign was framed as grandiose, and with potential benefits that would last for generations.

The Four Pests Campaign implemented a multifaceted approach to control rat populations. The large-scale use of rat poison played a pivotal role, with poisoned baits strategically distributed in both urban and rural areas to effectively target rats. Complementary to this poisoning strategy, an extensive implementation of traps was employed, providing a localized method to capture and eliminate rats, thereby augmenting the broader impact of the poison campaign. Furthermore, citizens were actively encouraged to enlist the natural predatory instincts of cats in controlling rat populations. Recognizing cats as effective hunters and deterrents, this measure sought to harness feline assistance as a complementary means to address the pervasive rat issue during the campaign.

Sparrows were perceived as a significant threat to grain stores. In an effort to reduce sparrow populations on a large scale, citizens were mobilized to participate in a mass extermination campaign. To further deter sparrows from consuming grain, people actively engaged in creating loud noises, disrupting the birds and making it challenging for them to rest. Simultaneously, the campaign encouraged the destruction of sparrow nests as a means to impede their reproduction, contributing to the broader objective of decreasing sparrow populations. Shooting sparrows using guns and other methods was implemented to achieve a significant reduction in their numbers.

Control of fly populations, with the widespread use of chemical insecticides served as a key component. Public spaces and known breeding grounds were systematically targeted with insecticide sprays, aiming to curtail the spread of diseases associated with flies. Complementing this chemical approach, a comprehensive public education campaign was initiated to promote cleanliness and proper waste disposal, targeting the root causes of fly breeding sites and serving as a synergistic measure alongside insecticide efforts to reduce fly infestations. Additionally, the strategic placement of traps designed to capture and contain flies in public spaces further diversified the campaign's toolkit for controlling fly populations.

Controlling mosquitoes focused on the elimination of stagnant water by improving water drainage systems. This measure targeted the core habitat of mosquitoes, seeking to disrupt their reproductive cycle and mitigate the spread of diseases by the vector.

In 1960 the campaign against sparrows ended and bed bugs became an official target. Approximations indicate that both the government and the general public were accountable for the demise of 1.5 billion rats, 1 billion sparrows, exceeding 220 million pounds of flies, and over 24 million pounds of mosquitoes.

Mao must have truly felt good about the accomplishments his country made towards conquering Mother Nature (*"man must conquer nature"*). *Wikipedia*

1964-1968 while attending the University of Idaho I fed and took care of rats used for nutrition studies. Research was being done comparing growth rates and reproduction performance of formulations of purified diets (all nutrients added were known). None of the purified diets performed as well as commercial rat food. The lab was trying to identify *"unidentified growth factors"* that were missing from the purified diets.

The use of the term *"Unidentified Growth Factors"* (UGF) dates back to around 1920, but most research work started from 1950 onwards. They were identified in fish extract, fish meal, fermentation products and their residues and lucerne (alfalfa) meal. Particularly good sources of UGF are de-hydrated soluble fish, distillers' feed and shrimp when added to the diet. Googling, I found the *UGF terminology is still present in the literature mostly along with the term nano (very small or minute) elements that they are sure they exist, but don't know what they are.*

Nanotechnology-driven smart agriculture has been considered as one of the highly potential approaches in improving crop productivity. Actually, plants serve as a potential pathway for the transportation of nanoparticles (NPs), closely resembling endogenous mineral nutrients. In modern agricultural production systems, rapid and uniform seed germination is required for successful seedling establishment and to finally yield achievement.

The increasing application of nanoparticles in diverse agricultural sectors has made it a crucial subject of study. Nanoparticle based studies have been fruitful in numerous fields for decades: Nanomedicine, nano industrial application, nano pharmacy and nano pesticides. Currently there has been advances in nanoparticle based studies on releasing seed dormancy and enhancing seed germination as well as seedling development has recently come to the limelight in the form of seed-nano-priming technology.

Are there "*unidentified growth factors*" involved in the germination of nano primed seeds? Seed priming is a process in which partial hydration of a seed is performed using natural/synthetic compounds such as vitamins, Polyethylene glycol to reduce nematode damage or water before sowing. Nano priming, a technique based on the combination of seed priming and nanoparticle treatment, has been a useful tool for enhancing seed quality, seedling establishment and crop yields as well as increasing tolerance to environmental stresses, compared to unprimed or other agents.[1]

Previous reports have shown improved chick growth where corn fermentation condensed solubility was added to a variety of "practical" chick rations. This effect was observed with both mash and crumbled diets. Additions of corn fermentation condensed solubility were made in these tests at the expense of either corn meal or a combination of corn meal and soybean oil meal. The work reported here deals with the effect on chick growth of replacing fish meal, condensed fish solubility and dried whey product with corn fermentation condensed solubilities. These replaced ingredients are widely recognized as sources of "*unidentified growth factors*" for chicks.[2]

Large variabilities in ammonia (NH3) released from animal manure and emitted from different livestock buildings are frequently reported, but the factors influencing the emissions were not sufficiently investigated.

Two "*unidentified factors*" influencing ammonia emissions were predicted using panel data analysis. They were most possibly related to variations in microenvironment and microbial activity inside manure pits. The results suggest necessary future research to identify physical properties of the new ammonia emissions factors in microbiological and biochemical processes.[3]

Crop rotation has been used by farmers for generations to improve grain yields by regenerating the soil and breaking the cycles of weeds, diseases and insect damage to crops. Our long-term study in eastern Nebraska showed that crop rotation had more agronomic and soil benefits compared to fertilizer-N alone. Fertilizer-N use, while beneficial, was no substitute for using crop rotation. In the long-term, rotating two or more crops can improve the soil and crop yields with less fertilizer-N cost.[4]

Dr. R. Kent Crookston stated at a BYU devotional: As you learned from my introduction, I am an agronomist. A considerable part of my career has been devoted to improving the production of corn. I begin my remarks with an insight that I have gained from my corn research, an insight that helps me to understand the key to obtaining blessings from heaven.

Let me show you a simple bar graph that shows corn yield as influenced by the previous crop. The best yield was obtained from corn that was grown on a field that had not been planted to corn for five years. The next best yield was from a field on which corn was grown alternately with soybeans. The most depressed yields were all from fields that had been planted to corn following a previous planting of corn for two, three, four, five, or ten years in a row.

The graph illustrates what is referred to among crop scientists as the rotation effect. Those of you who grow tomatoes have learned that they will not yield their best if you repeatedly grow them in the same spot in your garden year after year. A veteran Idaho potato farmer once said that the best rotation for potatoes was a thousand years of sagebrush and one year of potatoes.

There are two significant conclusions that my students and I gathered from our 20 years of research with corn. The first was that the rotation effect was unfailingly reliable. Rotated corn always, not just sometimes, but always gave the best yields. No matter the weather, no matter how we modified our management or inputs of fertilizers or pesticides, we could not lift the yield of continuous corn to the level of a first-year crop. Second, although we did gain some insights, we were never able to determine why that first-year yield boost occurred. We evaluated every physical and biological factor we could think of. We finally accepted that we were working with a law of nature and that we could not divert Mother Nature from her decreed course. It is about the laws of Mother Nature—or rather about the laws of Mother Nature's father...We might refer to Mother Nature's father as Grandfather Nature—or we might call him God (added - the creator of *unidentified growth factors*). [5]

The word "chiffon" started out as a French term for a rag or small piece of cloth. Several centuries ago, fabric and clothing manufacturers adopted it as the name of a light, airy fabric. This led to the use of "chiffon" as a generic or brand name for a number of other consumer products, ranging from cake and toilet paper to margarine, as a way of emphasizing their "fluffiness."

In the 1950s a Texas-based corporation that had been selling cotton and cotton products since the early 1900s, created a food division to find uses for hydrogenated cottonseed oil. Two years later, it began selling products made with this oil, including Seven Seas salad dressing and Chiffon margarine.

Chiffon was one of the first soft, tub-style margarine products. But by the 1960s there were many brands of soft margarines and Chiffon lacked notable name recognition among consumers. That changed in the 1970s, when the company began airing TV commercials for Chiffon that included a memorable character and a slogan that became a pop culture catchphrase: "It's not nice to fool Mother Nature."

These classic Chiffon ads featured the talented Hollywood character actress Dena Dietrich as Mother Nature. In this early Chiffon commercial, Mother Nature is given some Chiffon to taste. She likes it and identifies it as "my delicious butter."

The narrator then tells her: "That's Chiffon margarine, not butter...*Chiffon's so delicious it fooled even you, Mother Nature.*"

Perturbed at being tricked, Mother Nature responds with her signature line: *"It's not nice to fool Mother Nature."*

She underscores her displeasure by creating a flash of lightning and a loud peal of thunder and a wild elephant is seen charging the camera. *Wikipedia*

Did Mao's efforts live up to his call, "*man must conquer nature?*" Or did mother nature teach mankind the lesson expressed by the marketers of Chiffon margin, "*It's not nice to (try to) fool Mother Nature?*"

The birds were on the brink of extinction when, in April 1960, ornithologist Tso-hsin Cheng highlighted that sparrows didn't just eat grain, they also ate insects and because of their decline rice yields were depleting. Mao stopped the campaign against the birds. However, as there were almost no sparrows remaining, locust numbers exploded and food crops were destroyed. *Wikipedia*

The Four Pests campaign is now seen as a contributing factor to the Great Chinese Famine, where 20-45 million people died of starvation. (It's not nice to (try) to fool mother nature").

As for the Chiffon margarine name and product line, it has changed hands several times since; the first being in 1985, when Chiffon was sold to Kraft Foods. The Kraft U.S. and Canada table spreads division subsequently became part of Nabisco in 1995; who then sold the brand to ConAgra Foods in 1998. Con-Agra discontinued domestic U.S. and Canadian distribution of Chiffon margarine in 2002. Chiffon margarine can still be purchased in the Caribbean region, however, where it is marketed by Seprod Ltd. *Wikipedia*

Scientists are steadily reducing the number of "*unidentified growth factors*" and other "*unidentified factors*" into reliable scientific facts mostly by studying very small minute particles called "nano." They know that they exist but don't know what they are – yet. They're there just waiting for us to find them: "Ask, and it shall be given you; seek, and shall find; knock, and it shall be opened unto you: for every one that asketh receiveth; and he that seeketh findeth; and to him that knocketh it shall be opened." *Matthew 7:7-8.*

1– *Are There Unidentified Factors Involved in the Germination of Nanoprime Seeds? Front. Plant Sci. Physiology, 09 June 2020.*

2– *Effects of unidentified growth factor sources on feed preference of chicks, Poult Sci, July 1983.*

3– *Identified factors and predicted unidentified-factors affecting ammonia emissions from a swine building, Journal of Hazardous Materials, Volume 453, 5 July 2023, 131365.*

4– *More Diverse Crop Rotations Improve Yield, Yield Stability and Soil Health, Susan E. Wagner, 10/25/2021.*

5– *The Natural Law of Blessings, R. Kent Crookston, BYU College of Biology & Agriculture, 03/20/2011.*

CHAPTER 26

THERE AT THE RIGHT TIME

Over 64,000 people have died from landmines in Cambodia alone since 1979. But specially-trained rats, partly funded by Britain's UK aid budget, have been able to discover landmines much faster, before they put even more lives in danger.

Magawa was born in November 2013 at the APOPO (in English, Anti-Personnel Landmines Removal Product Development) headquarters in the Sokoine University of Agriculture in Morogoro, Tanzania. After being trained to sniff out landmines as a HeroRAT, he was moved to Siem Reap, Cambodia, in 2016 to begin landmine-removal work.

From 2016 to 2021, Magawa cleared more than 22.5 hectares (56 acres) of land in Cambodia. In that time, he found 71 landmines and 38 instances of other unexploded ordnance. Magawa was trained to sniff out TNT in explosives, allowing him to disregard scrap metal that would confuse metal detectors. He was able to search for landmines far faster than humans due to his exceptional sense of smell and light weight, which prevented him from detonating the mines. He received the PDSA Gold Medal Gold (medal is known as the animals' George Cross.

The PDSA Gold Medal is an animal bravery award that acknowledges the bravery and devotion to duty of animals. It was created by the People's Dispensary for Sick Animals (PDSA) in 2001, and is now recognized as the animal equivalent of the George Cross. The Gold Medal is considered as the civilian equivalent to PDSA's Dickin Medal for military animals. An animal can be awarded the PDSA Gold Medal if it assists in saving human or non-human life when its own life is in danger or through exceptional devotion to duty. The medal can also be awarded to animals in public service, such as police or rescue dogs, if the animal dies or suffers serious injury while carrying out its official duties in the face of armed and violent opposition.

The first ceremony, in November 2002, saw the Gold medal awarded to three dogs, including Endal, an assistance dog whose actions helped to save the life of his disabled owner. The Labrador Retriever service dog pulled his disabled owner into the recovery position after he was struck unconscious, then covered him with a blanket. He also retrieved his mobile phone and pushed it against his face. Endal only left his owner's side to fetch help once he had regained consciousness.

As of September 2023, the PDSA Gold Medal has been awarded to 31 different animals. All recipients were dogs until 2020, when a mine-sniffing African giant pouched rat named Magawa received the prize. The majority of recipients have been British.

Magawa was the most successful mine-sniffing rat in APOPO's history when he received his medal, and was described by the program's manager in Cambodia as a "very exceptional rat" upon his retirement. He retired from bomb sniffing in June 2021 owing to his old age, as is standard for APOPO's HeroRATs. He spent a number of weeks mentoring 20 newly-recruited rats before ultimately retiring to a life of "snacking on bananas and peanuts". Magawa died peacefully in early January 2022, and was the organization's most successful HeroRAT at the time of his death. *Wikipedia*

For many cancers, there's currently no screening method available: people don't know they're suffering from the disease until they start to experience symptoms. And no variety of cancer currently has a reliable screening method for the disease in its earliest stages. Hopefuly, this means that someday in the not-too-distant future, dogs' noses will be saving many thousands of lives, whether it's through a mechanical nose or a real, live four-legged friend.

The use of dogs in detection of volatile organic compounds (VOCs), which are emitted through skin, breath, and bodily fluids, is not new. However, the approach has not yet been used on a widespread basis for detection or mass screening in the setting of a global COVID-19 pandemic. Dogs have been trained and used for detection of drugs and explosives on either articles or people in airports or other locations and are used by government airport security, law enforcement agencies, and private companies throughout the world. Dogs have also been used in search and rescue operations and have been proven to be an invaluable tool to detect the scent of live or deceased humans. For medical detection, they have been used in multiple capacities, including assistance dogs (e.g., alerting for drops in blood sugar called hypoglycemia in diabetics or onset of seizures).

Several diseases, such as Parkinson disease; bacterial, and viral, including influenza, infections, and several types of cancer have been documented to have unique VOC profiles by either chemical sensors (gas chromatography, mass spectrometry) or biological sensors (dogs). Dogs can detect VOC signatures through their sense of smell of different biological fluids, such as urine, saliva, sweat, and breath samples. One study in type 1 diabetes showed that the dogs, when trained on limited samples, did not respond to hypoglycemia in new samples on which they were not trained. Although the sensory capability of dogs is well known, the training of the dogs to identify an odor that is specific to COVID-19, but still generalize the odor across a wide variety of individuals is a challenge. Due to requirements for sufficient numbers of both positive and appropriate control samples, the necessary diversity of samples to represent the population to be screened, the appropriate handling and storage of samples to preserve the odor, prevent disease transmission and avoid sample contamination, there exists a need to standardize research protocols and conduct regular double-blind testing to determine each dog's sensitivity and specificity for COVID-19. [1]

Exactly how are dog's superpowers of smell put into practice by research centers and healthcare providers around the country? Cancerous cells produce a very specific odor. In fact, in the late stages of the disease, even human noses can detect it. With a sense of smell that researchers estimate is between 10,000 and 100,000 times superior to ours, dogs can detect this smell far earlier in the disease's progress - even while the cancer is still "in situ," or has not spread from the site where it was first formed. Remarkably, they don't even need to smell the growth directly. Dogs can detect this scent on waste matter like breath.

That makes the work of training a dog to detect cancer a lot simpler says Dina Zaphiris, founder of the In Situ Foundation. She developed the first protocol for training cancer-detecting dogs. Having trained 52 dogs to detect cancer, she now trains dog handlers from around the world. The goal is to help to spread this life-saving knowledge to all who need it.

Each In Situ dog trains for up to eight months. During this time, they smell samples of breath, plasma, urine, and saliva collected by doctors and sent to the foundation. After smelling more than 300 unique samples, dogs are able to distinguish between a healthy sample and a cancerous one. They also learn to "generalize" the smell, meaning they can transfer what they know about the smell from previously-tested samples to new, similar samples.

At In Situ, has trained dogs to work with research teams at hospitals and universities, distinguishing healthy samples from cancerous samples for teams at Duke University and the University of California, Davis. Now, In Situ is preparing to roll out the first-ever hospital-backed program to use cancer-detecting canines among the public, providing early screening for firefighters in California, who are at high risk of developing cancer because of all the toxins they're exposed to in fires.

Elsewhere, cancer-detecting dogs are being trained not to work directly on early screening for the public, but rather to help researchers gather data they will use to build a "mechanical nose"—a device that will detect odors just like a dog's nose, without the need to train multiple dogs or account for the unpredictabilities of working with living beings. [2]

At first, Sept. 19, 1985, seemed like a normal day in Mexico City, as millions of good, hardworking people busily began their morning. Then, around 7:19, a powerful 8.1-magnitude earthquake jolted the city, and life changed in an instant. Thousands of people lost their lives. Thousands more were injured. Large sections of the city were cut off from electricity and water. Hundreds of buildings collapsed, trapping people under piles of rubble.

Tragedy can bring out the best in people, and that's what happened on that day in Mexico City, as caring people organized themselves into search-and-rescue teams.

Marcos Efrén Zariñana from Cuautla, Morelos, about 100 kilometers south of Mexico City, was one of those volunteers. Marcos was visiting Mexico City that day to pick up a uniform for a marathon he'd been preparing for. His short stature, thin build and runner's determination made him an ideal rescuer. With his ability to crawl into places that others couldn't reach, Marcos earned the affectionate nickname la Pulga, Spanish for "the Flea." But the size of his frame wasn't nearly as important as the size of his heart. Marcos rescued 27 people who were buried under the rubble in Mexico City's Tlalpan neighborhood.

And la Pulga didn't stop there. The 1985 earthquake completely changed Zariñana's life. After helping and serving the victims and their families during the earthquake, he decided to continue training to become a certified rescue worker. In addition to this selfless work, Zariñana worked as a highway patrolman in his native Cuautla.

Over the next 28 years, he traveled to 10 countries that had requested his help after disasters. In all, he rescued 160 people. Duc to his selfless service, Marcos was named a national hero in Mexico. He passed away at the age of 79.

What do we learn from la Pulga's life? For one thing, we learn that sometimes God puts us in just the right place at just the right time. When Marcos traveled to Mexico City, he thought he was preparing for a marathon; he didn't know he would end up saving lives. And we don't always know how God might use us to rescue someone in need. But we can always be ready. When we seek to follow the Lord's two great commandments — to love God and to love our neighbor (see Matthew 22:36–39) — that love will lead us to opportunities to help. As it did for Marcos, (Endal, the En Situ organization, and scientists) - love (and caring) can become our call to action. [3]

1– *The Promise of Disease Detection Dogs in Pandemic Response: Lessons Learned From COVID-19, Disaster Med Public Health Prep. 2021 Jun 8:1–6.*

2– *Dogs Detecting Disease: Meet America's Cancer-Sniffing Canines, Mary Robins, 01/17/2024.*

3– *Music & the Spoken Word: To the rescue, recorded Mexico City, June 2023.*

CHAPTER 27

OBSERVATIONS OF THE SABBATH

On July 24, 1847, the pioneer company of our people came into the Utah valley. An advance group had arrived a day or two earlier. Brigham Young arrived on Saturday. The next day, Sabbath services were held both in the morning and in the afternoon. There was no hall of any kind in which to meet. I suppose that in the blistering heat of that July Sunday they sat on the tongues of their wagons and leaned against the wheels while the brethren spoke. The season was late, and they were faced with a gargantuan and immediate task if they were to grow seed for the next season. But President Young pleaded with them not to violate the Sabbath then or in the future.

Can you possibly imagine how tempting it must have been for our pioneer forefathers to break the Sabbath day? Their survival depended upon the food they could grow and harvest. Yet their leaders counseled them to exercise faith in the promises of the Lord and to respect the Sabbath day.[1]

Most of us only think about Eric Liddell as 'the man who wouldn't run on Sunday', about whom the Oscar winning movie 'Chariots of Fire' was made. He was known as the 'Flying Scotsman' after the record-breaking locomotive and was the first of his country to win Gold during the 1924 Paris Olympics.

Committed Christian Eric Liddell refused to race on the Sabbath day and was forced to withdraw from the 100, 4x100 and 4x400 metres, his best event was the 100 metres. Instead, Liddell raced in the 400 metres and little was expected of him. As Liddell went to the starting blocks for the race, an American slipped a piece of paper in his hand with a quotation from 1 Samuel 2:30, "Those who honour me I will honour."[3]

Shabbat—also known as Sabbath—is the day of the week reserved for rest and worship in Judaism and Christianity. Jews observe Shabbat on Saturdays, beginning Friday nights with lit candles and shared meals. In addition to resting from work at their jobs during that time, Orthodox Jews also refrain from a number of other activities that are considered work, such as driving and switching lights off or on.

Seventh-day Adventists also take Sabbath seriously, worshiping, avoiding work, and spending time with other church members on Saturdays. Most Christians worship on Sunday, and their observance of a day of rest varies from church to church and even from Christian to Christian.

In the past, the regular practice of Sabbath has included so-called "blue laws" (Sunday laws) which once kept many stores closed on Sundays. The laws restricted or banned some or all activities on specified days mostly on Sundays in the western world. They were particularly past to promote the observance of a day of rest. Such laws may restrict shopping or ban sale of certain items on specific days. Blue laws are enforced in parts of the United States and Canada as well as some European countries, particularly in Austria, Germany, Switzerland, and Norway, keeping most stores closed on Sundays.[1]

The U.S. Supreme Court has held blue laws as constitutional numerous times, citing secular bases such as securing a day of rest for mail carriers, as well as protecting workers and families, in turn contributing to societal stability and guaranteeing the free exercise of religion. The origin of the blue laws also partially stems from religion, particularly the prohibition of Sabbath desecration in Christian Churches following the first-day Sabbatarian tradition. Both labor unions and trade associations have historically supported the legislation of blue laws. Most blue laws have been repealed in the United States, although many states continue to ban selling cars and impose tighter restrictions on the sale of alcoholic drinks on Sundays. *Wikipedia*

The word Sabbath comes from the Hebrew shabbath, meaning "day of rest." Flavius Josephus, an oft-quoted scholar in the first century, stated that the Sabbath was a day "set apart from labor; [and] dedicated to the learning of our customs and laws" so that the people might learn a good thing and avoid sin.

What is the origin of the Sabbath day? We often think that it originated with Moses when he gave the Israelites the Ten Commandments. In Exodus, chapter 20: Remember the sabbath day, to keep it holy. Six days shalt thou labour, and do all thy work: But the seventh day is the sabbath of the Lord thy God: in it thou shalt not do any work, thou, nor thy son, nor thy daughter, thy manservant, nor thy maidservant, nor thy cattle, nor thy stranger that is within thy gates: For in six days the Lord made heaven and earth, the sea, and all that in them is, and rested the seventh day: wherefore the Lord blessed the sabbath day, and hallowed it (*Exodus 20:8–11*).

Elder Bruce R. McConkie states that Sabbath observance is an eternal principle, and he notes five occurrences in the scriptures when observance of the Sabbath day was required by the Lord:

- First: "From the day of Adam to the Exodus from Egypt, the Sabbath commemorated the fact that Christ rested from his creative labors on the 7th day" (*Genesis 2:2–3, Exodus 20:8–11*).

- Second: "From the Exodus to the day of his resurrection, the Sabbath commemorated the deliverance of Israel from Egyptian bondage" (*Deuteronomy 5:12–15*).

- Third: "From the days of the early apostles to the present, the Sabbath has been the first day of the week, the Lord's Day, in commemoration of the fact that Christ came forth from the grave on Sunday" (*Acts 20:7*).

- Fourth: "The Latter-day Saints keep the first day of the week as their Sabbath . . . because the Lord so commanded them by direct revelation" (*section 59 of the Doctrine and Covenants*).

- Fifth: "Sabbath observance was a sign between ancient Israel and their God whereby the chosen people might be known" (*Nehemiah 13:15–22, Isaiah 56:1–8, Jeremiah 17:19–27, Ezekiel 46:1–7, and Exodus 31:12–17*).[1]

Elder Donald L. Hallstrom of the Seventy (January 2006) offered a present-day example of observing the sabbath where he recounted the experiences of Brother Toshio Kawada and his wife Miyuki:

"Like all of us, Toshio Kawada of the Obihiro Ward, Sapporo Japan Stake, has had to make crucial choices when faced with life's difficulties. He joined the Church in 1972, and he and his wife, Miyuki, were sealed in the Laie Hawaii Temple in 1978. They have two sons...

More than 20 years ago, when his family was still very young, Brother Kawada was working for his father as a dairy farmer. Tragically, one day the large barn where they kept their milk cows and all their equipment burned down. Financially devastated, his father went to the farmers' union for a loan but was turned down. Subsequently, his father and older brother filed for bankruptcy. Although not legally responsible, Brother Kawada felt obligated to help pay back all the debts.

As Brother Kawada was pondering a solution to his problem, he decided to plant carrots. He had grown potatoes, but he did not know how to grow carrots. He planted the seeds and prayed earnestly for his carrots to grow.

All this time, Brother Kawada faithfully served in the Church, kept the Sabbath day holy, and paid his tithing. When he and his family dressed in their best clothes and went to their Sunday meetings, many neighbors scoffed at them. It was difficult to lose one day a week in their fields, especially at harvest time. It was not always easy for them to pay their tithing, but they offered it to the Lord obediently and cheerfully.

Fall came and Brother Kawada's carrots turned out to be unusually sweet and large, with an exceptionally rich color. He had an abundant harvest and went to the farmers' union for help, but they refused to sell his carrots through their distribution system. He fasted and prayed and felt inspired to try to find a produce distributor in Tokyo— something that is very difficult to do without introductions or connections.

Brother Kawada was blessed to find a large distributor in Tokyo. Since then, he has been very successful and has repaid all his father's debts. He currently has a large agricultural operation with many employees, and he is teaching young farmers how to effectively organize their businesses.

Even in exceptionally trying circumstances, Brother Kawada chose to be true to the promises he made in his baptismal, priesthood, and temple covenants.

Let me read you some of Brother Kawada's own words from his testimony: "Sometimes we worked until midnight on Saturday to keep from breaking the Sabbath. We went to church the next day, often without much sleep. Once we came home from church, and a cow had gotten caught in the pasture fence and died.

There were times when we had millions of yen worth of damage to our cut hay because it had lain in the rain on the Sabbath. We knew accidents didn't happen because it was Sunday. If you worry about that kind of thing, you would never be able to keep the Sabbath. Accidents can happen anytime…

We planted carrots with great success. Finally, we were getting some kind of order in our lives. With carrots, it didn't matter if it rained or we took every Sunday off. We could make our own decisions. We could serve more easily in any calling we were called to.

In our business, we use a lot of part-time help. When we are really busy, our employees suggest that we work Sundays. I tell them that we just don't work on Sundays. When our workers know that, they work hard and rarely take days off. On Sundays the younger workers spend the day with their children, and the older workers visit with their grandchildren." *Toshio Kawada, in Hallstrom, "Using Agency"*

Celisa Young commented: "I've always thought of the Sabbath as a strict tithe of time, a day designated for all things church. My dad used to humorously refer to Sunday as 'the day of all the rest' due to the ironic onslaught of meetings and to-dos. It can be easy to get lost in it all. Against the booked-out backdrop of calendars and lists, simplicity resurfaces through scripture: 'The sabbath was made for man, and not man for the sabbath: Therefore, the Son of Man is Lord also of the sabbath' (Mark 2:27–28).

Christ, the one who promises us rest, is Lord of the Sabbath. The Sabbath is His gift to us. A gift of rest. My daughter is eager to grow. She is discernibly frustrated when she can't crawl, grab things, sit up, or stand on her own. And she seems to fear that, while she naps, she'll miss out on all the excitement of this colorful, sensational world! She wants to do everything, and she wants to do it Right. Now.

How I wish I could reassure her that all those milestones and more will be met sooner than she thinks! And how I wish I could reason with her that, if she takes time to rest, her body will be able to grow in the ways it needs to. I'm sure the Lord wishes the same for us and our spirits.

Yes, the Sabbath is a day of worship, a day to go to celebrate truth and study scripture and sing hymns and remember covenants. But it's also a gift. It's naptime for your spirit! Like our bodies, our spirits need rest in order to grow and thrive.

'If thou turn away … from doing thy pleasure on my holy day and call the sabbath a delight, the holy of the Lord, honorable, and shalt honor him …Then shalt thou delight thyself in the Lord; and I will cause thee to ride upon the high places of the earth, and feed thee with the heritage of Jacob thy father: for the mouth of the Lord hath spoken it' (Isaiah 58:13–14).

This upcoming weekend, it might be worth asking yourself, 'How can I make my Sabbath more restful?" Put the textbook down. Close the scheduling app. Leave emails for later. Take a break from the news. Let chores wait one more day. Simplify meal prep. Let yourself breathe. Accept the gift of rest!

If your Sundays are inherently busy due to a demanding calling or job, it is still possible to find and enjoy rest. President Russell M. Nelson encourages: 'Ask [the Lord] to enlighten your mind and send the help you need. Each day, record the thoughts that come to you as you pray; then follow through diligently…. As you let God prevail in your life, I promise you greater peace, confidence, joy, and yes, rest.'

Rest is within reach for even the busiest hands and minds. Peace, confidence, and joy are all forms of spiritual rest—rest from stress, insecurity, and sorrow. As a new, sleep-deprived mom, I'm learning that growth and rest are just two different names for the same mentality: Assurance. A 'consider-the-lilies' dash of assurance goes a long way between naps."[2]

Eric Liddell ran with that piece of paper in his hand containing the quotation from 1 Samuel 2:30 and not only won the race but broke the existing world record with a time of 47.6 seconds. Did the Sunday "day of rest" before the 400 metre race help him win the race in record time? If he had run the three races scheduled on Sunday would the three together affected his performance on that day and resulted in him not breaking the existing world record on Monday? I doubt any of this crossed his mind: For he knew that "For in six days the Lord made heaven and earth, the sea, and all that in them is, and rested the seventh day: wherefore the Lord blessed the sabbath day, and hallowed it." (Exodus 20:8–11)

The Tour de France is considered by some to be the hardest major sporting event. It consists of a three-week long race comprising 21 stages with a total distance of around 3,500km (2,188 miles). Racing for three weeks takes a heavy toll on the body, even for professional cyclists. Hence, they have realized over time that there is a need for rest days. The rest day is the day where there is no racing at the Tour de France. In 2023, there were two rest days. The first rest day was after Stage 9 on 10 July, and the second was after Stage 15 on 17 July. Both rest days were on a Monday. Since 1999, there have been two rest days on

Mondays in week two and week three (note they are seven days a part).

Later in his life, Liddell achieved a greater prize than in 1924 when he won Olympic Gold. After the Olympics, Liddell returned to China where he was born to work as a missionary. His family, originally from Scotland, worked in China during the time of the Boxer Rebellion. Liddell worked as a teacher at a school for Chinese boys at which he taught chemistry and organized sports. He married in 1934 and in 1936 China prepared for war as Communist and Nationalist tensions increased. Liddell was asked by the London Missionary Society to give up his work in Tientsin, and work as a village evangelist in Siao Chang. This was a dangerous area. Liddell could not take his wife and two daughters with him and he was forced to leave them behind when he went to work there. He was able to visit on occasion, but it was a long journey. Visits were not frequent.

The hymn "Be Still My Soul" is said to have been the favourite of Eric Liddell during his imprisonment as a missionary during World War II. He was known to have taught this hymn to others in the prison camp. This popular revival hymn was written by a German Katharina von Schlegel (1697-1768) when the Lutheran Pastor Philipp Jacob Spencer began encouraging congregational singing. Approximately 100 years later it was translated into English by Jane L. Borthwick a devoted religious and social worker in the Free Church of Scotland. Psalm 46:10. *"Be still, and know that I am God; I will be exalted among the nations, I will be exalted in the earth."*

In 1944 during imprisonment and World War II, Liddell was not well. The doctors did not have the resources to diagnose the real nature of the problem. A few days before his death, Eric walked to the hospital grounds and asked the band to play "Be Still, My Soul". On February 21, 1945, he began coughing uncontrollably, and as friends came to his aid, he lay back and uttered the words *"It is surrender"*. An autopsy later revealed that Liddell had a large tumour on the left side of his brain. He died never having seen his third child, Maureen Liddell. This man was truly committed to the cause of Christ. He had the opportunity to leave China but he chose to stay. He poured his life into the work of reaching the lost in China. He worked for a prize far greater than gold, even Olympic gold.

From Eric's Discipleship Manual:

- Victory over all the circumstances of life comes not by might, nor by power, but by a practical confidence in God and by allowing His Spirit to dwell in our hearts and control our actions and emotions.

- Learn in the days of ease and comfort, to think in terms of the prayer that follows, so that when the days of hardship come you will be fully prepared and equipped to meet them.

- Father, I pray that no circumstance however bitter or however long drawn out, may cause me to break Thy law, the Law of Love to Thee and to my neighbor. That I may not become resentful, have hurt feelings, hate, or become embittered by life's experiences, but that in and through all I may see Thy guiding hand and have a heart full of gratitude for Thy daily mercy, daily love, daily power, and daily presence.[3]

Help me in the day when I need it most to remember that:
- *All things work together for good to them that love the Lord.*
- *I can do all things through Him that strengthened me.*
- *My grace is sufficient for thee, for my strength is made perfect in weakness.*

January 16, 1902 – February 21, 1945…Eric Liddell

1– *The Law of the Sabbath, Earl C. Tingey, 08/06/1995.*
2– *You don't just deserve Sunday rest, your soul needs it. Here's how to find it, Celisa Young, 05/01/2024.*
3– *Eternal Prospectives Ministries, The Little-known Story of Olympian Eric Liddell's Final Years, 2018.*

CHAPTER 28

GENEROSITY

John A. Johnson, Ph.D. shares his thoughts on selfless service: "One of the most extolled virtues of all time is selfless service to others. The blessedness of giving rather than receiving is one of the most popular and most quoted verses in the Bible, and John F. Kennedy's call for service is one of the most recognized lines from any presidential inaugural address. The value of selfless service is found in many religions and spiritual traditions around the world. Indian religions refer to selfless service with the Sanskrit word seva, which means helping others in need without the thought of receiving any reward or repayment in return. Seva is thought to advance a person›s spiritual growth or development.

So, is it really possible for an ordinary person to serve others without expecting reward or recognition, or does one have to be a saint to engage in such service? According to wellness expert Daniel Scott, the answer is that we all have the capacity for selfless service. He writes: (former psychology professor-turned-spiritual teacher, and a founder of the Seva Foundation) Ram Dass explains this beautifully: 'Helping out is not some special skill. It is not the domain of rare individuals. It is not confined to a single part of our lives. We simply heed the call of that natural impulse within and follow it where it leads us.'

I agree that nearly every person has a natural impulse to help another human being who is in need. Yet I also believe that there are substantial individual differences in the strength of this impulse to help others and the likelihood of acting on this impulse consistently. It is one thing to drop a dollar into the hat of a homeless person I happen upon; it is quite another to devote my entire life to assisting the homeless or volunteering for similar selfless service.

I am skeptical about whether most of us can help others consistently without expecting some kind of reward. I'm not saying that we necessarily need a return favor from the person we help or recognition from society. All I am saying is that, at the very least, we expect to feel good about ourselves after helping someone. I think that expecting to feel good (or to avoid feeling bad) is the anticipated reward that that motivates most charitable acts. Consider the following example.

You are walking down the street and notice that a stranger's parking meter has expired. You decide to put some change in the meter so the person doesn't get a parking fine, and then you walk away. Because the owner of the car does not know you, he or she will not be able to thank you or return the favor in any way. But, did you really receive no reward for your random act of kindness? Didn't you feel good about yourself for helping the stranger? Wasn't feeling good a rewarding experience? Let me put it another way. If you did not expect to feel good after putting the change in the meter, would you have helped the stranger to avoid the parking fine?"[1]

Years ago, a little girl named Annie Sullivan was placed by her family in an insane asylum located just outside of Boston. Annie was wild and uncontrollable, so the doctors placed her in a cage in the basement of the facility. She became even more volatile. At times she would attack anyone who approached her cage, at other times she didn't even acknowledge that they were present. She was considered a hopeless case and seemed destined to spend the rest of her miserable existence in that cage in the basement.[2]

Dr. Frank Mayfield was touring Tewksbury Institute when, on his way out, he accidentally collided with an elderly floor maid. To cover the awkward moment Dr. Mayfield started asking questions. He was told that the maid had worked there almost since the place was open. She told Mayfield that she did not know much about the place but took him by hand and led him down to the basement under the oldest section of the building. She pointed to one of what looked like small prison cells, their iron bars rusted with age, and said this was the cage where they used to keep Annie Sullivan. Annie was a young girl who was brought in here because she was incorrigible – nobody could do anything with her. She'd bite and scream and throw her food at people. The doctors and nurses couldn't even examine her or anything. She would see them trying with her spitting and scratching at them.

The maid was only a few years younger than Annie and used to think how she would hate to be locked up in a cage like that. She wanted to help her, but didn't have any idea what she could do. The doctors and nurses couldn't even examine her. She'd see them trying with her spitting and scratching at them.

Annie was a young girl who was brought in here because she was incorrigible—nobody could do anything with her. She'd bite and scream and throw her food at people. The doctors and nurses couldn't even examine her. She'd see them trying with her spitting and scratching at them.

The maid didn't know what else to do, so she just baked her some brownies one night after work. The next day she brought them in. I walked carefully to her cage and told Annie that she baked the brownies just for her. She put them on the floor and told her she could come and get them if she wanted. Then she "got out of there just as fast as she could" because she was afraid Annie might throw them at her. But she didn't. She actually took the brownies and ate them. After that, she was just a little bit nicer when she was around. And sometimes she could talk to her. Once, she even got her laughing.

One of the nurses noticed this and she told the doctor. They asked the maid if she'd help them with Annie. She said she would if she could. So that's how it came about. Every time they wanted to see Annie or examine her, the maid went into the cage first and explained and calmed her down and held her hand.

This is how they discovered that Annie was almost blind.

After they'd been working with her for about a year— and it was tough sledding with Annie—the Perkins institute for the Blind opened its doors. They were able to help her and she went on to study and she became a teacher herself.[3]

Johnson continues: I question the notion of pure altruism—of doing something to benefit another person without expecting anything in return. As I said, at the very least, when we do good deeds we expect to feel good about ourselves, or to avoid negative feelings like guilt or shame. Often, we actually expect more. We usually expect in return at least a smile, a "thank you," or other token of appreciation. Think about it: How long would you keep giving to a friend if he or she never showed appreciation? How long would that friendship last?"

On the other hand, it is also a fact that people sometimes to extend themselves in extraordinary ways, making enormous sacrifices of time, energy, and resources to assist others, way beyond what they might receive in return. In the most dramatic cases, people sometimes even give their lives to help other people. "Selfless service" is one of the seven core values of the U.S. Army. A soldier who dies to protect others is not going to hear a thank-you in return for the ultimate sacrifice.

Evolutionary psychologists have long puzzled over how to explain altruism because it is not obvious why a set of genes could encourage self-sacrificial behavior without going extinct. The only way in which it is mathematically possible for any kind of selflessness to evolve is for selfless individuals to associate more frequently with other selfless individuals than with non-selfless individuals.[1]

Annie came back to the Tewksbury Institute to visit, and to see what she could do to help out. At first, the Director didn't say anything and then he thought about a letter he'd just received. A man had written to him about his daughter. She was absolutely unruly—almost like an animal. She was blind and deaf as well as 'deranged.' He was at his wit's end, but he didn't want to put her in an asylum. So, he wrote the Institute to ask if they knew of anyone who would come to his house and work with his daughter.[3]

The Bible consistently pushes for altruism, advocating for believers to help others without seeking recognition. Through these teachings, we clearly see that altruism isn't just a good idea – it's a biblical mandate. For instance, Matthew 6:1-4. In this passage, Jesus tells his followers not to make a show of their righteousness in front of others but instead, to do good deeds quietly and humbly. He says "So when you give to the needy, do not announce it with trumpets…but when you give to the needy, do not let your left hand know what your right hand is doing." This verse speaks volumes about the Bible's stance on altruism.

Let's also consider Proverbs 19:17 which states "Whoever is kind to the poor lends to the LORD, and he will reward them for what they have done." Here again we see God encouraging His people to be generous and kind-hearted without any expectation of acknowledgment or repayment from those they help.

Then there's Hebrews 13:16 - "And do not forget to do good and share with others…" The language here is clear; sharing and doing good are non-negotiables for believers. But notice there's no discussion about getting credit or applause for these actions.

In Acts 20:35 where Paul quotes Jesus saying "It is more blessed to give than receive." This statement embodies pure altruism - finding joy in giving rather than receiving.

And the most important - John 13:34-35 says, "A new command I give you: Love one another. As I have loved you, so you must love one another. By this everyone will know that you are my disciples, if you love one another."

According to Latter-day scriptures, the Spirit of Christ is a gift from God that helps people in all aspects of life. It is always present and cannot leave, so everyone already has it. The Spirit of Christ is also a source of truth and a way for God to lead and direct his children. We all have "natural impulses" and a "god-shaped hole" available for our spirit and reserved 24/7 to help us if we will sincerely ask.

The letter to the Director of Tewksbury Institute was about Helen Keller. When Helen Keller received the Nobel Prize, she was asked who had the greatest impact on her life and she said, "Annie Sullivan." But Annie said, "No Helen. The woman who had the greatest influence on both our lives was a floor maid at the Tewksbury Institute."[2]

Are there any "Little Annie's" in your life? While we will never know the full extent of the little acts of kindness that we do from time to time, we can be assured that their benefits will far exceed the cost of a plate of brownies or a few minutes of our time that we have spared for others. We can also be assured that Someone is watching and will bless our small sacrifices in ways that we can never know.[3]

1– *Selfless Service, Part I: Is Selfless Service Possible? Psychology Today, John A. Johnson, Ph.D., 05/08/2013.*

2– *And now you know... the rest of the story, Paul Harvey.*

3– *Helen Keller, Anne Sullivan, and the Nobel Prize Parable, A popular tale claims that an act of kindness greatly impacted the lives of Helen Keller and Anne Sullivan Macy, Dan Evon, 10/05/20021.*

Helen Keller & Anne Sullivan

CHAPTER 29

WHO'S THE HAPPIEST

Few choices are more important than whether to have children, and psychologists and other social scientists have worked to figure out what having kids means for happiness. Some of the most prominent scholars in the field have argued that if you want to be happy, it's best to be childless. Others have pushed back, pointing out that a lot depends on who you are and where you live. But a bigger question is also at play: What if the rewards of having children are different from, and deeper than, happiness?

The early research is decisive: Having kids is bad for quality of life. In one study, the psychologist Daniel Kahneman and his colleagues asked about 900 employed women to report, at the end of each day, every one of their activities and how happy they were when they did them. They recalled being with their children as less enjoyable than many other activities, such as watching TV, shopping, or preparing food. Other studies find that when a child is born, parents experience a decrease in happiness that doesn't go away for a long time, in addition to a drop in marital satisfaction that doesn't usually recover until the children leave the house.

As the Harvard professor Dan Gilbert puts it, "The only symptom of empty nest syndrome is nonstop smiling."

After all, having children, particularly when they are young, involves financial struggle, sleep deprivation, and stress. For mothers, there is also in many cases the physical strain of pregnancy and breastfeeding. And children can turn a cheerful and loving romantic partnership into a zero-sum battle over who gets to sleep and work and who doesn't.

But, as often happens in psychology, although some research provided simple findings—in this case, "having children makes you unhappy"—other efforts arrived at more complicated conclusions. For one, the happiness hit is worse for some people than for others. One study finds that fathers ages 26 to 62 actually get a happiness boost, while young or single parents suffer the greatest loss. And crucially, there are geographic differences. A 2016 paper looking at the happiness levels of people with and without children in 22 countries found that the extent to which children make you happy is influenced by whether your country has child-care policies such as paid parental leave. Parents from Norway and Hungary, for instance, are happier than childless couples in those countries—but parents from Australia and Great Britain are less happy than their childless peers. The country with the greatest happiness drops after you have children? The United States.

Children make some happy and others miserable; the rest fall somewhere in between—it depends, among other factors, on how old you are, whether you are a mother or a father, and where you live. But a deep puzzle remains: Many people would have had happier lives and marriages had they chosen not to have kids—yet they still describe parenthood as the "best thing they've ever done." Why don't we regret having children more?

One possibility is a phenomenon called memory distortion. When we think about our past experiences, we tend to remember the peaks and forget the mundane awfulness in between. Our experiencing selves tell researchers that we prefer doing the dishes—or napping, or shopping, or answering emails—to spending time with our kids ... But our remembering selves tell researchers that no one—and nothing—provides us with so much joy as our children. It may not be the happiness we live day to day, but it's the happiness we think about, the happiness we summon and remember, the stuff that makes up our life-tales.

But other theories about why people don't regret parenthood actually have nothing to do with happiness—at least not in a simple sense. One involves attachment. Most parents love their children, and it would seem terrible to admit that you would be better off if someone you loved didn't exist. More than that, you genuinely prefer a world with your kids in it. This can put parents in the interesting predicament of desiring a state that doesn't make them as happy as the alternative.

When one person said raising her sons was the best thing she'd ever done, she was not saying that they gave her pleasure in any simple day-to-day sense, and not saying that they were good for her marriage. She's talking about something deeper, having to do with satisfaction, purpose, and meaning. It's not just her. When you ask people about their life's meaning and purpose, parents say that their lives have more meaning than those of nonparents. A study found that the more time people spent taking care of children, the more meaningful they said their life was—even though they reported that their life was no happier.[1]

The 2022 edition of the General Social Survey (GSS)—the nation's preeminent social barometer—reveals that marriage and family are strongly associated with happiness. The GSS shows that a combination of marriage and parenthood is linked to the biggest happiness dividends for women. Among married women with children between the ages of 18 and 55, 40% reported they are "very happy," compared to 25% of married childless women, and just 22% of unmarried childless women.

Nevertheless, it is important to note that unmarried mothers are the least likely to be very happy: with just 17% of them indicating they are very happy. These results parallel findings from 2020 and 2021 during the pandemic that we reported last year in The Atlantic. In earlier surveys, we found that women who were married with children were generally the happiest and the least lonely.

But what about men? Is the link between happiness, marriage, and parenthood similar for men? Indeed, the 2022 General Social Survey indicates that marriage is also linked to greater happiness for men ages 18-55. And here again, married fathers are happiest.

Specifically, 35% of married men ages 18-55 who have children report being "very happy," followed by 30% of married men who do not have children. By contrast unmarried childless men, and especially unmarried fathers are the least happy—with less than 15% of these men saying they are "very happy." In other words, married men (ages 18-55) in America are about twice as likely to be very happy, compared to their unmarried peers.

These results parallel other recent research from the University of Chicago indicating that for both men and women, marriage is "the most important differentiator" of who is happy in America. Meanwhile, falling marriage rates are a chief reason why happiness has declined nationally, according to that same study. The research found an astounding 30-percentage-point happiness gap between married and unmarried Americans.

Other factors do matter—including income, educational achievement, race, and geography—but marital status is most influential when it comes to predicting happiness in the study. What's more, other research indicates that the United States is witnessing a growing happiness divide between the most educated and least educated Americans, and marriage is likely the biggest driver of that decline.

Social psychologist Jean Twenge attributes the growing happiness divide in America along class lines to a faster decline in marriage among those with less education and income. In Twenge's view, the growing class divide in happiness clearly has many causes, including income inequality. Still, relationships are also crucial for happiness, and for many people, marriage is their primary and most stable relationship.

This new research provides further evidence that happiness is linked to American family life. In particular, and contrary to the views articulated by many on social media, the mainstream media, and the American public, marriage and parenthood do not appear to be obstacles to living a happy life. Instead, these two traditional markers of adulthood are associated with a happier life. As difficult as marriage and parenthood can be, in general, men and women who have the benefit of a spouse and children are the most likely to report that they are "very happy" with their lives, according to the most recent round of the General Social Survey.[2]

Raising children, then, has an uncertain connection to pleasure but may connect to other aspects of a life well lived, satisfying our hunger for attachment, and for meaning and purpose. The writer Zadie Smith describes having a child as a "strange admixture of terror, pain, and delight." Smith, echoing the thoughts of everyone else who has seriously considered these issues, points out the risk of close attachments: "Isn't it bad enough that the beloved, with whom you have experienced genuine joy, will eventually be lost to you? Why add to this nightmare the child, whose loss, if it ever happened, would mean nothing less than your total annihilation?" But this annihilation reflects the extraordinary value of such attachments; as the author Julian Barnes writes of grief, quoting a friend, "It hurts just as much as it is worth."[1]

When my kid's mom was diagnosed with terminal cancer her primary thoughts of disappointment was that she wasn't going to have the opportunity to see her grandchildren born or be involved with their growing experiences. She spent the last two and one-half years of her life visiting, buying gifts, and going on vacations with our children and grandchildren. Unfortunately, only one was old enough to still remember her. At home she would spend most of her free time finishing scrap books, blankets etc. for her children and future grandchildren.

There are two plaques on our wall that say, "Home is where your story begins", "Live, laugh and love" and one that is nearby is a picture of Christ that says "I never said it would be easy – I only said it would be worth it." One of our family's favorite songs that ties together, at least for me, "Who's the Happiest" is "Families can be together forever" found in Mormon Hymnal #300:

"I have a fam'ly here on earth. They are so good to me. I want to share my life with them through all eternity. Fam'lies can be together forever, through Heav'nly Father's plan. I always want to be with my own family, and the Lord has shown me how I can. The Lord has shown me how I can.

While I am in my early years, I'll prepare most carefully, so I can marry in God's temple for eternity. Fam'lies can be together forever through Heav'nly Father's plan. I always want to be with my own family, and the Lord has shown me how I can. The Lord has shown me how I can."

Fairy tale, I don't think so…my faith, hope and the pure love of Christ (Charity) helps keep me plugging along with a smile on my face even though raising a family has often felt like "It hurt just as much as it was worth it."

1– *What Becoming a Parent Really Does to Your Happiness, The Atlantic, adapted from the Book "The Sweet Spot: The Pleasures of Suffering and the Search for Meaning", Paul Bloom, 11/02/2021.*

2– *Who Is Happiest? Married Mothers and Fathers, per the Latest General Social Survey, By W. Bradford Wilcox | Wendy Wang, Institute for Family Studies, 09/13/2023.*

CHAPTER 30

HELP YOUR FELLOWMAN
SIT IN THE SUN

Kenneth E. Behring (1928-2019): Born in Freeport, Illinois, father worked in a lumber yard making 25 cents an hour, and his mother cleaned houses. Started working a variety of jobs around town starting at age seven: mowing lawns, caddying, transporting milk, selling newspapers, working at a grocery store, and at a lumberyard. He became a salesperson at Montgomery Ward at age 16, and started a side business selling sporting goods in town while attending Monroe High School.

A high school football player, he received a partial football scholarship to the University of Wisconsin–Madison, but dropped out of college due to an injury that left him unable to play football, and therefore ineligible for his scholarship. Out of college, Behring, a car buff, worked as a salesperson at a Chevrolet and Chrysler auto dealership. At age 21, he started Behring Motors, a used car business in Monroe.

In 1988, he and partner purchased the NFL's Seattle Seahawks football team from the Nordstrom family for $80 million. After the 1995 season, they transferred the team's operations to the Rams' former facilities in Anaheim, California. The team continued to play in Seattle at the Kingdome. He had failed to properly apply for relocation, on top of having his plans for a full move being scuttled when lawyers discovered that the Seahawks were locked into the Kingdome through 2005; in addition, the NFL threatened fining him $500,000 each day if he did not return the team from Southern California. He was forced to sell the Seahawks to Microsoft in 1997 for $200 million, who elected to keep the team in Seattle.

He has been listed several times on the annual Forbes 400 list of richest Americans. In 1997, his last year on the list, he ranked #395, with an estimated net worth of $495 million. He has since been described in the press as a billionaire.

He founded the Wheelchair Foundation in Blackhawk, California in 2000, to provide free wheelchairs for people with physical disabilities in developing nations unable to afford one. As of September 2013, the Wheelchair Foundation had given away over 940,000 wheelchairs in 152 countries around the globe.

Mr. Behring received an honorary doctorate degree during a commencement address at Brigham Young University and shared these words with the graduating class:

I'm going to tell you some stories about lives that have crossed mine, and then I'm going to tell you what I think those stories mean.

It is really amazing how things work out. Because I have a big airplane that flies across the world at 35,000 feet, I came into contact with people who see the world by crawling on their stomachs and elbows. I owe this blessing to The Church of Jesus Christ of Latter-day Saints. Although I'm not a member of the Church, about three years ago I was asked if I had room on my plane to drop off 15 tons of canned meat for refugees in Kosovo. Then the Church asked, "And is there any chance that you might have a little extra room to drop off some wheelchairs in Romania?"

I had never really thought about wheelchairs before. But after that trip I could think of little else. When we dropped off the chairs, the doctor told me that disabled people in third world countries—such as many of the children in refugee camps whose legs have been blown off by land mines—are often just discarded and abandoned. Often families hide the disabled in the back room because they're ashamed. They don't even want their neighbors to know. Some of you on your missions overseas may have seen such things.

I've met people who have spent 25 years in a bed in a room with no windows. I met a girl who had spent the last 23 years lying flat on a mattress, looking at the ceiling without the ability to move or to be easily moved. Imagine not being able to see the outdoors unless someone carries you. No wonder so many dream that they're birds.

I wish you could meet the people I've met. They have taught me to use the word love much more freely than I would have thought possible.

When we were in North Vietnam, we put an elderly lady in a wheelchair. She asked the interpreter if she could thank me. She came over and said, "I'm 85 years old, and I've wanted to die, but I have not been able to." I didn't know what to say. Then she moved closer and took my hands. She looked at me and smiled. Then she said, "But now I don't want to die."

A young Guatemalan man's leg was swollen. He wanted to know if he could borrow a wheelchair to get him around so that he could come up with the money to have his leg taken off. It had gangrene, and he had 30 days to have it removed. The doctor wanted $100 to cut the leg off and another $25 to put him to sleep. I gave him the $125. He counted it out, and he handed me $25 back. He said, "That's okay. I don't need to be put to sleep." I gave the money back to him. Three days later I got a call from down there. He had had his leg off and was getting around in a wheelchair. His wife had found a job, he was in the house taking care of the children, and they were going to be a very happy family.

When these people come to us, some are driven, some are carried, some come by wheelbarrow or hand truck. Some crawl. In Zimbabwe a fellow crawled on his elbows for 17 kilometers to get to us. We put him in the wheelchair, and he was going around and around with a big smile on his face. After a while he pulled himself out of it and sat on the ground. We asked him why. He said, "I've had my turn." He didn't realize he could keep it. This year he came back with his children to show us that he had cared for the chair so well that it was just like new.

We gave a chair to a woman in South Africa who had not gotten one on a previous trip. She said to me, "I've prayed every day for two years that God would send you back with a chair, and here you are." When you give people these chairs, they grab your hand, they cry, they thank you, they very often say a prayer. And they always smile.

Most of us think of a wheelchair as a confinement, but to millions of people it is not confinement, it is freedom— freedom to move, to go to school, to get a job. A chair is hope, self-reliance, independence. Most important, it is dignity.

In a way a wheelchair is to the body what the education you have received is to the mind. You would be overwhelmed by how much a little chair with wheels can mean—how it can change lives. A young South American woman who was going to school—just like you have been—got hit by a truck. She spent the next 11 years in bed. We gave her a wheelchair. The next day she came back and said she had reenrolled and was starting her studies the next day.

People go from not smiling to smiling. As soon as we put one young boy in a chair, he took off for a water fountain and started splashing the water. He splashed himself, he splashed other people, then he went and felt a leaf on a tree. These are such simple pleasures that we take for granted.

There is another story that means a lot to me. We had a woman from Mexico who has worked for us for 12 years. She heard we were going to Mexico City to deliver wheelchairs. She informed us that she had a nephew in Mexico City whose name was Angel. He had a terminal disease. He had first lost his eyesight and had now lost his mobility. She asked if we could give him a wheelchair so he could be mobile during the limited time he had to live. I said yes and told her to have his parents come to our distribution. His parents found us and were crying. They said that Angel had received his wheelchair and wanted to thank me. They brought him in his wheelchair, and I spoke to him so he would know where I was. He then took my hands and looked up with his blind eyes into my eyes and said, "I'll see you in heaven." I was not able to even answer him.

These people's stories may seem far removed from this beautiful campus, so what do they have to do with you graduates? I think these stories reveal a number of truths about life and how we live it. Graduates, there is so much need out there in so many different ways. In terms of wheelchairs alone, between 100 and 130 million people worldwide cannot afford a wheelchair and need one. China needs 20 million chairs. India needs 30 million chairs. Next year we will give away 200,000 wheelchairs in 100 countries. Our goal is to provide one million chairs by 2005 (total > 940,000). The Church is really helping us with this ministry of mobility.

This wheelchair mission is the greatest thing that has ever happened to me. I used to give money to good causes because I felt obligated to give back. Many people give because they feel obligated—which is good—but they don't feel the giving with their hearts. If I have any wisdom worth this honorary doctorate that you have so kindly given me, it is this: Giving is not a duty; it is a joy.

I wish every one of you graduates could lift someone into a wheelchair and look into his or her eyes. There are no barriers of race or religion or culture when your eyes meet. I want you to feel such joy. I want you to feel such humanity. Your lives are going to need similar experiences to be truly rich.

Let me close with one last story. When I was in Yugoslavia, this man was telling me about his teenage son. The man said he saw his son step on the land mine that blew him onto another one, which then blew him onto another one. By the time the father got to him, most of his life was gone. The man frantically found an old pickup truck to take the boy to a place where he could receive blood. The young man stayed 11 months. Although he lived, he lost an eye, his hearing in one ear, and both legs up to his hips.

The man said that although they were refugees, they had a house and they had food to survive. And now with this wheelchair he could give his son what he wanted most, and that was to go out and sit in the sun.

Ladies and gentlemen, I don't think that the desire of a human being to sit in the sun is too much to ask. As you graduates leave here today full of brightness and possibilities, I ask that you not forget those who lie in the lonely depths of darkened rooms—immobilized perhaps physically, perhaps mentally, perhaps by poverty or despair.

As you leave this university to make your way in the world, I ask one thing of you. I don't care how rich you become. I don't care what position of power you someday hold. I don't care what you invent or create or build. I ask one thing of you.

I ask that along life's path you take the time now and then to help your fellowman sit in the sun.

Thank you.

Whoever brings blessing will be enriched, and one who waters will himself be watered…Whoever is kind to the poor lends to the LORD, and he will reward them for what they have done...The generous will themselves be blessed, for they share their food with the poor. Proverbs 11:25, 19:17, 22:9

1– *This Ministry of Mobility, Kenneth E. Behring (1928-2019), founder Wheelchair Foundation, BYU commencement address, 08/15/2002.*

CHAPTER 31

HANDCART TRAVELERS

Many of these early converts of the Church of Jesus Christ of Latter-day Saints emigrated from Europe and were too poor to buy oxen or horses and a wagon. They were forced by their poverty to pull handcarts containing all of their belongings across the plains by their own brute strength. President David O. McKay related an occurrence about a group which took place some years after their heroic exodus: "A teacher, conducting a class, said it was unwise ever to attempt, even to permit them (the Martin handcart company) to come across the plains under such conditions. (According to a class member,) some sharp criticism of the Church and its leaders was being indulged in for permitting any company of converts to venture across the plains with no more supplies or protection than a handcart caravan afforded.

An old man in the corner ... sat silent and listened as long as he could stand it, then he arose and said things that no person who heard him will ever forget. His face was white with emotion, yet he spoke calmly, deliberately, but with great earnestness and sincerity: In substance (he) said, "I ask you to stop this criticism. You are discussing a matter you know nothing about. Cold historic facts mean nothing here, for they give no proper interpretation of the questions involved. Mistake to send the Handcart Company out so late in the season? Yes. But I was in that company and my wife was in it and Sister Nellie Unthank whom you have cited was there, too. We suffered beyond anything you can imagine and many died of exposure and starvation, but did you ever hear a survivor of that company utter a word of criticism? Not one of that company ever apostatized or left the Church, because everyone of us came through with the absolute knowledge that God lives, for we became acquainted with him in our extremities.

I have pulled my handcart when I was so weak and weary from illness and lack of food that I could hardly put one foot ahead of the other. I have looked ahead and seen a patch of sand or a hill slope and I have said, I can go only that far and there I must give up, for I cannot pull the load through it. I have gone on to that sand and when I reached it, the cart began pushing me. I have looked back many times to see who was pushing my cart, but my eyes saw no one. I knew then that the angels of God were there.

Was I sorry that I chose to come by handcart? No. Neither then nor any minute of my life since. The price we paid to become acquainted with God was a privilege to pay, and I am thankful that I was privileged to come in the Martin Handcart Company." (Relief Society Magazine, Jan. 1948, p. 8.)

Here then is a great truth. In the pain, the agony, and the heroic endeavors of life, we pass through a refiner's fire, and the insignificant and the unimportant in our lives can melt away like dross and make our faith bright, intact, and strong. In this way the divine image can be mirrored from the soul. It is part of the purging toll exacted of some to become acquainted with God. In the agonies of life, we seem to listen better to the faint, godly whisperings of the Divine Shepherd.

Elder James E. Faust relates this story: Stillman Pond was a member of the Second Quorum of Seventy in Nauvoo. He was an early convert to the Church, having come from Hubbardston, Massachusetts. Like others, he and his wife, Maria, and their children were harassed and driven out of Nauvoo. In September 1846, they became part of the great western migration. The early winter that year brought extreme hardships, including malaria, cholera, and consumption. The family was visited by all three of these diseases. Maria contracted consumption, and all of the children were stricken with malaria. Three of the children died while moving through the early snows. Stillman buried them on the plains. Maria's condition worsened because of the grief, pain, and the fever of malaria. She could no longer walk. Weakened and sickly, she gave birth to twins. They were named Joseph and Hyrum, and both died within a few days.

The Stillman Pond family arrived at Winter Quarters and, like many other families, they suffered bitterly while living in a tent. The death of the five children coming across the plains to Winter Quarters was but a beginning.

The journal of Horace K. and Helen Mar Whitney verifies the following regarding four more of the children of Stillman Pond who perished: "On Wednesday, the 2nd of December 1846, Laura Jane Pond, age 14 years, … died of chills and fever." Two days later on "Friday, the 4th of December 1846, Harriet M. Pond, age 11 years, … died with chills." Three days later, "Monday, the 7th of December, 1846, Abigail A. Pond, age 18 years, … died with chills." Just five weeks later, "Friday, the 15th of January, 1847, Lyman Pond, age 6 years, … died with chills and fever. Four months later, on the 17th of May, 1847, his wife Maria Davis Pond also died. Crossing the plains, Stillman Pond lost nine children and a wife. He became an outstanding colonizer in Utah, and became the senior president of the thirty-fifth Quorum of Seventy. (See Leon Y. and H. Ray Pond, comps., "Stillman Pond, a Biographical Sketch," in Sterling Forsyth Histories, typescript, Church Historical Dept. Archives, pp. 4–5.)

According to Kate B. Carter, *Heartthrobs of the West,* 12 vols (SLC: Daughters of the Utah Pioneers, 1939-51), 2:108: Driven from Nauvoo at the point of a bayonet; driving one hundred and fifty miles looking through a knothole; losing his wife and nine of his eleven children – would it surprise any of us if the record showed that at this point Stillman raised his fists and shook them at the heavens, crying, "Enough! I will endure no more?"

But no He went on to Utah and, as President Faust notes, 'became an outstanding colonizer in Utah.' … Stillman Pond did not lose his faith. He did not quit. He went forward. He paid a price, as have many others before and since, to become acquainted with God."

Into every life there come the painful, despairing days of adversity and buffeting. There seems to be a full measure of anguish, sorrow, and often heartbreak for everyone, including those who earnestly seek to do right and be faithful. The thorns that prick, that stick in the flesh, that hurt, often change lives which seem robbed of significance and hope. This change comes about through a refining process which often seems cruel and hard. In this way the soul can become like soft clay in the hands of the Master in building lives of faith, usefulness, beauty, and strength. For some, the refiner's fire causes a loss of belief and faith in God, but those with eternal perspective understand that such refining is part of the perfection process.

In our extremities, it is possible to become born again, born anew, renewed in heart and spirit. We no longer ride with the flow of the crowd, but instead we enjoy the promise of Isaiah to be renewed in our strength and "mount up with wings as eagles" (Isa. 40:31).

The proving of one's faith goes before the witnessing, for Moroni testified, "Ye receive no witness until after the trial of your faith" (Ether 12:6). This trial of faith can become a priceless experience. Stated Peter, "That the trial of your faith, being much more precious than of gold that perisheth, though it be tried with fire, might be found unto praise and honour and glory at the appearing of Jesus Christ" (1 Pet. 1:7). Trials and adversity can be preparatory to becoming born anew.

A rebirth out of spiritual adversity causes us to become new creatures. From the book of Mosiah we learn that all mankind must be born again—born of God, changed, redeemed, and uplifted—to become the sons and daughters of God. (See Mosiah 27:24–27.)

President Marion G. Romney, speaking for the Lord, has said of this marvelous power: "The effect upon each person's life is likewise similar. No person whose soul is illuminated by the burning Spirit of God can in this world of sin and dense darkness remain passive. He is driven by an irresistible urge to fit himself to be an active agent of God in furthering righteousness and in freeing the lives and minds of men from the bondage of sin." (In Conference Report, 4 Oct. 1941, p. 89.)

Unfortunately, some of our greatest tribulations are the result of our own foolishness and weakness and occur because of our own carelessness or transgression. Central to solving these problems is the great need to get back on the right track and, if necessary, engage in each of the steps for full and complete repentance. Through this great principle, many things can be made fully right and all things better. We can go to others for help. To whom can we go? Elder Orson F. Whitney asked and answered this question: "To whom do we look, in days of grief and disaster, for help and consolation? … They are men and women who have suffered, and out of their experience in suffering they bring forth the riches of their sympathy and condolences as a blessing to those now in need. Could they do this had they not suffered themselves?

"… Is not this God's purpose in causing his children to suffer? He wants them to become more like himself. God has suffered far more than man ever did or ever will, and is therefore the great source of sympathy and consolation." (Improvement Era, Nov. 1918, p. 7.)

Isaiah, before the Savior's birth, referred to him as "a man of sorrows" (Isa. 53:3). Speaking in the Doctrine and Covenants of himself, the Savior said: "Which suffering caused myself, even God, the greatest of all, to tremble because of pain, and to bleed at every pore, and to suffer both body and spirit—and would that I might not drink the bitter cup, and shrink" (D&C 19:18). *The Refiner's Fire, Elder James E. Faust, April 1979.*

CHAPTER 32

SEA STARS

Most people who live near ocean shores are familiar with starfish (or sea stars, as they are more properly called) for they are often seen dead on the shore. The more common starfish are colored bright orange, red or brown. They are a true star shape, with five tapered arms extending out to rounded points from the center. But there are many varieties, some with as many as 50 spidery arms. The surface of the arms are rough and usually spiny.

A very colorful variety is the brittle star which moves rapidly through the water by thrashing its arms vigorously. This variety got its name because its brittle arms are easily shattered by crabs and large fish that then eat the broken pieces. Using suction cups (or pads) on the underside of each arm, they pull themselves over the ocean bottom, onto a rock, a piling, or other object.

It is with these sensitive arms and the suction cups that starfish probe for and capture food. When a shellfish, such as a clam or oyster, is found, the suction cups of one arm grasp it firmly on one side and another arm clings to the other side. Then a contest takes place -- the clam pulling its two shell halves tightly together and the starfish trying to pull them apart. In the end it is always a hopeless battle for the shellfish, as its enemy will relentlessly pull on the two sides for an hour or more, until the victim has no more strength left to resist. When the shells finally open, the starfish pulls its stomach (located on its underside) over the clam or oyster, surrounding it, and slowly digests it. *God's Creations, Stars of the Seas.*

Starfish are radially symmetrical, star-shaped organisms of phylum Echinodermata and the class of Asteroidea. Aside from their distinguished shape, starfish are most recognized for their remarkable ability to regenerate, or regrow, arms and, in some cases, entire bodies. While in most species it requires a portion of the central body to be intact in order to regenerate arms, a few tropical species can grow an entirely new starfish from just a portion of a severed limb. While the overall morphological processes have been well documented in many starfish, little is known regarding the underlying molecular mechanisms that mediate their regeneration. Moreover, some researchers hope starfish may one day serve as inspiration for therapeutics aiming to expand the extent to which humans can repair and replace damaged cells or tissues. *Wikipedia*

In the early 1900s starfish were devouring the oysters in the fishing village of Narragansett, Rhode Island, seriously impacting their economy. The townsfolk came up with a brilliant solution. On a designated day, everyone in town headed to the beach with machetes in hand. The fishermen hauled in starfish and dumped them on the shore. The remaining villagers chopped up the sea stars. Then the fishermen dumped them back into the bay.

The Villagers thought that the chopped-up sea stars thrown into the bay would not only solve the problem but that the oysters would feed on the starfish's carcass. However, they didn't realize that each chopped-up piece that contained the sea star's core, created a new starfish. Instead of ridding themselves of starfish, their troubles increased exponentially.

It is suspected this story has been stretched a bit through the years and may be more fictional than factual. But it reveals a powerful principle. Sometimes when we try to fix our problems, we only make matters worse.

There once was an old man who lived near the beach. Every day he would wake up and the first thing he would do was to take a walk along the shore. One morning he noticed that the receding tide had left behind dozens of more starfish than were usually on the beach. He wandered if this was the result of high wave swells from winds of a distant storm.

The man looked sadly at the situation. This was a special moment for seagulls and other animals of pray; but the remaining suffering starfish would soon die out of the water. The chances of another high tide rescuing them was remote. As he walked among them, "How sad!" he thought. However, he couldn't think of an inspiring solution.

In the distance he saw a young person doing something near the water's edge. As the old man approached, he saw that it was a boy surrounded by numerous starfish lying on the sand. He was running around in the sand and seemed sweaty and distressed. The old man watched, intrigued, as the boy picked up starfish after starfish and threw them as far as he could over the breaking surf. After some time, the old man approached the boy and said, "Son, do you realize there are thousands of starfish on this shore? Certainly, what you are doing can make no real difference."

After respectfully listening, the boy reached down and picked up another starfish and hurled it into the ocean. Then, looking thoughtfully at the old man, the boy said, "It made a difference to that one." And he continued to throw more starfish back into the water. *"The Star Thrower", Loren Eisley*

Interesting: The fishing village of Narragansett's lacking knowledge about starfish and their attempts at fixing the problem - made it worse. On the other hand, the boy, knowing he couldn't save the hundreds of starfish stranded on the sand had his mind set: "It makes a difference to the ones I save by throwing them into the breaking surf."

The inspiring stories shows us the value of preparation, small actions and perseverance. Sometimes we don't prepare ourselves adequately for the task and make things worse or think the value in modest tasks we perform aren't worth the effort. This happens because we aren't focusing our behavior on the value of things. Instead, we focus on the result. It's as if we saw the world in terms of quantity and size, instead of meaning and essence.

Every great deed begins with small actions. In fact, beginnings tend to be hard and costly. Hence, someone who has a hard time seeing the meaning of a flower will find it difficult to understand nature. Therefore, someone who dismisses the meaning of a small sacrifice will most likely not make an effort. We strengthen our characters through small restrictions and discrete discipline. The first big obstacles for big dreams are the little signs of skepticism from the people around you. Giving meaning to the small is an inspiring way of living.

Perseverance is, above all, a descendant of values. You need to have real conviction to resist the difficulties and setbacks which are always present when you set a valuable goal. The worst part is that often we let ourselves be invaded by a totalitarian thought. A thought which tells that if you don't have "everything", then you have "nothing." In turn, this mental scheme is poisonous for your motivation.

If you associate your big dreams and aspirations with human values, it will be much easier for you to find the strength you need to keep moving forward. On the other hand, if you concentrate solely on immediate results, it's likely that frustration will become your shadow. Great cathedrals are built brick by brick, stone by stone. The fishing village, inspiring legend of the boy and the starfish tells us that small actions and being prepared do make sense and have meaning. The truth is that it's worthwhile to start seeing life this way.[1]

We are told in Proverbs 23:7 that "as he thinketh in his heart, so is he." Related to that is this old saying: Sow a thought, and you reap an act; Sow an act, and you reap a habit; Sow a habit, and you reap a character; Sow a character, and you reap a destiny.[2]

Natural symbolisms of the Starfish (sea stars) are: The star shape (infinite divine love), perceptual anatomy (heightened awareness and perception), crown or pentagram shape (five elements: earth, air, fire, water and space), and their aid in sustaining ocean ecosystems (seek balance and harmony).

Its spiritual realm: Renewal, to have faith, embodies hope, intuition, extrasensory perceptions, and finding our own path.

1– *Institute of Mercy, 2020.*

2– *The Dayspring 10, mo. 3 (March 1881): 40; quoted by Samuel Smiles in Life and Labor (1887).*

CHAPTER 33

IF ANTS CAN – WHY NOT US

The Matabele ants, also known as African diver ants, are aptly named after an African tribe that destroyed everything in their path as they swept through south and central Africa in the 1800's on raids and military campaigns. Matabele ants are likewise rather formidable; they go to war with termites the same way the Matabele tribe use to overwhelm their enemies. Even humans are not exempt, as they have a ferocious bite and 10 or more bites can paralyze a human arm.

Matabele ants live in colonies that can grow to sizes in excess of 20 million members. The ants are often seen on the march in search of food, especially once their supply has diminished. When the colony is on the march they move as one entity in a single column, with the larger soldier ants on the edge of the column providing protection for the smaller worker ants. The ants create a rattling or hissing noise as they move, but will do this especially when threatened.

While marching in their columns, smaller search parties break off in search of food and prey. Once food has been located, a pheromone is released to attract the rest of the column which quickly overwhelms it. The soldier ants possess formidable pincers which are easily able to puncture flesh or can be used as a defensive weapon. They are one of the world's largest ants reaching a size of 20 millimeters or more.

Another defensive weapon, which is not often utilized, is the sting it possesses, which is sometimes used to dissuade any intruders or predators. The pincers are effectively utilized in the efficient dismemberment of their prey which includes grasshoppers, moths or even considerably larger prey such as mice and birds.

Matabele ants are specialists at feeding on termites. They attack the termite colony, neutralizing the soldiers and then killing the workers. They steal the eggs and nymphs within the termite colony to take back to their colony as food. The ants form tightly structured armies and gather in large numbers to raid the termite nests. In Botswana there is an abundance of termite mounds and it is probable that the Matabele ants play a major role in controlling termite numbers within this region.

Reproduction is carried out exclusively by a lone queen in the colony in which mated workers are absent. During mating season, winged queens and drones are formed. In terms of size the drones are larger than the soldiers while the queens are much larger. Like most ants, workers and soldiers of the colony are sterile and therefore are non-producing females. The ants mate on the wing, and the queens go off to establish new colonies.

In regions like Botswana, these ants can be seen as a menace to humans as not much can be done about their abundant existence. When passing through a village the ants bring about a problem or a risk. There have been documented cases of kids being consumed by the ants often dying of asphyxiation. The ants do however serve a purpose in that they get rid of and keep away pests like large rats, crop pests and other insects. *Botswana Wildlife Behavior*

When Matabele ants lay siege to a termite colony they eat by the hundreds, braving the potentially life-threatening bites of large soldier termites that defend them. What they found interesting about these ants is they carry their wounded home after a raid and it turns out their battlefield rescues are just part of the story. Back in the nest, ants take turns caring for their injured comrades, gently holding the hurt limb in place with their mandibles and front legs while intensely "licking" the wound for up to four minutes at a time.

This discovery marked the first time non-human animals have been observed systematically nursing their wounded back to health. They found out not only did the ants have such a sophisticated treatment of the injured - but that it was actually necessary.

They saw that once in the nest, the ants carefully examine injured comrades, probing them with their antennae more than twice as often as healthy nest-mates. This behavior proved vital: 80 percent of experimentally injured ants died within 24 hours if kept by themselves. But if cared for by their nest-mates for even an hour, only a tenth died. Interestingly, 80 percent, that died, survived without treatment if placed in a sterile environment, so Frank believes infections are the main cause of death and this "licking" behavior may help prevent them.

While animals have frequently been observed treating their own wounds, there were only a few anecdotes of animals treating one another prior to this discovery, including an instance of a captive capuchin monkey tending to her infant's head wound.

In his earlier work, it was discovered that injured ants release a pheromone that acts like a signal flare, alerting the raiders that there's a man down. But this time, there was noticed another strategy: playing up their injuries. When no help was in sight, injured ants made a beeline for the nest. But when nest-mates were near, they stumbled and fell, appearing "more injured" as a way to attract aid.

Ants only did this if their injuries were not life-threatening. Mortally wounded ants—ones where scientists removed five legs instead of two—were mostly left to die by raiding parties in field and lab experiments. Such triage makes sense, as it ensures ants don't waste their resources caring for lost causes; the injured that recover continue to raid, despite their lost limbs. It was found they comprised more than a fifth of the raiding party even though they're only five percent of the total colony.

Even dousing the injured ants with the rescue pheromone, their comrades still left them behind. Careful video analysis revealed why: It wasn't that the healthy ants refused to rescue the gravely injured ants. The dying ants refused to cooperate, flailing their legs around when probed or picked up, forcing their helpers to abandon them.

In humans in cases where a triage system is necessary, the decision [about] who will receive help is made by the doctor: a top-down regulated system. In the ants it's exactly the opposite.[1]

If God's creation the lowly ant can show compassion one to the other caring for the sick and the needy – why does natural man struggle with this concept. Spending time caring for the needs of fallen ant comrades, 80 percent of the dying return to health and are able to continue the battles they face in their lives?

Compassion is good for your brain and our body. When we respond to ourselves and others to us, with awareness, courage, kindness, and love: We can navigate life's challenges effectively, together. Ways to build a more compassionate mind include breathing and meditation practices and journal exercises.

Our brains are organized around nurturing and generosity. We evolved cooperative, caring brains in order to care for our vulnerable young, and because we were more likely to survive if we worked on teams. Being kind is built into our nervous system, and part of our nature: It is who we are.

If you zoom out the challenges, losses, milestones, and growth resulting in the highs and lows of your life up to this point: compassion makes a lot of sense. Compassion also makes sense considering the scope of the suffering of all humans across our planet.

Compassion is different from love or kindness: It's willingly turning towards pain with courage, acceptance, and care. And, it's often compassion towards the people we don't love or even like (including ourselves) that has the most impact.

When we respond to ourselves and others with awareness, courage, kindness, acceptance, flexibility, and love, we can navigate life's challenges more effectively, together.[2]

If God's creation the lowly ant can show compassion one to the other caring for the sick and the needy – why does natural man struggle with this concept? Just spending time caring for the needs of fallen ant comrades, 80 percent of the dying return to health and are able to continue the battles they face in their lives. Pretty much all of God's communication with man concerns this subject:

Put on then, as God's chosen ones, holy and beloved, compassionate hearts, kindness, humility, meekness, and patience. Proverbs 10:9 (ESV)

Thus says the Lord of hosts, Render true judgments, show kindness and mercy to one another, do not oppress the widow, the fatherless, the sojourner, or the poor, and let none of you devise evil against another in your heart. Zechariah 7:9

Put on then, as God's chosen ones, holy and beloved, compassionate hearts, kindness, humility, meekness, and patience, bearing with one another and, if one has a complaint against another, forgiving each other; as the Lord has forgiven you, so you also must forgive. Colossians 3:12-13

Where is my wand'ring boy tonight—The boy of my tend'rest care,
The boy that was once my joy and light, The child of my love and prayer?
Once he was pure as morning dew, As he knelt at his mother's knee;

No face was so bright, no heart more true, And none was so sweet as he.
O could I see you now, my boy, As fair as in olden time,

When prattle and smile made home a joy, And life was a merry chime!
Go for my wand'ring boy tonight; Go, search for him where you will;

But bring him to me with all his blight, And tell him I love him still.
O where is my boy tonight? O where is my boy tonight?

My heart o'erflows, for I love him, he knows; O where is my boy tonight?

("Where Is My Boy Tonight?" words and music by Reverend Robert Lowry, 1877)
1– *Self-Sacrificing Ants Refuse Treatment of Their Wounds, National Geographic, Christie Wilcox Ph.D., 02/13/2018.*
2– *How to Build a More Compassionate Mind, Psychology Today, Diana Hill, Ph.D., 06/10/2021.*

CHAPTER 34

YOU ARE NOT LISTENING

In Kate Murphy's book, *You're not listening*, she draws together a barrage of statistics and research to persuade us that we have unthinkingly descended into a dystopian reality. Over the past century, she asserts, the average amount of time people devoted to listening to one another during their waking hours has gone down by almost half, from 42% to 24%. In a 2018 survey of 20,000 Americans, almost half said they did not have meaningful in-person social interactions; meanwhile American life expectancy is declining due to suicide, opioid addiction, alcoholism and other so-called diseases of distress often associated with loneliness.

Feeling lonely affects your health as much as being an alcoholic or smoking 14 cigarettes. Thirteen-year-olds who are heavy users of social media increase their risk of clinical depression by 27% and are 56% more likely to say they are unhappy than their peers who spend less time on Facebook, YouTube and Instagram. A study conducted by Microsoft found that since the year 2000, the average attention span dropped from 12 to eight seconds.

The dubious precision of much of this research is slightly irritating and makes you question the methodology, but clearly something has changed, and no one can really dispute the argument that our affection for our phones is eating into the time that we might previously have spent listening to the people to whom we are closest. Murphy's descriptions of modern life are acute. "If anyone tells a story longer than 30 seconds, heads bow not in contemplation but to read texts, check sports scores or see what's trending online." Even toddlers understand this, she points out, describing a friend's child who has repeatedly thrown his parents' mobiles into the toilet. "No other objects, just the cell phones. He knows precisely what keeps Mom and Dad from listening to him."

And it's not just mobile phones that are damaging our capacity to listen, she argues, but a culture of "aggressive personal marketing" where "to be silent is to fall behind. To listen is to miss an opportunity to advance your brand and make your mark ... Listening is often regarded as talking's meek counterpart," she writes. "Value is placed on what you project, not what you absorb ... The very image of success and power today is someone miked up and prowling around a stage or orating from behind a podium. Giving a TED talk ... is living the dream." We are wrong to downplay the importance of listening, she argues, reminding us that the ancient Greek philosopher Epictetus said: "Nature has given men one tongue but two ears, that we may hear from others twice as much as we speak." Evolution gave us eyelids so we can close our eyes but no corresponding structure to close off our ears, she adds, suggesting listening is essential to our survival.[1]

We live in a world that seems to have stopped listening. Sound bites have replaced conversation; texting has displaced telephone calls; rhetoric has supplanted dialogue; and multitasking has divided our attention. So often, listening isn't on the list of things to do and so it gets overlooked.

Famed solo percussionist and composer Dame Evelyn Glennie, who performed with the Tabernacle Choir during the 2002 Winter Olympics, began losing her hearing at age 8, and by 12 she was deaf. But though she could no longer hear, she found that she could still listen. "Listening to music," she contends, "involves much more than simply letting sound waves hit your eardrums." She describes listening in her legs and feet, her face, her neck and chest. She performs around the world and, in one sense, never actually hears either her music or the applause it inspires. But she feels it and sees it and understands it deeply. Her goal, she says, "is to teach the world to listen" the way she does.

Evelyn Glennie's insights apply not just when listening to music but also when listening to people. So many cry out, "Listen to me," but only those who truly know how to listen can even hear them. Listening is much more than hearing with our ears. It requires shifting the focus from ourselves to someone else. It takes time and often is not convenient. With our ears, but also with our eyes, our minds, our hearts, and our actions, we say, "I'm listening. I'm hearing and thinking about what you are saying. You matter to me."

In this loud and noisy world, think how much it means to someone when you really listen, when you take time to understand their woes and challenges, their joys and excitement, their dreams and aspirations. Consider the gift of love you give when you show that you care by truly listening.[2]

At a College of Nursing BYU Speech, Troy W. Carlton, stated that twenty-five years ago he found himself in his first nursing course at St. Benedict's Hospital in Ogden, Utah. His clinical instructor lined him and other students up against the wall to inspect there clean, white, crisp nursing uniforms early that first morning. With stethoscopes around their necks and confidence abounding, they were assigned their first patients. Troy could hardly wait to care for his patients—to do those skills that he had practiced so long and so hard in the nursing lab. The students were excited to take their first blood pressure, give their first medication, and start their first IV.

He remembers his first patient, a man in his fifties who had been diagnosed with bladder cancer—a terminal disease. Completing the technical skills with precision and, after giving what he thought was good care, he walked out into the hallway to be met by his instructor, Dr. Farr. She asked how he was doing. He reported all the tasks he had completed, including giving her a report of the patient's current blood pressure and pulse.

With a worried look she asked him if he had taken the time to talk to the patient and really listen to understand his concerns and worries about his health problems. She told him to go back into the room and not come out until he had talked and then listened intently to his patient.

With his "tail between my legs", he turned around and headed back into the patient's room. He felt uncomfortable as he entered. He could not remember what was said to break the tension, but he soon found out this patient's physician had told him of his terminal condition that morning. The man shared with him his concern and his fears about the terminal diagnosis. How was he going to be able to talk about this to his wife? He told Troy he was scared of being in pain. He shared his concerns about leaving his wife and told him how important she had been to him. Tears came to his eyes as he spoke about how much he wanted to be with his children and grandchildren, to go fishing and camping with them. We spoke for a long time that day. At times no words were spoken, but communication occurred soul to soul.

Even though he felt he had been scolded by Dr. Farr that morning, he was taught an important and valuable lesson that day: to be still and listen. He said that lesson has helped him more throughout his nursing career than anything else he has learned since. Years later he relived this experience as he sat at the edge of his Grandpa Carlton's bed, watching each day bring him closer to his death. He had the great opportunity of caring for him when his health began to decline. Troy had lived next door to his grandpa most of his life, but it was not until this period that he actually took the time to really listen to him. He learned much more about him, his life, and his love and concern for my grandmother and other family members. Those cherished moments will be forever remembered.

In the world today listening has become more complex. In the information age in which we live we are bombarded with constant information, facts, and messages that we must continually process. E-mail, the Internet, cell phones, pagers, text messaging, instant messaging, and virtual electronic communications are all great innovations.

"Communication technology will make strangers of neighbors and neighbors of strangers. We can now know more about what is going on across the globe than we do about what is going on across the street."[3]

Two friends were walking along the side of a busy street, when one asked the other if he could hear a cricket? The friend replied, how can you possibly hear a cricket with all of this noise? A few steps later they saw the cricket on a tree branch.

His friend thought it was incredible and that his friend had superhuman ears. The first replied "My hearing is as normal as yours. Watch."

At that moment, he tossed a few coins to the ground, and all the people within ten meters turned to see where the tinkling sound was coming from. The friend concluded by saying: "As you can see, it all depends on what one chooses to listen to." *David Fischman, Espejo del Líder (2017)*

Wherefore, my beloved brethren, let every man be swift to hear, slow to speak, slow to wrath:

For the wrath of man worketh not the righteousness of God. Wherefore lay apart all filthiness and superfluity of naughtiness, and receive with meekness the engrafted word, which is able to save your souls. *James 1:19-21*

1– *You're Not Listening, What You're Missing & Why It Matters, Kate Murphy, Book, Guardian review, 01-07-2020.*

2– *Evelyn Glennie: How to Truly Listen," & Are You Listening? Music & the Spoken word, #4358, 03/24/2013.*

3– *Listen to Find the Sweet Assurances of the Spirit, BYU Speeches, Troy W. Carlton, 07/12/2005.*

CHAPTER 35

ENEMIES CAN BE
OUR FRIENDS

If we change our perspective so that caring for the poor and the needy is less about giving stuff away and more about filling the hunger for human contact, providing meaningful conversation, and creating rich and positive relationships, then the Lord can send us someplace.

At Brigham Young University many years ago, there was a great athletic coach named Eugene L. Roberts. He grew up in Provo and, as a youth, sort of drifted aimlessly with the wrong kind of friends. And then something remarkable happened. He wrote: Several years ago when Provo City was scarred with the unsightly saloon and other questionable forms of amusement, I was standing one evening upon the street waiting for my gang to show up when I noticed that [the Provo] tabernacle was lighted up and that a large crowd of people were traveling in [that] direction. I had nothing to do so I drifted over there and drifted in. I thought I might find some of my gang, or at least some of the girls that I was interested in. Upon entering, I ran across three or four of [my] fellows and we placed ourselves under the gallery where there was a crowd of young ladies, who seemed to promise [some] entertainment.

We were not interested in what came from the pulpit. We knew that the people on [the] rostrum were all old fogies. They didn't know anything about life and they certainly couldn't tell us anything, for we knew it all. So we settled down to have a good time. Right in the midst of our disturbance there thundered from [the] pulpit the following [statement]: "You can't tell the character of an individual by the way he does his daily work. Watch him when his work is over. See where he goes. Note the companions he seeks, and the things he does when he may do as he pleases. Then you can tell his true character."

I looked up towards the rostrum because I was struck with this powerful statement. I saw up there a little dark-haired, fierce-eyed, fighting man whom I knew and feared; but didn't have any particular love for. . . . He went on to make a comparison. He said: "Let us take the eagle, for example. This bird works as hard and as efficiently as any other animal in doing its daily work. It provides for itself and its young by the sweat of its brow, so to speak; but when its daily work is over and the eagle has time of its own to do just as it pleases, note how it spends its recreational moments. It flies to the highest realms of heaven, spreads its wings, and bathes in the upper air, for it loves the pure, clean atmosphere, and the lofty heights.

"On the other hand, let us consider the hog. This animal grunts and grubs and provides for its young just as well as the eagle; but, when its working hours are over and it has [some] recreational moments, observe where it goes and what it does. The hog will seek out the muddiest hole in the pasture and will roll and soak itself in filth, for this is the thing it loves. People are either hogs or eagles in their leisure time."

Now . . . when I heard this short speech, I was dumbfounded. I turned toward my companions abashed for I was ashamed to be caught listening. What was my surprise to find everyone of the gang with his attention fixed upon the speaker. . .

We went out of the tabernacle that night rather quiet and we separated from each other unusually early. I thought of that speech all the way home. I classified myself immediately as of the hog family. I have thought of that speech for years. That night there was implanted in me the faint beginnings of an ambition to lift myself out of the hog group and to rise to that of the eagle. . .

There was implanted that same evening also the faint beginnings of an ambition to help fill up the mud holes in the social pasture so that those people with hog tendencies would find it difficult to wallow in recreational filth. And as a result of constant thinking about that speech I have been stirred to devote my whole life and my profession towards developing wholesome recreational activities for the young people, so that it would be natural and easy for them to indulge in the eagle type of leisure.

The man who made that speech which has affected my life more than any other one speech I ever heard was President George H. Brimhall. God bless him.

George Brimhall was the president of BYU a hundred years ago. He was the president who helped it transition from BYU Academy to become a university. And he was revered and admired for his ability to move people—the way he moved Eugene. He may have never realized that his talk in the Provo Tabernacle that day touched somebody like Eugene, but it completely changed Eugene's life, and Eugene became a respected teacher and a coach at BYU.

I have thought a lot about the following question, and you probably have too: What do I do in my leisure time? And am I going to be a hog or an eagle? Maybe you are like me because you might ask, What leisure time?... I believe that the Lord often isn't asking us for big, time-consuming gestures; He merely wants minutes of our time every day to help another person on their way...

Let me give a more modern example of a way to reach out to people that we might not traditionally think about. Most of you remember Sister Linda K. Burton, who was a general Relief Society president. In the April 2016 general conference, she quoted a scripture that is revered by Christians, Muslims, and Jews. It is from Leviticus 19. It says: And if a stranger sojourn with thee in your land, ye shall not vex him. But the stranger that dwelleth with you shall be unto you as one born among you, and thou shalt love him as thyself; for ye were strangers in the land of Egypt: I am the Lord your God.

Sister Burton asked us each to think about the strangers among us. Is there anyone who doesn't participate in society for some reason? Somebody who is on the periphery? Somebody who—because of language, background, disability, religion, family status, life choices, or anything else—is not fully participating within the circle? And can we think of them as brothers and sisters? Can we serve them?

Since Sister Burton gave that address in 2016, I have been in awe of how many examples have been shared relating to that great call to action. I want to share one with you. I took this story from the Deseret News. It took place in Lincoln Elementary in south Salt Lake City, which has students from fifteen different countries.

On the first day of school, the Hamed brothers, who recently had arrived from Syria, were greeted by Principal Milton Collins. He is this larger-than-life personality, and he does this crazy bobcat (the Lincoln Elementary mascot) growl - I can't imagine what that sounds like. He makes sure every kid has a backpack, and he tells them, "Oh, by the way, high fives are mandatory. Whenever you see me in the hall, you must give me a high five." And if students feel bullied, they are to go straight to an adult.

Milton Collins's job is to be the principal - he is doing his job - but he is going beyond his job in order to be an unforgettable force for good in the lives of kids. They have experienced bombs, hunger, the death of loved ones, and uncertainty. And now, on the first day of school, they are scared to death. They don't know if they are going to fit in or if they are going to have any friends. And their parents are even more scared than they are. As true disciples of Jesus Christ, we should have with us all of our lives the habits of having fearless courage, of being willing to serve and help people with their problems, and of thinking of others in terms of their being our brothers and sisters.

The big humanitarian crises that are going on right now and the ones that have happened in the past when people have been driven out of their homes and lands are, at the heart, failures to remember that we are brothers and sisters and that God is the Father of us all. That is the root cause of what is happening in the world. And when we respond in a humanitarian way, we can send bushels of food, we can dig wells, we can build latrines, we can put up schools and health care centers, and we can settle people into apartments. But if we don't do something about people feeling like strangers instead of like our brothers and sisters, then the whole thing is in vain and will just feed the cycle of emotional and spiritual misery...

What would it look like if each of us were our own well-stocked humanitarian organization? Instead of just giving out tangible goods in foreign locations, what if we had the richness of dispensing healing, friendship, respect, peaceful dialogue, sincere interest, protective listening of children, birthday remembrances, and conversations with strangers? What if that was what your humanitarian organization did? This kind of humanitarian work can be done by anybody and it can be done at any time. And you don't need warehouses or fundraising or transportation. You can be perfectly responsive to any need that comes to you, wherever you are...

King Benjamin taught: that to serve others is to serve God - or, as Jesus Himself said, "As I have loved you . . . love one another." There are many, many organizations and people who do enormous amounts of good in the world with their limited resources and their Benjamin-like desires to serve their fellow beings and to serve God. I am privileged to work with many of them, and I get to see what is being done in the world. I am going to speak to you from my own experience now about what I have seen that accomplishes the most lasting good. If you want to be involved in humanitarian service, this is the way - and I hope this is the thing that you will remember from the forum today. You are the gift. You yourself are the gift. It is not the clothing, the hygiene kits, the school desks, or the wells. It is you.

We live in a world that is coming apart, that is being pulled apart, so that the unity of community and respect for other people's beliefs, tolerance of differences, and protection of the minority voice are being shredded. It is extremely destructive to all of us when everyone outside of our narrow clan becomes an enemy we vilify. As those forces in our society rise up, then so must an answering strong sentiment and skill set on the opposite side...

The Lord wants to use you. There is a work for you to do, and it is specific to you and your abilities. Nobody will be the ambassador that you will be. But you need to be clean to do it. Jesus can lift you out of the mire and set you on your way. Repent, and He will forgive. And remember that, in the same way as the Savior, you yourself are one of the best gifts that you can give to other people in need.[1]

I classified myself immediately as of the hog family. I have thought of that speech for years. That night there was implanted in me the faint beginnings of an ambition to lift myself out of the hog group and to rise to that of the eagle. . .

1– *Turning Enemies into Friends, Sharon Eubank, Director of LDS Charities -Counselor General Relief Society Presidency, 02/23/2018.*

CHAPTER 36

TEARS

Most of us think of tears as a human phenomenon, part of the complex fabric of human emotion. But they're not just for crying: All vertebrates, even reptiles and birds, have tears, which are critical for maintaining healthy eyesight. A recent study in the journal Frontiers in Veterinary Science, reveals that non-human animals' tears are not so different from our own. The chemical similarities are so great, in fact, that the composition of other species' tears may provide insights into better treatments for human eye disease.

Previously, scientists had studied closely only the tears of a handful of mammals, including humans, dogs, horses, camels, and monkeys. In the new study, Brazilian veterinarians analyzed the tears of reptiles and birds for the first time, focusing on seven species: barn owls, blue-and-yellow macaws, roadside hawks, turquoise-fronted Amazon parrots, broad-snouted caimans, loggerhead sea turtles, and red-footed tortoises.

Tears, which are emitted from tear ducts (in humans and some other mammals) or other similar glands, form a film over the eye that's composed of three ingredients:

mucus, water, and oil. The mucus coats the eye's surface and helps to bind the film to the eye, the water is a natural saline solution containing crucial proteins and minerals, and the oil prevents the eye from drying out. Tears help with vision by lubricating the eye and clearing it of debris. They also protect the eye against infection and provide nutrition to the cornea, the eye's clear outer layer, which lacks blood vessels. The broad-snouted caimans—an alligator relative with "beautiful eyes," can keep their eyes open without blinking for up to two hours. People, by contrast, blink every 10 to 12 seconds.

Surprisingly, given that birds, reptiles and mammals have different structures for producing tears, all the species' tears—including those of humans—had a similar chemical makeup, with similar amounts of electrolytes, although bird and reptile tears had slightly higher concentrations. This difference may be because they live in water and air, which may be disruptive to the surface of the eye—higher levels of electrolytes in their tears may be needed to protect against inflammation.[1]

In addition to the general ability to secrete ions by kidneys and the gut, a number of vertebrate species that are exposed to an extra salt load also have extra possibilities to secrete salt from the body, mainly in the form of sodium and chloride ions. Many fish species thus have chloride cells on their gills or the boney flap covering the gills, which in marine fish excrete salt. Marine cartilaginous fish, reptiles and birds have proper salt-secreting glands, which are inactive until stimulated by a salt load, for example from eating or drinking marine prey and water. In cartilaginous fish, NaCl is secreted by an unpaired gland, the rectal gland, in the tissue dorsal to the posterior intestine. Marine birds and turtles have a pair of flat, crescent-shaped salt glands close to the eyes, the supraorbital glands, which excrete extra salty "tears." Marine lizards may have nasal glands that empty into the nasal cavity, where the fluid is prevented from running backwards and being swallowed by a ridge structure. Some marine snakes have an extra efficient ion extrusion from their salivary glands. In crocodile species, tongue salt glands excrete hyperosmotic fluid2.

Humans are the only known species to produce "emotional tears"; the expression "crocodile tears," which refers to a person's phony display of emotion, comes from the tendency of crocodiles to release tears as they eat.

Crocodile tears, derives from an ancient belief that crocodiles shed tears while consuming their prey, and as such is present in many modern languages, especially in Europe where it was introduced through Latin. While crocodiles have tear ducts that do generate tears, the tears are not linked to emotion. The fluid from their tear ducts functions to clean and lubricate the eye, and is most prominent and visible when crocodiles have been on dry land for a while. In the case of crocodiles and saltwater crocodiles, the tears and (added - "salt glands under the tongue) help rid the excess salt that they take in with their food.

It is difficult to trace the origin of this particular myth, but it's easy to see why it has become so popular – for an apparently remorseless creature such as a crocodile to actually weep over its victims is a memorable irony which has inspired considerable prose and created the phrase which is still popular today.

In 2006, neurologist Malcolm Shaner, assisted by Kent Vliet, a researcher at the University of Florida, decided to test the story that crocodiles or their close relatives; alligators and caimans were likely to "weep" while feeding. Studying animals in Florida's St. Augustine Alligator Farm Zoological Park, Vliet recorded seven caimans feeding. He chose to use caimans rather than crocodiles because at the sanctuary they could be observed feeding on dry land. Five of the seven animals were seen "weeping", leading to the conclusion that the story describes a real phenomenon. The researchers suggest that the "weeping" may be caused by the hissing of warm air during feeding, which is forced through the sinuses, stimulating the animals' tear glands into emptying fluid into the eye. *Wikipedia*

Charles Darwin provided excellent illustrations of attributing human forms or personalities (anthropomorphism) in the human mind's capacity to see the same kinds of covert emotional states in the behavior of non-human animals as it does in the behavior of other humans. This is unlikely to have an exact correspondence given that animals have their emotions in physiological terms (but no feelings, according to their lack of a complex conscious behavior). However, when we perceive that an animal is experiencing a concrete emotion or feeling we attribute a human feature to the animal, in which case we are indeed applying our anthropomorphism to the animal. In addition, our daily experience interacting with different types of animals has a long history and this process can provide advantages to the animal, since individual differences in anthropomorphism predict the degree of moral care and concern afforded to an agent and, moreover, empathy towards animals and humans is correlated.

Moreover, in line with this interest in the anthropomorphization of animals, some authors have explored its neural basis to show that we use the same neural mechanisms to attribute emotions to the facial expressions of humans and non-human animals.

"Emotional tears" are a special form of non-verbal communication that are unique to humans. Non-human animals do not generate tears to express emotions, though they do display their emotional state in other ways.

Human "emotional tears" have adaptive advantages; among these, we have hypothesized that tears are an honest biological signal with a clear purpose of inhibiting aggression towards the crier in social contexts. In a study researchers extended the universality of this hypothesis by using animal faces to which were artificially added visible tears.

By means of this experimental methodology they provided empirical support for the notion that the presence of artificial tears on the face of an animal results in the human observer perceiving it to be less aggressive, possibly through a process of implicit anthropomorphization. In addition, such tears increase the perceived friendliness of the animal, and this influences the perception of its aggressiveness.

Moreover, the results showed that how much an individual likes animals, how many animals he/she is living with, and how important animals are for the individual, is clearly affected by our perception of the friendliness of the animal, which increases with the presence of tears.

Considering the results as a whole, it seems that the presence of tears improves the social relationship between humans and animals. Given that animals do not cry in natural conditions, the results observed here are presumably a consequence of some anthropomorphization process between the human observer and the animal, which leads us to propose that tears are the main element in this improved social communication. In conclusion, our results further endorse the notion of tears as an important human biological signal that is essential for non-verbal communication.[3]

As a phenomenon that is unique to humans, crying is a natural response to a range of emotions, from deep sadness and grief to extreme happiness and joy. Thinkers and physicians of ancient Greece and Rome posited that tears work like a purgative, draining off and purifying us. Today's psychological thought largely concurs, emphasizing the role of crying as a mechanism that allows us to release stress and emotional pain.

Crying is an important safety valve, largely because keeping difficult feelings inside - what psychologists call repressive coping - can be bad for our health. Studies have linked repressive coping with a less resilient immune system, cardiovascular disease, and hypertension, as well as with mental health conditions, including stress, anxiety, and depression. Crying has also been shown to increase attachment behavior, encouraging closeness, empathy, and support from friends and family.

But is crying good for your health? The answer appears to be yes. Medical benefits of crying have been known as far back as the Classical era. Thinkers and physicians of ancient Greece and Rome posited that tears work like a purgative, draining off and purifying us. Today's psychological thought largely concurs, emphasizing the role of crying as a mechanism that allows us to release stress and emotional pain. Crying is an important safety valve, largely because keeping difficult feelings inside — what psychologists call repressive coping — can be bad for our health. Science has proven that chronic, low-grade inflammation can turn into a silent killer that contributes to cardiovascular disease, cancer, type 2 diabetes and other conditions.

Studies have linked repressive coping with a less resilient immune system, cardiovascular disease, and hypertension, as well as with mental health conditions, including stress, anxiety, and depression. Crying has also been shown to increase attachment behavior, encouraging closeness, empathy, and support from friends and family.

Scientists divide the liquid product of crying into three distinct categories: reflex tears, continuous tears, and emotional tears. The first two categories perform the important function of removing debris such as smoke and dust from our eyes, and lubricating our eyes to help protect them from infection. Their content is 98% water.

It's the third category, emotional tears (which flush stress hormones and other toxins out of our system), that potentially offers the most health benefits. Researchers have established that crying releases oxytocin and endogenous opioids, also known as endorphins. These feel-good chemicals help ease both physical and emotional pain. Popular culture, for its part, has always known the value of a good cry as a way to feel better - and maybe even to experience physical pleasure. The millions of people who watched classic tearjerker films such as West Side Story or Titanic (among others) will likely attest to that fact.

"I know a man ain't supposed to cry," goes the lyric of a popular song, "but these tears I can't hold inside." These words succinctly summarize many a man's dilemma about emotional expression. From early on, boys are told that real men do not cry. When these boys grow up, they may stuff their feelings deep inside and withdraw emotionally from their loved ones, or self-medicate with alcohol or drugs, or even become suicidal. Many men therefore need to learn the skills of how to reconnect with their emotions.

There are times when crying can be a sign of a problem, especially if it happens very frequently and/or for no apparent reason, or when crying starts to affect daily activities or becomes uncontrollable. People suffering from certain kinds of clinical depression may actually not be able to cry, even when they feel like it.

As challenging as it may be, the best way to handle difficult feelings, including sadness and grief, is to embrace them. It is important to allow yourself to cry if you feel like it. Make sure to take the time and find a safe space to cry if you need to. Many people associate crying during grief with depression, when it can actually be a sign of healing. Teaching boys and young men that it's okay to cry may reduce negative health behaviors and help them have fuller lives.[4]

James S. Gordon writes: "I begin many days by crying. I'm not depressed, it's not something I intend to do and I'm not a sad person. It just happens, often when I'm reading the morning paper. And it's been going on for several years.

When I cry, I sometimes think of Gregory and Bill, who were puzzled and intrigued by their own later-life tears.

Almost 40 years ago, anthropologist Gregory Bateson - a pioneer in cybernetics and architect of the double bind theory of schizophrenia - wondered aloud to me if he were becoming more sensitive and affectionate as he moved into old age, more prone to tears. A few years later, playwright William Alfred, my former Harvard tutor and long-time friend, said something similar: poems which had once touched him now brought him to tears, Jonathan Swift's birthday tributes to Stella, for instance, as well as movies that Bill once recognized as "corny" — I remember the adaptation of Emile Zola's "Therese Raquin" with Simone Signoret — with scenes that creakily tugged at the emotions.

And now, in my 70s, it's happening to me and I'm trying to understand. Sometimes the cause is deeply personal dreams. I'll wake just as a little girl I love and helped raise, but haven't been able to see in years, simply dissolves. Other mornings, my eyes open and dear friends, long-since deceased, who have, for a moment, come alive again, disappear. Movies about fathers and sons, and about family or friends who overcome obstacles and grow close, make me cry. The other day it was "The Way," in which Martin Sheen's frozen heart slowly melts as he carries his dead son's ashes on the Camino de Santiago, the pilgrim's route in Northern Spain. I become emotional, even more often, observing the dramas playing out on the world's stage.

I cry when I read about our Congress' utter inability to work together, or learn from experience, devolving routinely now into the repeated triumph of unexamined ideology over compassion and common sense. And I cried - this time with joy - reading New York Times Opera critic Anthony Tommasini's account of a long-ago summer spent listening, enraptured, to Leonard Bernstein conduct Igor Stravinsky.

What's clear is that after I cry, I feel better. My face and shoulders are more relaxed. I feel a little lighter and more energized. Sometimes I find myself smiling or even dancing.

I've looked for studies on increased emotionality or sensitivity in older men and haven't found anything conclusive. The research I've seen tells me that as we grow older, women are more likely to be empathetic than men.

There are suggestions that hormonal changes may make aging men more emotional, or that as we age we care less about maintaining a stoic posture. And there are certainly studies which correlate emotional expression with the effects of depression, social isolation and dementia. As a psychiatrist, these assertions seem plausible but not sufficiently documented and ultimately unsatisfying. They certainly don't do justice to the human experience.

It's pretty clear to me that my emotional mornings (and sometimes afternoons and evenings) aren't, as I've said, about depression (I've been there and this is definitely not depression, isolation or even unhappiness). I am continually and happily with many people. Nor does it seem to be dementia. My brain, so far as I can tell, is functioning pretty well; certainly Gregory's and Bill's were. So what's going on?

Gregory, gifted observer of patterns, may have put his finger on it. Men may, as they age, indeed become more sensitive. I've noticed the changes in classmates at high school, college and medical school reunions, and in e-mails we sometimes exchange, as well as in myself. The competitiveness, the real or assumed toughness of our youth is, as we age, being balanced; our Yang tempered by Yin.

Perhaps social scientists will eventually find a way to exhaustively quantify the changes. Right now, though, it's important simply to know what I and other men are seeing and feeling. We are more willing to admit to and feel the terrible pain of our losses; to weep in celebration of our own and other's loving connections; to know and feel the threat that individual and collective greed and selfishness, and the fear that feeds them, pose to all of us and to generations beyond us. That our tender emotions are hopeful signs, not of weakness or pathology, but of a necessary and welcome growth — in our compassion, wholeness and, perhaps, our wisdom.[5]

In their 80s, I gave my parents a list of questions about their life stories. One of the questions was asking them negative experiences that affected their lives. Each of them wrote that they did not have any bad experiences – life had been remembered as all good. I never remember my father shedding tears during my early life or until after he retired at the age of 75. I did notice a mellowing personality, that he was more touched during special moments and occasionally I noticed what appeared to be a welling of tears.

During my career I occasionally questioned if I could shed tears. My life seemed to be more anxiety and fear of failure than seeking my "God-shaped hole"- a place where only God can fill the needs of my heart and soul.

According to *Tithely*: For some people, feeling the influence of their "God-shaped hole" can be a physical sensation, as our bodies are designed to respond to God's presence. When the Holy Spirit enters our bodies there may be a feeling of warmth, being embraced, a tingling or electricity sensation, physical balance or mental stability. These sensations are often accompanied by an intense feeling of peace and love. They may find themselves experiencing more joy, peace, and patience, even in difficult situations. These relatively-tangible signs are the fruits of the Spirit, where Galatians 5:22-23 tells us, "The fruit of the Spirit is love, joy, peace, forbearance, kindness, goodness, faithfulness, gentleness and self-control."

Like James S. Gordon I'm not being treated for depression and as I have aged, I have become more sensitive. I am continually and happily with many people. No one has questioned me about having dementia. My brain, so far as I can tell, is functioning pretty well. I find myself occasionally crying after being touched by unexpected events. Usually, they are from events that take me through my "God-shaped hole" that brings sudden feelings from the fruits of the Spirit.

In my youth I often had experiences that made me believe there was a larger and easier way to enter His "God-shaped hole. My mature years have been a time when God seemed to have backed off and/or it took more effort and desire on my part to be in tune with His spirit. A time for me to exercise my "Moral Agency" and think and do pretty much as I pleased. Now I'm receiving little snippets of what fruits He has in store for us. Helping me get my life in order for the big day and encouraging me to endure to the end. Experiencing the unknown is bound to get a little dicey - as I go into that "God-shaped hole" and through the veil.

1– *'Crocodile tears' are surprisingly similar to our own, National Geographic, Virginia Morell, 08/13/2020.*

2– *Salt Glands, D.B. McMillan & R. J. Harriss, An Atlas of Comparative Vertebrate Histology, 2018.*

3– *When animals cry: The effect of adding tears to animal expressions on human judgment, PLoS One. 2021; 16(5): e0251083.*

4– *Is crying good for you? Harvard Health Blog, Leo Newhouse, 03/01/2021.*

5– *I'm not a depressed or sad man. Washington Post, But the older I get, the more often I cry, James S. Gordon, 10/15/2015.*

CHAPTER 37

LEGACY

In the 1960's I went to grandma Leva Rich's home with a new voice recorder: I asked her a series of questions about her life experiences living on a ranch, Pingree Idaho, and raising my mother. She was a talented piano player and when a young woman was given an opportunity to go to Hollywood and develop her talents. Instead, she stayed in the area, played the piano during silent movies at the local theater and married my grandfather, a rancher.

When video cameras became available, I filmed the home I grew up in and "special" memories around the area; reciting stories of my youth. The 8-track movie was acceptable, but the voice overlay was unable to be understood. I hadn't compensated for the Idaho wind blowing into my mike.

When my parents were in the 80's, I send them a list of questions about their lives. They took it like a college assignment and shared many details that are of value to my family (I included the questions and answers in *Thoughts on my Thoughts*…book II). However, their answers have led to more questions that their passing has prevented me from really getting into their deeper thoughts – not just their experiences. Important to me is what "floated their boat", their memories of the ups and downs in their lives and raising me?

Journals have been encouraged by my faith. The things I have written down that could be classified as a "journal" have been of some value helping me write more accurate stories about my life. However, I question if anyone in my family would ever take the time to try and read my hand written thoughts placed in a journal.

Old videos show the physical features, record the voices, relate some experiences, but do not give much insight into who they really are. Even legacy videos can only give snippets of one's life and the story told be more fluff than reality.

That's one of several reasons why I started accumulating stories about my life and eventually started writing books. It's there for anyone who cares to read it, it involves my ups/downs, internal thoughts and what "floated my boat." I also tie in most of my experiences with mother nature and her Creator – which is my fascination, career and intertwined with my shared personal thoughts and experiences.

Consider two scenarios. In the first you have a life filled with love and meaning and enough money to get by comfortably. However, after you die, something terrible is revealed about you – which may not even be true – and people come to despise you. In the second, you have a life of relative hardship and obscurity, but after you die, it is revealed that you were an incredibly talented artist and your reputation is assured forever. Which option would you choose?

If you picked the second, you aren't alone, as Brett Waggoner at the University of Otago, New Zealand, discovered when he carried out this thought experiment. It may seem like a counterintuitive choice, but it reveals our deep concern for legacy. Across time and cultures, people seem to have acted with a desire to etch their names into the history books. From the pharaoh Khufu's Great Pyramid of Giza to acts of scientific discovery, works of art, sporting achievements and public philanthropy.

Nevertheless, such behavior is something of a paradox. Why devote so much time and energy to being warmly recalled when you won't be around to see the benefits?

Researchers trying to answer this question have come up with some surprising answers. Some suggest it gives individuals an evolutionary advantage. Others see it as a sort of glitch in the way we think – a mistake based on various cognitive biases. Meanwhile it is becoming clear that our desire to be positively remembered is far more than just self-aggrandizement nurtured in the correct way, it could be leveraged to tackle long-term, global issues including climate change, biodiversity loss and inequality.

Humans, along with every other species on Earth, can leave a genetic legacy. If we successfully reproduce, our biological descendants continue our evolutionary journey. They are the physical manifestation of a process that has been unfolding on our planet for more than 3.5 billion years, since the first living organism emerged. But while we share this evolutionary drive for genetic legacy, humans seem peculiarly concerned about a more symbolic form of legacy – that is, how our peers and strangers will remember us after we die.

Perhaps this has something to do with the fact that we are more deeply aware of our own mortality than any other animal. We know that one day we will die. That being the case, say some evolutionary psychologists, there is a good reason to think about legacy. Your posthumous reputation could affect the reproductive success of your direct relatives. If so, then legacy seeking behaviors might be an adaptation to give our biological kin favorable conditions for finding a mate and reproducing.

This idea is bolstered by yet-to-be-published research by Waggoner and Jesse Bering, also at the University of Otago. They found that people's hypothetical dating choices were negatively influenced by familial transgressions, such as the knowledge that serious crimes have been committed by a close biological relative of the prospective date, even one not involved in their upbringing. This they argue, suggests we operate a type of "folk heritability", where people carry not only the genetic inheritance of their relatives, but also the social burden of their ill deeds. Other research revealing that people are more motivated to avoid negative legacy than to pursue a positive one lends more weight to the idea.

This all sounds very reasonable, but it fails to consider another aspect of mortality awareness it can make us anxious or even terrified. According to what psychologists call terror management theory, the knowledge that we will die, combined with our survival instinct, creates an inherent tension, and we have developed certain belief systems to cope with this. Religion and the assertion that the soul transcends death are, perhaps, the most obvious. If you believe in the afterlife, a desire for a positive legacy makes some sense because, in a way, your soul will be around to see how your legacy unfolds.[1]

Separate bodies of research suggest that young children have a broad tendency to reason about natural phenomena in terms of purpose and an orientation toward intention-based accounts of the origins of natural entities. This study explored these results further by drawing together findings from various areas of cognitive developmental research to address the following question: Rather than being "artificialists" in Piagetian terms, are children "intuitive theists" (a person who believes in the existence of a god or gods, specifically of a creator who intervenes in the universe) —disposed to view natural phenomena as resulting from nonhuman design? A review of research on children's concepts of agency, imaginary companions, and understanding of artifacts suggests that by the time children are around 5 years of age, this description of them may have explanatory value and practical relevance.

Given findings regarding children's beliefs about purpose and their ideas about the intentional origins of nature, is it possible that children are intuitive theists insofar as they are predisposed to develop a view of nature as an artifact of nonhuman design? A review of cognitive developmental research reveals that by around 5 years of age, children understand natural objects as not humanly caused, can reason about nonnatural agents' mental states, and demonstrate the capacity to view objects in terms of design. Finally, evidence from 6- to 10-year-olds suggests that children's assignments of purpose to nature relate to their ideas concerning intentional nonhuman causation. Together, these research findings tentatively suggest that children's explanatory approach may be accurately characterized as intuitive theism—a characterization that has broad relevance not only to cognitivists or the growing interdisciplinary community studying the underpinnings of religion, but also, at an applied level, to science educators because the implication is that children's science failures may, in part, result from inherent conflicts between intuitive ideas and the basic tenets of contemporary scientific thought. In conclusion, the question of whether children and adults are intuitive theists provides fertile ground for future research.[2]

They are the last words of Steve Jobs (1955-2011), reported by his sister, the novelist Mona Simpson, who was at his bedside. In her eulogy, a version of which was published in the New York Times, she spoke of how he looked at his children "as if he couldn't unlock his gaze." He'd said goodbye to her, told her of his sorrow that they wouldn't be able to be old together, "that he was going to a better place." In his final hours his breathing was deep, uneven, as if he were climbing.

"Before embarking, he'd looked at his sister Patty, then for a long time at his children, then at his life's partner, Laurene, and then over their shoulders past them. Steve's final words were: 'OH WOW. OH WOW. OH WOW.'" The caps are Simpson's, and if she meant to impart a sense of wonder and mystery she succeeded. "Oh wow" is not a bad way to express the bigness, power and force of life, and death. And of love, by which he was literally surrounded.

I wondered too, after reading the eulogy, if I was right to infer that Jobs saw something, and if so, what did he see? What happened there that he looked away from his family and expressed what sounds like awe? I thought of a story told by a friend, whose grown son had died, at home, in a hospice. The family was ringed around his bed. As Robert breathed his last an infant in the room let out a great baby laugh as if he saw something joyous, wonderful, and gestured toward the area above Robert's head. The infant's mother, startled, moved to shush him but my friend, her mother, said no, maybe he's just reacting to . . . something only babies see.

Anyway, I sent Ms. Simpson's eulogy to a number of people and spoke to some of them, and they all had two things in common in terms of their reaction. They'd get a faraway look, and think. And if they had a thought to share, they did it with modesty. No one said, "I think I can guess what he saw," "I know who he saw," or "Believe me, if he saw anything it was the product of the last, disordered sparks of misfiring neurons." They were always modest, reflective. One just said, "Wow." Modesty when contemplating death is a good thing. When words leave people silent and thinking they are powerful words. *Is it "Something Only Babies See", Peggy Noonan, WSJ, 12/27/2011.*

My day-old child lay in my arms;
With my lips against his ear,
I whispered strongly; "How I wish?
I wish that you could hear."
"I've a hundred wonderful things to say;
(a tiny cough and a nod)
"Hurry, hurry, hurry and grow;
So, I can tell you about God."
My day-old baby's mouth was still;
And my words only tickled his ear.

But a kind of light passed through his eyes;
And I saw this thought appear.
"How I wish I had a voice and words;
I've a hundred things to say.
Before I forget I'd tell you of God!;
I left Him just yesterday."
Day-Old Child, Carol Lynn Pearson 10/10/2009

The darkness of death can always be dispelled by the light of revealed truth. "I am the resurrection, and the life," spoke the Master (John 14:27). "Peace I leave with you, my peace I give unto you." (John 14:27). "For as in Adam all die, even so in Christ shall all be made alive." (1 Corinthians 15:21-22). "For we saw him, even on the right hand of God; and we heard the voice bearing record that he is the Only Begotten of the Father." (D&C 76:22-23). "And said, Verily I say unto you, except ye be converted, and become as little children, ye shall not enter into the kingdom of heaven." (Matt 18:3).

But in many countries a significant number of people don't believe there is any existence after death. Here, the puzzle of legacy deepens. What motivates these so-called extinctivists to leave a legacy when they think they won't be there to enjoy it? Terror management theory might say that, to mitigate their death anxiety, extinctivists cultivate their legacy to create a sort of symbolic immortality. Our identities are intertwined with the narratives we tell about ourselves and what happens at the end of our life is a major feature in our story. As we get older, we tend to become increasingly concerned with having meaningful interactions with younger generations and passing down values and beliefs that have served us. We may believe that when we die, the lights go out, but the knowledge of our actions and values rippling through the future gives us at least some psychological respite from the expiration date placed on us. In this view, legacy offers all of us, no matter what our beliefs, a way to make life more meaningful by transcending death.

But there could be a simpler explanation for why extinctivists are motivated to build a legacy: perhaps, deep down, we all entertain some sort of notion of life after death. After all, nobody can consciously experience the absence of consciousness, making it effectively impossible to imagine our own death without being a conscious spectator. Indeed, research by Bering and his colleagues suggests that belief in continued existence of the mind following death is a default state for all of us. In one study, for example, children watched a puppet show where an alligator ate an anthropomorphized mouse. Older children were unlikely to ascribe any psychological functions to the dead mouse. However, the youngest children, who were 3 or 4 years old, took a different view. While they understood that the dead mouse no longer had biological needs, they stated that it still had emotions, contradicting the notion that afterlife belief is something we learn. The findings, which have been replicated across both secular and religious schools, suggest that belief in the continuity of consciousness after death is an intuitive position, with religious belief systems taking advantage of this quirk in our thinking. "I think a lot of (legacy motivation) has to do with these cognitive (processes)," says Bering.

And this isn't the only example that could motivate a desire for legacy. An extremely large body of literature points to the evolutionary benefits that our species gets from living in groups. We have evolved to seek close connections with our peers and admiration from them because our physiological and emotional well-being depends on it. As a result, when something socially gratifying happens, it activates the reward circuits in our brains. For example, you get a buzz when you give money to a charity, even though you are completely disconnected from the material benefits that the donation will provide. Since legacy, as it is most often conceptualized, refers to a person's posthumous reputation, the drive to leave one could be an artefact of this evolved psychology. It may not be logical to seek to be admired when you are dead, but the act of building a legacy could make you feel good while you are alive.

What all this suggests is that the human desire to be positively remembered beyond the grave is complicated. "There is a juxtaposition between our higher-order cognitive faculties and not being able to properly think about our own deaths, combined with our basic evolved psychology to be concerned about our social status, how other people regard us, feeling valued and having a good reputation," says Bering. "This, spills over into our thinking about the afterlife that propagates the legacy drive."

Our motivation on this front varies enormously. Among people who feel this drive strongly, though, it can have a big impact on their behavior. On the surface, seeking a legacy seems quite egotistical – it is about projecting yourself into the future. Nevertheless, some researchers are exploring the idea that the legacy drive could be harnessed for the greater good to help tackle issues such as climate change, the biodiversity crisis and wealth inequality.

"We are looking at how the legacy move can help attenuate intergenerational discounting or promote beneficence on behalf of future generations," says Kimberly Wade-Benzoni at Duke University in North Carolina. Intergenerational discounting is a psychological term for how we weigh the benefits of our actions to future generations relative to those to the current generation, favoring the latter. In other words, she believes the desire for legacy can help us overcome some psychological biases that undermine our ability to address long-term problems. People generally find it hard to defer rewards in the here and now to the future. The further away in time a problem is, the fewer resources we are willing to devote to solving it. We also struggle to give resources to others, particularly if they aren't embedded in our social network. However, more than a decade of positive legacy can enable people to overcome these barriers, leading them to make sacrifices in the present for the benefit of future generations.

The context in which we think about death is important when we make intergenerational decisions. Being shown images of a car accident, or walking past a cemetery tends to elicit a death anxiety response. When people become aware of their mortality in this way, it increases their in-group identity – including nationalism and religious affiliation - encouraging them to distance themselves from outside beliefs and cultures. As a result, their legacies become primarily concerned with helping those who belong to their group – their families, for example. But when we reflect on our death in a more contemplative way this generates a different reaction. Wade-Benzoni and her colleagues asked people to write about their own legacy before doing a task in which they chose to allocate resources to others. Doing this made them more generous with what they were willing to leave to people. It also widened the scope of who they were willing to leave their resources to. "It increases their circle of moral concern, and their intergenerational wealth allocations are shifted from relation to collective," she says. In other words, they become more mindful of helping the broader community.

Nevertheless, the legacy building actions of any single individual can't solve problems that require social collaboration at large scales. On top of the intergenerational hurdle, there is also a social dilemma. It's not just the trade – off between you and the future other, you also need to get people in your generation cooperating in order to get the sacrifice to make a difference.

It seems that thinking about legacy can help us here too. Mark Hurlstone at Lancaster University, YK, and his colleagues found that when the legacy motive was activated by asking a group of participants to read a paragraph about leaving a positive legacy, their investments into a public program of tree planting increased. Similarly, Lisa Aval at Columbia University in New York and her colleagues found that priming people to think about their legacy increased their concern for the environment and climate change and led to them donating more money to an environmental charity.

Waded-Benzoni thinks that the symbolic aspect of legacy is what can make it a collective endeavor. It isn't necessarily the case that everyone is concerned with their own ego being attached to their legacy: just being part of something larger than yourself can be enough. Some people want to be anonymous. They just want to know that, somehow, their existence and life had some kind of meaning and impact. That it wasn't all for nothing.[1]

Atheists, philosophers, historians, podcasters, Holocaust survivors, writers, therapists, military veterans, ministers, and psychologists concur with biologists: building lasting relationships and connections with other people is the only way to live happy and meaningful lives.

Author and atheist Alain de Botton, whose essay is on marriage relationships; survivor Viktor Frankl; Christian social worker Brene Brown; war veteran and journalist Sebastian Junger; historian of Mormon's theology Samuel Brown; Congregationalist historian and archivist Margaret Bendroth; Methodism's founder John Wesley; and BYU's psychology professor Brent Slife do not, on the surface, seem to have much in common. But they all landed in the same spot: asserting that building relationships with others, loving others, is the most important work of humanity – not the product but the purpose of life. In Slife's words at a forum, loving others must be "an end, not…a means." And John Wesley's words, "The gospel of Christ knows of no religion but social; no holiness but social holiness."[3]

The Prince of Darkness and his perpetrators may have been released to confuse our purpose of life. However, looking from an eternal perspective – legacy may be a mute subject. Like it or not we all may have a legacy that has been developing for a long time:

Eternal perspective provides peace "which passeth all understanding." (Philip. 4:7.) In speaking at a funeral of a loved one, the Prophet Joseph Smith offered this admonition: "When we lose a near and dear friend, upon whom we have set our hearts, it should be a caution unto us. ... Our affections should be placed upon God and His work, more intensely than upon our fellow beings." (Teachings of the Prophet Joseph Smith, p. 216.)

Life does not begin with birth, nor does it end with death. Prior to our birth, we dwelled as spirit children with our Father in Heaven. There we eagerly anticipated the possibility of coming to earth and obtaining a physical body. Knowingly we wanted the risks of mortality, which would allow the exercise of agency and accountability. "This life [was to become] a probationary state; a time to prepare to meet God." (Alma 12:24.) But we regarded the returning home as the best part of that long-awaited trip, just as we do now. Before embarking on any journey, we like to have some assurance of a round-trip ticket. Returning from earth to life in our heavenly home requires passage through—and not around—the doors of death. We were born to die, and we die to live. (See 2 Cor. 6:9.) As seedlings of God, we barely blossom on earth; we fully flower in heaven. *Doors of Death, Pres. Russel M. Nelson, 04/1992*

1– *The Legacy Paradox, New Scientist, Conor Feehly, 14/10/2023.*

2– *Are Children "Intuitive Theists"? Reasoning About Purpose and Design in Nature, Psychological study, Deborah Kelemen Boston University, 2004.*

3– *Of Dead Cats and Dead People: How Family History Can Save the World, Amy Harris - BYU Ass Prof Dept of History, 18/07/2017.*

CHAPTER 38

WHEN I DIE - I WANT TO GO WHERE THEY WENT

Companion animals play major roles in the lives of many children. Indeed, in her 2008 book *The Powerful Bond Between People and Pets*, psychologist Elizabeth Anderson wrote, "Nothing less than alchemy (form of chemistry) is involved when animals and children get together, and the resulting magic has healing properties that work well."

But is it generally true that pets are linked to the psychological well-being of children? Yes, according to a review of 22 studies of the impact of companion animals on child development. While some of the findings are mixed, the authors concluded that growing up with pets is linked to higher self-esteem, cognitive development, and social skills.

Are Pets Linked to Positive Child Development? What is it about living with pets that makes kids better off? The authors of the review suggest several possibilities. These include the impact of pets on reducing stress, providing social support and companionship, and improving children's communication skills. But a new study suggests a different answer, and I expect the results will be controversial.

Research from the journal Anthrozoös, was conducted by a group of high-powered statisticians from the RAND Corporation. All of the members of the research team had pets or grew up with pets, and they anticipated that their analyses would demonstrate the positive impact of companion animals on child development. To answer these questions, the investigators turned to a large existing data set, the California Health Interview Survey. This is an ongoing project that assesses the health and well-being of Californians. For the survey, telephone interviews are conducted with randomly selected adults, adolescents, and parents of children under 11. In addition to information on health and behavior, the survey includes items related to socioeconomic status and demographic factors such as race, ethnicity, and sex. In the 2003 administration, participants were also asked whether their household included a cat, a dog, or both.

To study the impact of pets on children, the researchers used the responses from households with at least one child between the ages of 5 and 11. Parents were asked a series of questions related to their children's physical and mental health. Data from 5,191 children were included in the study; 2,236 lived in homes with a dog or cat, and 2,955 lived in households that did not include any animals.

As expected, the researchers found that children living with pets were generally better off than children who did not have a pet. Children raised in families with pets were reported by their parents to:

- have better general health

- be more obedient
- be more physically active
- be less moody
- have fewer behavior problems
- have fewer learning problems
- Interestingly children with pets were more likely to have been diagnosed with an attention deficit disorder or hyperactivity.
- The pattern of generally better physical and mental health among pet-owning kids was true for children living with cats and with dogs. So, it would be easy for us to conclude that pets are good for kids.

However, that conclusion would be wrong. The problem is that homes with and without pets were different in many ways other than the presence of an animal. For example, the researchers found that kids with pets were:

- less likely to be on free school lunch programs
- less likely to be from households that moved frequently
- more likely to have parents who spoke English
- more likely to be white rather than African-American, Hispanic, or Asian
- more likely to have parents born in the United States
- more likely to live in a house rather than an apartment
- more likely to have parents who were in good health

In short, children in homes with dogs or cats were wealthier and had a host of socioeconomic factors on their side. Could these advantages be the real explanation for the apparent relationship between pet ownership and improved health and well-being in children?

To answer this question, the RAND researchers turned to a sophisticated statistical technique called the "double robust regression approach." Here is a brief description from their report: "We obtained a double robust estimate of exposure effect by adjusting for all covariates used in the propensity score model in our regression model, weighted by the propensity score weights."

If you don't understand any of this, don't worry: You just need to know that this method of analysis enabled the researchers to examine the effects of pet ownership that remained after adjusting for 20 demographic and socioeconomic differences between households with and without pets.

Virtually all differences between pet-owning and non-pet-owning kids disappeared when factors such as race, homeownership, parental health, and wealth were taken into account. This includes differences in the rates of ADD/ADHD. In short, the analysis showed that kids with pets are better off — but not because they have companion animals. It's because they are likely to come from more prosperous homes and not to be members of minority groups.

Dr. Herzog stated, "When I read this report, I realized that these findings applied to me. I was raised in a solidly middle-class suburb where practically every family had a well-kept lawn and a dog. Unlike many kids today, I had a stable home and parents who were amazingly tolerant of my scaly animal friends. Indeed, my father constructed cages for Fred and my other snakes and lizards, and my mother did not complain about my menagerie, even the time she had to get me out of my high-school English class to retrieve an escaped king snake she stumbled upon while vacuuming the living room. Sure, my siblings and I had pets, as did all our friends. But we also had lots of advantages that less well-off children lacked. I found the argument that the health and psychological benefits of pet-keeping to children are largely attributable to differences in wealth and social class convincing.

Ironically, the researchers from RAND are less sure. In an e-mail to me, Dr. Layla Parast who was involved in the study wrote: 'We all were truly surprised by the results, and unlike other work that we do at RAND (on, for example, health insurance or hospital performance, etc.), we had a very personal and emotional investment in this topic.'

She pointed out that the data set did not have information on how long pets lived in the households, and thus they could not check for possible long-term effects of pets on kids. As she added: 'Perhaps if we could measure that, we would see something different. I feel like I can see the positive effects of interactions with animals on my 2-year-old son: it helps him learn kindness and compassion, to the point where he tries to hug and feed every animal we see — including a skunk and raccoon in our backyard.'"[1]

I don't think I need to ask the Sullivan's if their family was better off having pets in their home. In January 2023 I euthanized their last pet with them present. A few days later they delivered individual handmade boxes for each member of the staff filled with candy and a note written inside: "Camden Pet Hospital has been our veterinarian of choice for over 28 years!!!!!!! Thank you for being here for us and our beloved pets!!!!!!!! I regret that we will not be getting a new dog... I am distressed about that but my age and health dictate no more pets... we'll enjoy our families' and friends' pets instead. I'll be thinking of you often since we travel up and down Camden a lot!!!!!!! B & J Sullivan"

My reply:

Dear Mr. & Mrs. Sullivan,

Thank you for the goodies and nice comments you made about the years you have spent allowing us to care for your beloved pets. In 1976 I began practice at Camden Pet Hospital with the desire to plant deep roots into this community and build relationships with special people that love their animals as I love working with them.

This March it will be fifty years since receiving my veterinary license, my children are grown and have moved away with my grandchildren and I still have family I visit on a daily basis (the folks still living in the area whom I care for their pets). There is hardly a day at work that I don't have special experiences like we recently had together.

A client of mine, that recently retired, told me that when he joined the San Jose Police Department an officer told him, "You will know when to quit when your job becomes a four-letter word." His four-letter word came last year. I don't know what that word was, but I'll tell you the current four-letter word I feel still working at Camden. It's LOVE because of families like yours that have helped make my life the best it could be and I still have enthusiasm at 77.

My wife and I recently acquired a new dog (BeBe). Before we picked her up, because of our ages, we asked the question if we shouldn't first check our will to be sure she would always be well cared for.

Enclosed is an article I wrote about whether animals go to Heaven. I believe like Will Rogers, "If there are no dogs (animals) in Heaven, then when I die I want to go where they went."

Recently, a group of university students were discussing their spiritual beliefs. They talked about what they believed in, what they felt the purpose of life might be. One young man stated, "I believe in nothing except myself. I believe only in me." A lively—but respectful—discussion followed, as many of his classmates questioned his view of life.

Young people are often encouraged to believe in themselves, and a healthy sense of self-worth is valuable, even essential. But several of the college students who were part of the conversation that day sensed that something was missing from their friend's outlook. It seemed narrow to them, a hollow, even empty way to live. He had the right, of course, to believe—or disbelieve—as he liked. But his words led many of his friends to ponder what they believe, and they found themselves arriving at the opposite conclusion: that for life to have joy and meaning, there simply has to be more than just "me"—more than the here and now.

Many people come to this same conclusion by observing the beautiful world around them. Nature, it seems, is an excellent teacher of faith. The stunning vistas, from mighty rivers to small streams, from magnificent mountains to a single wildflower, from the wide starry sky to the intricacies of a butterfly wing—all of it tends to humble us away from self-centeredness. The variety of trees and plants and animals, both the beautiful and the unusual, seems to declare that God's hand is in this world.

But perhaps even more wonderful than the earth's natural beauty are the people who call it home. Think about the variety of people you see—each one with a unique, fascinating story, and every one a testament to the beauty of life.

All this did not happen by random chance. Each of us is placed here for a purpose. God loves His children. He wants us to find joy and fulfillment, and He knows we're not likely to find it alone. So, He surrounded us with other people, both loved ones and strangers, so that we can help each other, learn from each other, and grow together. That is why we are here, together, in this wonderful world.[2]

Who knows, maybe I may end up like Dr. Paul Wise and be around a while longer continuing to enjoy nature and those that have become close to me: In 1918, Daylight Saving Time was observed for the first time in the United States, Babe Ruth still played for the Boston Red Sox, and Germany

WALTER R. HOGE, DVM

signed an armistice agreement with the Allies, ending World War I.

Dr. Paul Wise was born that same year, on Sept. 5 to be exact. At age 100, he continues to practice veterinary medicine. On Fridays and Saturdays, Dr. Wise can be found at Evers Veterinary Clinic in Chico, California, running the low-cost vaccination clinic, a part-time position he's held since 1981. Reached by phone at his home and asked to comment on his prodigious work ethic, Dr. Wise quipped, "Oh, for heaven's sakes. I guess all you have to do is live to a hundred and still be able to walk to be famous."

After growing up on a small farm in Hotchkiss, Colorado, Dr. Wise moved to Santa Ana, California, to study engineering at the junior college. While working nights and weekends at the local veterinary hospital, he realized that the life of an engineer wasn't for him. "I decided I liked what (the hospital owner) was doing better than what I was planning to do," he explained.

Dr. Wise enrolled in Colorado State University College of Veterinary Medicine & Biomedical Sciences, graduating in 1950. With his veterinary degree in hand, Dr. Wise returned to the Santa Ana hospital, no longer a kennel worker but an associate. And there he remained for seven years before opening his own practice, Grand Avenue Pet Hospital, also in Santa Ana.

In 1972, Dr. Wise retired and sold his practice to two veterinarians "fresh out of the Army." It turns out that retirement, like a career in engineering, wasn't in the cards for Dr. Wise. "I retired for one full year, and my wife (Lorraine) said, 'I know I married you for better or for worse, but not for lunch every day.' I took that as a clue she wanted me out of the house part of the time," he recalled.

Dr. Wise followed the advice of his wife, now deceased, and found ways to keep himself busy. Then, in 1981, Dr. Hank Evers hired the "retired" veterinarian, now in his early 60s, to run the vaccination clinic at Evers Veterinary Clinic. The late Dr. Evers opened the Chico small animal hospital with his wife, Marilyn, a licensed veterinary technician. The practice has passed to his daughter, Dr. Susan Evers.

"The agreement my father and I had was to always have a position for Dr. Wise as long as he wanted to work," Dr. Susan Evers said. "Veterinary medicine is his passion, and working recharges him. His dedication, loyalty, and encouragement are priceless.

"Since my father's death, I value Dr. Wise's advice even more. He is a sincere, kind person and a mentor to many. He is an adopted member of my personal and veterinary family and loved by everyone he comes in contact with."

For anyone considering becoming a veterinarian, Dr. Wise offers a bit of wisdom gained from a career of 68 years and counting: "If you're not interested in a life where no two days are alike, then you'd better not go into veterinary medicine."[3]

1– *Animals and Us, Why Kids With Pets Are Better Off, a controversial study helps explain the impact of pets on child development, Hal Herzog Ph.D., 2017.*

2– *What a Wonderful World, Music & the Spoken word, #4,692, 201.*

3– *Still Practicing After All These Years, by R. Scott Nolen, JAVMA V253 #12, page 1526, 12-15-2018.*

CHAPTER 39

THE BEST IS YET TO COME

I am curled in the fetal position on the sidewalk outside my house. I have finished work for the day and walked home from the local train station. I walked up to the front of my house, then paused on this spot on the sidewalk. I don't want to go inside. Inside the house, there are dishes to do, rooms to clean, digital devices to police, mouths to feed, and teenagers to parent. Late summer shadows are creeping across the valley. Feeling chilly, I try to absorb every photon. As long as I don't go inside, perhaps I can avoid the reality of my life.

But even if the chaos inside the house were fixed, what will fix me? Inside my body, just below my right-side rib, I can feel the bulge of a tumor growing exuberantly within my liver. I feel like I'm running out of time, and I'm so sad. My sister-in-law, Beth, comes out of the house and quietly sits next to me on the sidewalk. Tears slide down my cheeks and sink into the concrete. "It's too much," I say. "I want another life." "It's okay," Beth says.

Much of the time, we feel adequate in rising to meet the daily challenges before us. We have the gospel. We know the plan. We've got the training, the education, the good habits, and the work ethic. We've got friends, family, and ministering sisters and brothers. We know God will prepare a way, as for Nephi, and that God has prepared us, as with Esther. And yet, sometimes we simply feel to sit down in the road of life and weep. Life can be really hard.

As Latter-day Saints, we proudly claim the gift of agency. We are proud to have sided with Christ in the premortal struggle over agency in heaven. We feel sorry for the hosts of spirit sisters and brothers who chose to follow Lucifer because they were too frightened at the prospect of living life in a physical body, subject to the laws of nature and the agency of others.

Lucifer promised that "one soul shall not be lost" and requested "only" that he receive God's full power in order to accomplish his goal of steering God's children unerringly through life. Whenever we were about to put a foot wrong, he would intervene and put us right. We would not be allowed to make stupid, self-defeating choices, even when pushed to our limits by the raw, elemental forces of life in the physical world.

As a novice parent, I am sometimes quite envious of "Satan's plan." Satan's kids would all get accepted at Ivy League colleges because they would always choose to do their homework and develop their talents before playing video games. Satan's kids wouldn't have brain health issues or life-altering physical injuries because Satan would manipulate chemicals in the brain and the laws of physics to keep the mind and body humming along beautifully. Satan's kids would never leave towels on the floor and would never leave an important job unfinished. It wouldn't just be unthinkable; it would be un-doable.

As a parent with a life-threatening illness, I can easily say that the pain of parenting is far more acute than the pain of impending death. I don't know if this makes people feel better or worse. People often say, apologetically, when telling me about a trial in their life, "I know it's nothing compared to what you're going through . . . " The truth is, in all of our lives, including my life, quite often impending doom ranks far below more quotidian anxieties—for instance: the anxiety of hoping a kid will make the right choices; or an acute attack of seasonal allergies; or even the sting of the sudden realization: "Oh shoot! I missed [Child]'s [activity]!" But, no doubt about it—for me, the pain that comes when someone you love is suffering is far, far worse than any sort of threat to one's own health or life.

Amidst life's everyday stresses sometimes it is quite easy for us to wish that God will take the helm, not simply whispering suggestions or sending us charts and maps or even cheering enthusiastically from a few paces back, but seizing the wheel of the ship in an iron grip and just taking over for an extended period of time, flattening the waves and working around storms. Perhaps we could keep this divine autopilot on until the kids are grown, or until I'm free of health difficulties, or even, until the very end, when the ship triumphantly sails back into the heavenly marina.

The appeal of "Satan's plan," in which the living is easy, teaches us another fundamental truth: Life is hard, though we wish it were easy. We wish we could get from point A to point B without having to traverse the steep, often treacherous terrain that connects those two points. We wish we could become skilled navigators without facing many terrifying storms on our own.

This, too, was Lucifer's ambition. He wanted to have the power of God, power that would make him godlike to his mortal sisters and brothers, without going through the period of learning and trial that would naturally develop that power in him. In proposing his plan, therefore, he was hoping to be the first to take a shortcut—to receive the capacity of godliness all at once, not cultivate it over time and throughout much difficulty. He offered us, and himself, the path of least resistance.

But our Heavenly Parents had a different plan. It was so fraught and full of struggle, it required the active assistance of a Savior, Jesus Christ, who would reach out and bring us back from the abyss. We would inevitably suffer physical degradation and die. Christ would create a way for us to live again. We would inevitably make the wrong choices, harming others and our own spirits. Christ would heal those harms and give us opportunities to try again. And Christ would show us the way, if we would only follow Him—a path with no shortcuts. He offered us, and Himself, the path of most resistance.

The truth of life's difficulty and the truth of our desire to be free from difficulty are made even harder to bear by a third truth: life's unfairness. If only the good always prospered and only the evil always came to an ignominious end! If only every child were born into a situation in which they were loved, treasured, and cared for all alike! If only violent, bone-shattering car accidents happened to people who were growing old and tired of life and not to young, vibrant people in life's prime!

Seriously, universe!? I find myself saying frequently. This is what you're going to do!? Here, too, the plan of salvation has offered us the path of most resistance. Instead of everyone being born on an exactly level playing field, so we know everything we do well or poorly is entirely because of our own merit, many of the circumstances in our lives are varied beyond any hope of control. It will never be possible for us to tick all the boxes, to be certain that we have fulfilled all requirements, in any measurable or comparable way.

Thus, how we spend our time and care is between us and those around us. What we do with our life is between us and God. It's not a competition. It's an opportunity to fully inhabit the physical and spiritual dimensions that make us like our divine Mother and Father, so we can begin to grow into their capacity and wisdom... *Truths to heal your heart when life feels not just hard—but too hard, excerpted from 'Sacred Struggle' by Melissa Wei-Tsing Inouye, 2023.*

Editor's note: After a long battle with cancer, Melissa Wei-Tsing Inouye recently passed away (04/23/2024). We share this excerpt from her book Sacred Struggle as a tribute to her incredible life of scholarship and discipleship, for which we will be forever grateful. Our hearts and prayers are with Melissa's family.

CHAPTER 40

CABBIE DRIVER AND
THE OLDER WOMAN

There are moments so packed with meaning that they shimmer through time. Some inspire awe by exposing the splendor of nature. Some deliver a flash of insight to solve what seems like an intractable problem. They are inherently transformative; they instantaneously expand awareness and alter one's sense of self. Psychologist Abraham Maslow coined the term peak experiences to suggest the inner magnificence of such rare and distinctive events.

But there are also moments of great meaning that are more social in nature, that arise spontaneously in the space between people. Such moments can shed an illuminating light on the deepest dimensions of a person's being. Arriving unheralded, they may accurately reveal a person's strengths, expose vulnerabilities, unveil core convictions, divulge life values. They beget a profound state of knowing with searing speed. Such moments carry credibility precisely because they are not anticipated or prescribed. They are, however, transformative. With their mix of insight and intensity, they give life new direction, forever altering the connection people have with each other and, often enough, with themselves. Of the various kinds of turning points life presents, the most powerful of all may be character-defining moments. They go to the heart of who we are.[1]

There has been a touching story circulating throughout the internet about a conscientious cab driver who discovered that his fare was a woman who was leaving her small apartment for the last time and going to a hospice to die. TruthOrFiction.com received a lot of emails from readers who gave them four or five different sources for this story including a man who claimed that he was the source—none of which has turned out to be correct.

The truth is that this is from the pen of inspirational writer Kent Nerburn. He told TruthOrFiction.com that the story is true and happened to him in Minneapolis, Minnesota in the early 1980's. At the time he was working as a driver for the Yellow Cab company and worked what he called "the dog shift" overnight.

The story goes like this: I arrived at the address and honked the horn. After waiting a few minutes, I honked again. Since this was going to be my last ride of my shift I thought about just driving away, but instead I put the car in park and walked up to the door and knocked. "Just a minute", answered a frail, elderly voice. I could hear something being dragged across the floor.

After a long pause, the door opened. A small woman in her 90's stood before me. She was wearing a print dress and a pillbox hat with a veil pinned on it, like somebody out of a 1940's movie. By her side was a small nylon suitcase. The apartment looked as if no one had lived in it for years. All the furniture was covered with sheets. There were no clocks on the walls, no knickknacks or utensils on the counters. In the corner was a cardboard box filled with photos and glassware.

"Would you carry my bag out to the car?" she said. I took the suitcase to the cab, then returned to assist the woman. She took my arm and we walked slowly toward the curb. She kept thanking me for my kindness. I told her that it was nothing. I just try to treat my passengers the way I would want my mother to be treated. She told me that I was such a good boy. When we got in the cab, she gave me an address and then asked if I could drive through downtown even though it was not the shortest way. She said that she was in no hurry and didn't mind since she was on her way to a hospice.

I looked in the rear-view mirror. Her eyes were glistening. She mentioned that she didn't have any family left and in a soft voice she informed me that the doctor said "she didn't have much longer." I quietly reached over and shut off the meter.

For the next two hours, we drove through the city. She showed me the building where she had once worked as an elevator operator. We drove through the neighborhood where she and her husband had lived when they were newlyweds. She had me pull up in front of a furniture warehouse that had once been a ballroom where she had gone dancing as a girl.

Sometimes she'd ask me to slow in front of a particular building or corner and would sit staring into the darkness, saying nothing. As the first hint of sun was creasing the horizon, she suddenly said, "I'm tired. Let's go now." We drove in silence to the address she had given me. It was a low building, like a small convalescent home, with a driveway that passed under a portico. Two orderlies came out to the cab as soon as we pulled up. They were solicitous and intent, watching her every move. They must have been expecting her. I opened the trunk and took the small suitcase to the door. The woman was already seated in a wheelchair.

"How much do I owe you?" She asked, reaching into her purse. "Nothing," I said "You have to make a living," she answered. "There are other passengers," I responded. Almost without thinking, I bent and gave her a hug. She held onto me tightly. She said that I gave an old woman a little moment of joy and thanked me. I squeezed her hand, and then walked into the dim morning light. Behind me, a door shut. It was the sound of the closing of a life.

I didn't pick up any more passengers that shift. I drove aimlessly lost in thought. For the rest of that day, I could hardly talk. What if that woman had gotten an angry driver, or one who was impatient to end his shift? What if I had refused to take the run, or had honked once, then driven away?

On a quick review, I don't think that I have done anything more important in my life. We're conditioned to think that our lives revolve around great moments. But great moments often catch us unaware-beautifully wrapped in what others may consider a small one. What a wonderful reminder to live life to the fullest![2]

For decades, psychologists have subscribed to a five-factor model of personality, a product of research in which myriad personal characteristics seem to naturally cluster into five broad traits—openness to experience, conscientiousness, extraversion, agreeableness, and neuroticism, or the tendency to experience negative emotions and react poorly to stress. But in the early 2000s, Canadian psychologists Kibeom Lee and Michael Ashton identified a sixth major trait. They call it the H factor, for honesty-humility—two qualities that, their research shows, travel together.

The H factor, say Lee and Ashton in their 2012 book, The H Factor of Personality: Why Some People Are Manipulative, Self-Entitled, Materialistic, and Exploitive—And Why It Matters for Everyone, underlies people's "approaches to money, power, and sex. It governs their inclination to commit crimes or obey the law. It orients them toward certain attitudes about society, politics, and religion. It influences their choice of friends and spouse." In short, it captures something fundamental about a person's adaptation to a shared world: The H factor sums up a person's willingness to exploit others. Or not.

Notably, Lee and Aston report, "your level of H doesn't depend just on your genes and on your childhood—it also depends on your own free will." While their work has made character scientifically admissible, it has also opened the door to consideration of personal responsibility—at least for some aspects of human behavior—a concept de facto discredited by decades of biologic determinism. Until now, says Goodwin, "studying moral aspects of personality was deemed too subjective and value-laden." So alien was the topic that psychologists long considered morally relevant behavior strictly a response to situations, not a quality arising from anything within, certainly not from something as stable as a personality trait. Research now suggests it's the confluence of both.

Like other traits, character is seen as a disposition that drives a person to behave in consistent ways, but its specific mission is to allow us to evaluate the world and other people, to judge them. Character has an inherently moral cast. There are some fuzzy borders between moral attributes and the personality traits of conscientiousness and agreeableness, but moral features extend beyond self-interests to interpersonal and societal interests.

According to Penn's Goodwin, character is king in social cognition: It is the first and the most important thing people actually perceive in others. They are rapidly gathering information about a person's kindness, fairness, honesty, trustworthiness, and loyalty.

How could it be that no one was onto such prominent psychic players before? That's because, in the world of psych research, many of the components of character were discounted as features of situations, not people. And others were hidden behind theories of warmth and outgoing behavior.

Contemporary psychology holds that the impressions we form of others are snapped together from quick estimations of two features—their warmth and their competence. But warmth is a nebulous notion, Goodwin says. And when he analyzed just what characteristics people identify behind warmth—he asked subjects to think of individuals they knew close up and those they knew from afar, such as George W. Bush and Barack Obama—he found kindness, humility, compassion, fairness, gratitude, and empathy. They were the traits that most powerfully predicted the overall impressions subjects had of individuals. "We can mistake social skills for character," observes Goodwin. "We mistake the social for the prosocial."

Despite having been discounted as products of specific situations, honesty, trustworthiness, loyalty, justness, and courage contributed most of all to the impressions subjects formed of others. "Moral character is indeed the predominant determinant of global impressions," Goodwin concludes from his studies. It actually "drives how impressions are formed."

What's more, character traits are negatively dominant: A negative or immoral trait outweighs the presence of a positive moral trait on the impressions we form. One failure to recognize an injustice overshadows any number of good deeds. When it comes to moral character, says Goodwin, "people are judged by their weakest link." And a transgression in the moral domain may be less subject to forgiveness than slip-ups in other realms.

Of all the elements of moral character he studied, the ones that carry the most weight are the "pure" moral traits—honesty, justness, fairness, trustworthiness, courage—which have nothing to do with warmth. In our judgment of others, honesty outranks even kindness, a moral trait that canoodles with warmth. Absent honesty, no information about a person can be trusted.[1]

For we are taking pains to do what is right, not only in the eyes of the Lord but also in the eyes of man (*2 Corinthians 8:21*), Therefore each of you must put off falsehood and speak truthfully to your neighbor, for we are all members of one body (*Ephesians 4:25*), But the wisdom that comes from heaven is first of all pure; then peace-loving, considerate, submissive, full of mercy and good fruit, impartial and sincere (*James 3:17*), Do to others as you would have them do to you (*Luke 6:31*), Whoever walks in integrity walks securely, but whoever takes crooked paths will be found out (*Proverbs 10:9*), The Lord detests lying lips, but he delights in people who are trustworthy (*Proverbs 12:22*), An honest answer is like a kiss on the lips (*Proverbs 24:26*), The one whose walk is blameless is kept safe, but the one whose ways are perverse will fall into the pit (*Proverbs 28:18*), I know, my God, that you test the heart and are pleased with integrity. All these things I have given willingly and with honest intent. And now I have seen with joy how willingly your people who are here have given to you (*1 Chronicles 29:17*).

- Inspirational writer Kent Nerburn comments: "I didn't pick up any more passengers that shift. I drove aimlessly lost in thought. For the rest of that day, I could hardly talk. What if that woman had gotten an angry driver, or one who was impatient to end his shift? What if I had refused to take the run, or had honked once, then driven away?
  On a quick review, I don't think that I have done anything more important in my life. We're conditioned to think that our lives revolve around great moments. But great moments often catch us unaware-beautifully wrapped in what others may consider a small one. What a wonderful reminder to live life to the fullest!"[2]

- Hara Estroff Marano & Anna Yusim M.D.s thoughts: "The strength of a person's character also determines how well he or she will follow through on plans, goals, commitments, and values," Goodwin reports—which may explain why his team found that obituaries are especially rich in information about character. When it comes to summing up a life, character counts most of all. It not only shapes a lifetime's worth of behavior, it's what we seek as others' legacy, why we even bother to read about them.[1]

– These thoughts got me thinking about how, for some unknown reason, I always understood that when I died my whole life would pass before me as I headed for the veil. I don't know where I got that idea – but I do know that I've hoped that my earlier years would go by much quicker on the replay!

There are some studies suggesting that we do have a life review before passing on. Mike Snider reported on a study: "What may happen when we die? As the moment of death approaches, memories of your life may really flash before you, new research suggests. This idea of a quick binge of past memories just before dying is not new, as experiences such as these – and other phenomena including out-of-body experiences – have been documented among those who've survived near-death experiences.

Researchers have reported what they say may be the first evidence of such memory recalls in a human brain near death, in the peer-reviewed Frontiers in Aging Neuroscience. The patient treated was an 87-year-old man who came to the Vancouver General Hospital emergency room in 2016 after a fall. Three days after surgery to relieve a buildup of blood between the skull and the brain, the patient began having seizures and the medical team started an electroencephalogram (EEG) test to monitor his brain activity and treat the seizures.

During this recording, the patient suffered a heart attack. The researchers recorded 900 seconds of brain activity before and around the patient's death – the first-ever recording of a dying human's brain, said Dr. Ajmal Zemmar, who treated the patient in Vancouver General Hospital in 2016 and is now a neurosurgeon at the University of Louisville neurosurgeon, where he pursued the study.

In-depth analysis of the patient's EEG around the 30 seconds before and after the patient's heart stopped beating identified brain waves that normally happen in healthy human brains when we undergo memory recall, out-of-body experiences, meditation and similar experiences. These brain waves, also called oscillations, happening around the time of death suggest a potential "last 'recall of life' that may take place in the near-death state," researchers wrote.

The researchers expressed caveats, including injury, seizures, swelling and anesthesia that could make the interpretation of the data difficult. But there are similarities to the oscillations in healthy humans undergoing out-of-body experiences and evidence from rats where these brain waves were also seen after cardiac arrest in a 2013 study.

We are seeing for the first time that these same brain waves that in a healthy human are known to be responsible for dreaming, meditation and out-of-body experiences are now observed in the dying human brain," Zemmar said. In the past six years, Zemmar and the research team have sought to find another example of an EEG recorded at the time of death because scientific data from one case is very thin ice to draw conclusions from, he said. Unfortunately, no other case was found forcing the team to publish the single existing dataset from a dying human brain.

Zemmar said: "Something we may learn from this research is: although our loved ones have their eyes closed and are ready to leave us to rest, their brains may be replaying some of the nicest moments they experienced in their lives. Caregivers could take some solace in the findings. Medical personnel often must tell family members that a loved one "is unfortunately not going to make it. These situations, no matter how long you do the job, they never get easier.

One thing I'm hoping that this could do is that I could tell them, 'Your loved one is okay. They're not suffering. They're not having pain in the last moments of life. They're replaying memories that they had with you throughout life'. I think that would be something comforting in that … extremely difficult situation to lose somebody. For the rest of us, perhaps we will rest easier knowing there's the potential for what the researchers termed a 'last memory flashback' before we die."

When asked about spiritual advice on death, Zemmar said, "As scientists, we focus on interpreting data to understand nature and we share our conclusions with society. From here on in, everyone should decide for themselves how they like to imagine the spiritual side around death."[3]

1– *The Moments That Make Us Who We Are, Psychology Today, Hara Estroff Marano & Anna Yusim M.D., 07/02/2018.*

2– *This true story was originally published in a book by Kent Nerburn about his experience, titled Make Me an Instrument of Your Peace and published by Harper, San Francisco. Updated 7/10/07.*

3– *Does your life pass before you as you die? New brain research suggests you have flashbacks, Mike Snider, USA Today, 02-26-2022.*

CHAPTER 41

"MYSIDE BIAS" AND AAHA

Psychological studies have shown that: "The vaunted human capacity for reason may have more to do with winning arguments than with thinking straight."

Study #1: In 1975, researchers at Stanford invited a group of undergraduates to take part in a study about suicide. They were presented with pairs of suicide notes. In each pair, one note had been composed by a random individual, the other by a person who had subsequently taken his own life. The students were then asked to distinguish between the genuine notes and the fake ones.

Some students discovered that they had a genius for the task. Out of twenty-five pairs of notes, they correctly identified the real one twenty-four times. Others discovered that they were hopeless. They identified the real note in only ten instances.

As is often the case with psychological studies, the whole setup was a put-on. Though half the notes were indeed genuine—they'd been obtained from the Los Angeles County coroner's office—the scores were fictitious.

The students who'd been told they were almost always right were, on average, no more discerning than those who had been told they were mostly wrong.

In the second phase of the study, the deception was revealed. The students were told that the real point of the experiment was to gauge their responses to thinking they were right or wrong. (This, it turned out, was also a deception.) Finally, the students were asked to estimate how many suicide notes they had actually categorized correctly, and how many they thought an average student would get right. At this point, something curious happened. The students in the high-score group said that they thought they had, in fact, done quite well—significantly better than the average student—even though, as they'd just been told, they had zero grounds for believing this. Conversely, those who'd been assigned to the low-score group said that they thought they had done significantly worse than the average student—a conclusion that was equally unfounded.

Conclusion: "Once formed," the researchers observed dryly, "impressions are remarkably perseverant."

Study #2: A few years later, a new set of Stanford students was recruited for a related study. The students were handed packets of information about a pair of firefighters, Frank K. and George H. Frank's bio noted that, among other things, he had a baby daughter and he liked to scuba dive. George had a small son and played golf. The packets also included the men's responses on what the researchers called the Risky-Conservative Choice Test. According to one version of the packet, Frank was a successful firefighter who, on the test, almost always went with the safest option. In the other version, Frank also chose the safest option, but he was a lousy firefighter who'd been put "on report" by his supervisors several times.

Once again, midway through the study, the students were informed that they'd been misled, and that the information they'd received was entirely fictitious. The students were then asked to describe their own beliefs. What sort of attitude toward risk did they think a successful firefighter would have? The students who'd received the first packet thought that he would avoid it. The students in the second group thought he'd embrace it.

Conclusion: "Even after the evidence "for their beliefs having been totally refuted, people fail to make appropriate revisions in those beliefs." In this case, the failure was "particularly impressive," since two data points would never have been enough information to generalize from.

The Stanford studies became famous. Coming from a group of academics in the nineteen-seventies, the contention that people can't think straight was shocking. It isn't any longer. Thousands of subsequent experiments have confirmed (and elaborated on) this finding. As everyone who's followed the research—or even occasionally picked up a copy of Psychology Today—knows, any graduate student with a clipboard can demonstrate that reasonable-seeming people are often totally irrational. Scientists have been led to wonder: "How did we come to be this way?

Stripped of a lot of what might be called cognitive-science-ese, Mercier and Sperber's (authors of "The Enigma of Reason") argument runs, more or less, as follows: Humans' biggest advantage over other species is our ability to cooperate. Cooperation is difficult to establish and almost as difficult to sustain. For any individual, freeloading is always the best course of action. Reason developed not to enable us to solve abstract, logical problems or even to help us draw conclusions from unfamiliar data; rather, it developed to resolve the problems posed by living in collaborative groups. Reason is an adaptation to the hypersocial niche humans have evolved for themselves. Habits of mind that seem weird or goofy or just plain dumb from an "intellectualist" point of view prove shrewd when seen from a social "interactionist" perspective.

Consider what's become known as "confirmation bias," the tendency people have to embrace information that supports their beliefs and reject information that contradicts them. Of the many forms of faulty thinking that have been identified, confirmation bias is among the best catalogued; it's the subject of entire textbooks' worth of experiments.

One of the most famous of these involved an experiment where researchers rounded up a group of students who had opposing opinions about capital punishment. Half the students were in favor of it and thought that it deterred crime; the other half were against it and thought that it had no effect on crime. The students were asked to respond to two studies. One provided data in support of the deterrence argument, and the other provided data that called it into question. Both studies—you guessed it—were made up, and had been designed to present what were, objectively speaking, equally compelling statistics.

The students who had originally supported capital punishment rated the pro-deterrence data highly credible and the anti-deterrence data unconvincing; the students who'd originally opposed capital punishment did the reverse. At the end of the experiment, the students were asked once again about their views. Those who'd started out pro-capital punishment were now even more in favor of it; those who'd opposed it were even more hostile.

If reason is designed to generate sound judgments, then it's hard to conceive of a more serious design flaw than confirmation bias. Imagine, Mercier a mouse that thinks the way we do. Such a mouse, "bent on confirming its belief that there are no cats around," would soon be dinner. To the extent that confirmation bias leads people to dismiss evidence of new or underappreciated threats—the human equivalent of the cat around the corner—it's a trait that should have been selected against.

The fact that both we and it survive proves that it must have some adaptive function, and that function is related to our "hypersociability." Scientists prefer the term "myside bias." Humans, they point out, aren't randomly credulous. Presented with someone else's argument, we're quite adept at spotting the weaknesses. Almost invariably, the positions we're blind about are our own.[7]

The American Animal Hospital Association's Mission & Vision: "Established in 1933 by leaders in the veterinary profession, AAHA is the only organization to accredit companion animal veterinary hospitals. To become AAHA accredited, companion animal hospitals undergo regular, comprehensive onsite evaluations by AAHA veterinary experts who evaluate each practice on more than 900 standards of veterinary care. Today, more than 4,500 practice teams (12%–15% of veterinary practices in the United States and Canada) are AAHA accredited or pre-accredited.

The association also develops publications, educational programs, and resources designed to help companion animal hospitals thrive. The AAHA membership philosophy is team-focused, allowing every hospital team member, from veterinarians to receptionists, to benefit from AAHA's resources through one team member."

Communication concerning Camden Pet Hospital's most recent "comprehensive onsite evaluation" by AAHA on 10/31/2023 (just happened to be on Halloween eve). *March 3, 2023 comments to Nancy Itri, Manager Camden Pet Hospital:

Please thank our staff for the tremendous effort they made in their preparation and during the evaluation of CPH for continued AAHA accreditation. This is the first time in a long time that we had no seasoned staff members to prepare for the evaluation. I believe, you might have AAHA verify, that we have been a member since 1976.

I would appreciate if you would discuss with the Evaluation Team section MA38.2: "Surgical suites are constructed and utilized as separate, closed, single purpose rooms entered only for activities associated with aseptic surgical procedures to minimize contamination."

Recommendation: The extra scrub room located in the surgery suite includes a sink and running water. this is considered "in the surgery suite" and cannot pass this mandatory standard. Consider removing the water faucets and sink in this part of the surgery suite as an alternative to changing the door entry in this room.

Questions:

1– During past inspections the requirements changed, by AAHA, to install doors separating the surgery suite from the scrub room and it's use restriction to the scrubbing of hands by the surgeon only. The first requirement was that we place a split swinging door that after scrubbing, to prevent contamination, the doors could be opened by pushing against them with the surgeon's back.

Later the requirement changed to where we replaced the swinging door with a solid door. I don't remember if we were ever required to have the scrub area next to the surgery room.

2– Please inform me where I can find documentation that the limited use sink and running water separated from the surgery suite by doors is a concern for contamination of the surgery suite and risk of infection to the patient.

3– If we wall off our scrub sink and running water area from the surgery suite, as recommended, and place a doorway through the wall next to the sink and running water - we would need to exit the scrub area into the main hallway from the receptionist area, pass through doors into the main hospital treatment area and then pass through another set of doors into the surgical suite. Is this an acceptable approach for AAHA?

4– Do you recommend that we use the sink in the treatment area to scrub and then go through only one set of doors into the surgical suite?

5– Another choice is that we have a large rest room near the treatment room. Would they suggest we consider scrubbing there? In this scenario we would have only two sets of doors between the rest room and the surgical suite?

6– Please let me know if you have any other concerns voiced with your evaluation team from AAHA…

Thank you again for the effort made by our staff!

Walter R. Hoge, DVM MS Hospital Director

*Response July 6, 2023 (Director of Accreditation) – name withheld) Nancy & Manager Camden Pet Hospital

Since our meeting as an accreditation team and the meeting with fellow AAHA peers within the volunteer committee, it was decided to keep our stance on not allowing operating sinks within the confines of a surgical suite. This would mean any sink that is located past the threshold of a surgical suite entrance.

Not having visited your hospital (personally) yet for the re-evaluation, I would like clarification as you stated you wanted any update on our policy of having sinks near the surgical suite to ensure that we are supporting Camden Pet Hospital appropriately without making assumptions. I request that Camden Pet Hospital shut off the water to the sink in the surgery until the re-evaluation.

I look forward to hearing from you soon Dr. Hoge. (name withheld - Director of Accreditation)

American Animal Hospital Association

*October 26, 2023 heads up
Hogepoge <hogepoge66@gmail.com>
4:30 PM (1 minute ago)

Reply
to Rich

Subject: AAHA Accreditation Re-Evaluation On October 26

Good Morning Dr. Hoge and Nancy,

I wanted to let your practice know about a change coming up for your AAHA Re- Evaluation.

Due to some unforeseen issues, Director of Accreditation (name withheld) will not be available to accomplish the AAHA

Accreditation Re-Evaluation on Thursday, October 26, 2023.

The Practice Consultant Manager (name withheld), will be accomplishing the Re-Eval now.

She will arrive between 8:30 and 9:00am.

If you have any questions, please let me or (name withheld) know. Have a good week!

*October 26, 2023

    Had a nice visit with (name withheld). She evaluated two infractions Camden Pet Hospital had been asked to correct. The cold tray has been eliminated from use and I was informed that all infractions would be removed if we had a plumber plug the water line and remove the drain of the sink in the surgery room.

She also mentioned that the surgical scrub area could not be used next to the surgery suite because *sewer gas* from the sink (a disproven fact for > 100 years –see below) was considered to be a risk for sterility in the surgery room. This comment reminded me, as I recall, the same comment when we were required to place a solid door separating the scrub sink from the surgery room. At the time, I believe they quoted a study from Purdue University resulting in the change. I remembered this because Purdue is my alma mater.

Following is a study I've conducted about sinks and other paraphernalia used to help perform sterile surgery. At first, *sewer gas* was not included as a concern in the study. My thoughts were that AAHA's primary issue would be contamination from microbiomes found in sink drains.

*October 27, 2023

Reply

- I'm sorry I missed you yesterday. I understand that you had a kidney transplant and that it is wise for you to be careful traveling - which is a very good idea. I attached an article I wrote, called freezing, that you might find of interest. Care of tissues for transplant are going to change a lot in the near future...

- I'm also sending another article that I wrote concerning our hospital evaluation. A shortened version will be a chapter in my upcoming book. I would like you to submit this to the "specialists" at AAHA that you consult with when making policies on sterility and would like their comments:

1– Their assessment of the content and if there are errors that need to be corrected?

2– If they have comments about why AAHA has decided to continue with their recommendations on scrub sinks and surgical suites? Also, do they give me permission to include this in the book or decline?

3– If they will send me an in-depth review of their research into sterility and surgical suites they have used to formulate their current policies.

4– If they prefer I do or do not include AAHA's name in my book?

I wish you the best during your recovery and would like to visit you someday when you are in the area...even if I've pulled the plug and retired. CPH has been a member of AAHA since 1976 at my request from the owner, I've been at this location since that time, and this June I've completed my 50th year of practice. My five children have all married, have children and moved away. Many of my client-families are still seeing me at Camden. They help keep my brain plasticity and the brain fog away. Ever since I did research at Purdue University, I've been interested in the intricate workings of God's animal creations. They're predictable - and it's fascinating learning its secrets. Much more fun than dealing with the "natural man."

Thanking you in advance for your assistance in this matter,

Rich Hoge

Sewer gas is a complex, generally obnoxious smelling mixture of toxic and nontoxic gases produced and collected in sewage systems by the decomposition of organic household or industrial wastes, typical components of sewage. *Sewer gases* may include hydrogen sulfide, ammonia, methane, esters, carbon monoxide, sulfur dioxide and nitrogen oxides. Improper disposal of petroleum products such as gasoline and mineral spirits contribute to sewer gas hazards. Sewer gases are of concern due to their odor, health effects, and potential for creating fire or explosions.

During the mid-nineteenth century, when indoor plumbing was being developed, it was a common belief that disease was caused largely by miasmas, or literally "polluted air." (Malaria, a disease spread by mosquitoes that breed in marshy areas, got its name from the Italian words for "bad air" because people initially blamed it on marsh gas.) Originally, traps in drain pipes were designed to help keep this bad air from passing back into living spaces within buildings. However, during the Broad Street cholera outbreak in London, in the summer of 1854, physician John Snow, among others, worked to prove that polluted water was the culprit, not the foul smells from sewage pipes or other sources. Subsequently, even as the germ theory of disease developed, society was slow to accept the idea that odors from sewers were relatively harmless when it came to the spread of disease.

The cover of an 1882 of The Wasp with an illustration linking *sewer gas* and disease…

<u>Summaries</u> of cited articles sent to AAHA:

– Water is the foundation of life; because of that, wet environments pose a particular hazard of infection, promoting microbial growth and serving as a source for antibiotic resistant pathogens, and healthcare-associated infections. Tap water meets stringent safety standards in the United States, but it is not sterile.[1]

– Many recent reports have found multidrug resistant bacteria living in hospital sink drainpipes, putting them in close proximity to vulnerable patients. But how the bacteria find their way out of the drains, and into patients has been unclear... The goal is to determine precisely how the pathogens reach the patients, said Mathers. "This type of foundational research is needed to understand how these bacteria are transmitted so that we can develop and test potential intervention strategies that can be used to prevent further spread.[2]

- Ensure that faucets don't flow directly into the drain to minimize splashing/aerosolizing. Consider changing to deeper sink basins to prevent cross-contamination of hands and adjacent surfaces. Eliminate misuse of sinks to dispose of fluids and materials that can provide nutrition for bacterial biofilm growth. Ensure that patient care items are not stored adjacent to sinks to avoid cross-contamination…New research suggests that implementing a routine drain disinfection program with a product that kills bacteria in biofilm, can maintain proper contact time for the product to take effect, and can be easily applied on a routine schedule may provide sustained decolonization of the sink drain, thereby preventing transmission of potentially dangerous pathogens from sinks…The bacteria that live in our sink drains are shaped by what we are directly putting down them. While we expected that bacteria from the gut would have a greater impact, caused by the wider environment of a bathroom, it seems that by and large the bacteria living on the skin of our hands are feeding the community in the drains beneath sinks.

This means that we need to be very aware that what we are putting down our sinks is affecting the bacterial community underneath. These areas may not be reached during routine cleaning, and this could lead to communities containing hardier, resistant microbes… detection of active microorganisms within biofilms is problematic, because there is no single analytical method to detect all physiological types of bacteria…There have been numerous reports of bacterial species that enter the viable but non-culturable (VBNC) state. Reports indicate that the infectivity and pathogenicity could be retained after resuscitation in vitro and in vivo…The ability to revive after air drying is also an important issue in human health. Mycobacterium tuberculosis remains viable for around one week when dried as an aerosol on glass in physiological saline. It is known that the natural reservoirs of this non-primary pathogenic mycobacterium include aquatic environments like drinking water distribution systems.[3]

– Our efforts to reduce hospital acquired infections (HAIs) may have hit a challenging conundrum. On the one hand, we know that handwashing is essential to break the chain of transmission from infected (or colonized) host to vulnerable patient. On the other hand, one of the key tools in facilitating handwashing has recently demonstrated to play a role in transmitting pathogens. That tool? The sink. Many think sinks are beginning to tip the balance toward doing more harm than good.[4]

– The Takeaways: Key pearls to put into practice. The surgical gown cuff may allow skin bacteria from surgical team members to enter the surgical field. Operating room humidity should be kept low to reduce perspiration that can wick skin bacteria through the cuff… Clinical infections in dogs during this study were rare despite positive results in 41.6% of bacterial cultures.[5]

- Honey and vinegar, a traditional medicinal combination known as oxymel, dates to the ancient world. Apothecaries in the Middle Ages sold it, Hippocrates prescribed it and the physician-philosopher Ibn-Sīnā extolled its virtues.

In modern medicine both honey and acetic acid are used individually to treat infected wounds, but they are typically not combined. Honey stresses bacteria and fights infections with its high sugar content and acidity. Similarly, vinegar's active component, acetic acid, is a natural antiseptic that breaks down bacterial DNA and proteins.

Researchers have discovered that neither compound is particularly effective alone. Most of the bacteria lived when they applied low doses of honey and acetic acid separately to laboratory-grown formations called biofilms, made up of the common wound pathogens of Pseudomonas aeruginosa and Staphylococcus aureus. But when they put these low doses together, they noticed a large number of bacteria dying. Oxymel killed up to 1,000 times more bacteria in the biofilm than vinegar alone and up to 100,000 times more than honey alone.[6]

I submit the following recommendations to consider for surgical scrubbing areas in AAHA approved hospitals:

1– If possible, a hand surgery wash/scrub area should be dedicated and have contact only with the surgery room. If the sink is placed in the surgery room area, it would have less chance of contaminating the area than washing/scrubbing in a general use sink. Just think for a moment what organic material goes down a veterinary hospital treatment area sink. (a second choice would have the sink placed in an area close to the surgery entry door in a low traffic area and dedicated for surgery prep only).

A sink located in a designated sterile surgery area will have a reduced use rate than other sinks in the hospital and allow more time to dry biofilm in the faucet, sink and drain between uses – thus there is less of a chance contaminating the area when in use.

When a surgery designated sink is used, only antimicrobial wash/scrubbing liquids would go into the sink or drain – helping to reduce pathogens in these areas. Also, using oxymel (vinegar/honey mixture) just might become available for control of drain microbiome. Not only does it have anti-microbial characteristics but the sticky solution would attach to the drain better than other chemicals.

2– Currently, what sinks are AAHA members using to scrub for surgery? It has been mentioned that you recommend a hand "dirty" wash/scrub to be performed outside the surgery suite, the surgical team then goes through a door into the surgery room, rubs an FDA approved alcohol cleaner on their hands (for what length of time?) and dawn their gown and gloves. The question is what are they taking into the surgery room with them from exposure to their treatment/bathroom pre prep surgical area?

3– As a rule, veterinary hospitals don't have many sinks. Considering what goes into a treatment sink, I suspect that a bathroom sink is less contaminated.

WALTER R. HOGE, DVM

I also suspect that neither one is a good choice when preparing to enter an animal's body cavity or knee. For hospitals without a designated wash/scrub sink area I recommend considering: a wall mounted sink with contact only to the surgery room, in a corner or other distant area from the surgery table, with a splash zone around it and no mirror, or medicine cabinet or storage area or closed off area underneath. The sink would have no items on or in or under it. When not in use it would be in an area where it could be kept dry and the plumbing underneath monitored for leaks or moisture.

4– I request that during your AAHA inspections that your staff ask, in an informal non intimidating or threatening way, the procedure their surgical staff goes through preparing for surgery. I know for a fact that some, I suspect most, member hospitals are using the general use treatment room sinks for prep. Come to think of it, in most cases where else would they scrub but the bathroom?

I personally think that this type of study will be quite revealing to you and be of value during your study on recommendations for changes in AAHA policies on sterility in the surgery room. I also feel that the information gathered would make a great study to be shared with our members and as well as other members of the veterinary profession.

Scanning the literature, it is apparent to me that the human medical community hasn't developed protocols they are confident will prevent outbreaks of infectious disease. Unfortunately, the development of antibiotic resistant strains of microorganisms in hospitals are common.

5– And maybe none of this really matters: When I started working at my first practice the veterinarian washed his hands, did surgery without gloves and smoked a cigarette during the event. I didn't see any infections while I was there. Maybe someone should do a study on nicotine surgical scrubs and forget the rest.

Walter R. Hoge, BS, MS, DVM, Hospital Director
Camden Pet Hospital, 4960 Camden
Ave, San Jose, CA 95124

04-06-2023

Among the many, many issues our forebears didn't worry about were the deterrent effects of capital punishment and the ideal attributes of a firefighter. Nor did they have to contend with fabricated studies, or fake news, or Twitter. It's no wonder, then, that today reason often seems to fail us. As Mercier and Sperber write, "This is one of many cases in which the environment changed too quickly for natural selection to catch up."

Steven Sloman and Philip Fernbach are also cognitive scientists. They, too, believe sociability is the key to how the human mind functions or, perhaps more pertinently, malfunctions. They begin their book, "The Knowledge Illusion: Why We Never Think Alone" (Riverhead), with a look at toilets.

Virtually everyone in the United States, and indeed throughout the developed world, is familiar with toilets.

A typical flush toilet has a ceramic bowl filled with water. When the handle is depressed, or the button pushed, the water—and everything that's been deposited in it—gets sucked into a pipe and from there into the sewage system. But how does this actually happen?

In a study conducted at Yale, graduate students were asked to rate their understanding of everyday devices, including toilets, zippers, and cylinder locks. They were then asked to write detailed, step-by-step explanations of how the devices work, and to rate their understanding again. Apparently, the effort revealed to the students their own ignorance, because their self-assessments dropped. (Toilets, it turns out, are more complicated than they appear.)

Sloman and Fernbach see this effect, which they call the "illusion of explanatory depth," just about everywhere. People believe that they know way more than they actually do. What allows us to persist in this belief is other people. In the case of my toilet, someone else designed it so that I can operate it easily. This is something humans are very good at. We've been relying on one another's expertise ever since we figured out how to hunt together, which was probably a key development in our evolutionary history. So well do we collaborate, Sloman and Fernbach argue, that we can hardly tell where our own understanding ends and other's begin.

"One implication of the naturalness with which we divide cognitive labor," they write, is that there's "no sharp boundary between one person's ideas and knowledge" and "those of other members" of the group. This borderlessness, or, if you prefer, confusion, is also crucial to what we consider progress. As people invented new tools for new ways of living, they simultaneously created new realms of ignorance; if everyone had insisted on, say, mastering the principles of metalworking before picking up a knife, the Bronze Age wouldn't have amounted to much. When it comes to new technologies, incomplete understanding is empowering.

"This is how a community of knowledge can become dangerous," Sloman and Fernbach observe. The two have performed their own version of the toilet experiment, substituting public policy for household gadgets. In a study conducted in 2012, they asked people for their stance on questions like: Should there be a single-payer health-care system? Or merit-based pay for teachers? Participants were asked to rate their positions depending on how strongly they agreed or disagreed with the proposals. Next, they were instructed to explain, in as much detail as they could, the impacts of implementing each one. Most people at this point ran into trouble. Asked once again to rate their views, they ratcheted down the intensity, so that they either agreed or disagreed less vehemently.

Sloman and Fernbach see in this result a little candle for a dark world. If we—or our friends or the pundits on CNN—spent less time pontificating and more trying to work through the implications of policy proposals, we'd realize how clueless we are and moderate our views. This, they write, "may be the only form of thinking that will shatter the illusion of explanatory depth and change people's attitudes."[7]

Maybe my version of the toilet experiment discussing whether the scrub sink in Camden Pet Hospital's surgery suite was in danger of contaminating surgeries for the last 50 years was in too much depth for AAHA's examination committee. If the articles were in less technical terms, if the committee was inclined to evaluate the studies details enough for discussion, and the impact of implementing each one: They might have ratcheted down the intensity of their opinions so they could either agree or disagree less vehemently and make a more logical (in my view) conclusion as to whether or not the surgical sink had likely been belching out toxic infectious gases all the years it had been in use.

Elizabeth Kolbert's final comment on the cognitive buildup of man was: "One way to look at science is as a system that corrects for people's natural inclinations. In a well-run laboratory, there's no room for 'myside bias'; the results have to be reproducible in other laboratories, by researchers who have no motive to confirm them. And this, it could be argued, is why the system has proved so successful. At any given moment, a field may be dominated by squabbles, but, in the end, the methodology prevails. Science moves forward, even as we remain stuck in place.[7]

In my disagreement on whether the surgical sink could stay where it is: I feel the science is being done, evaluating the facts was of little interest and the "myside bias" filtrated throughout the room.

As for me, my last gasp attempting to contribute my little candle for a dark world to my profession flickered and died. As of February 29, 2024 I retired as a veterinarian and as AAHA's Hospital Director at Camden Pet Hospital. It was in my 50th year of practice and the surgical sink about 40th year of service. It is still in place, the water has been shut off, the sink drain plugged and just maybe it will have a chance of returning to service in the future.

One day I may walk into the surgery suite and notice that the sink is being used. When questioned, one may mention the covered jar of tongue depressors and a liquid in a plastic squeezable container sitting on the scrub sink. The plastic container may have written on it: "Oxymel – contents Honey and vinegar… apply with a tongue depressor around drain and pipe area after each use."

Just think about it: The scrub sink's odds of being useful again are better than mine.

1– *CDC Centers for Disease Control and Prevention, Health Care Associated Infections, Reduce Risk from Water, 24-7.*

2– *Multidrug resistant bacteria found in hospital sinks, Science News, 2017.*

3– *Effects of short-time drying on biofilm-associated bacteria, Annals of Microbiology, 57 (2) 277-280 (2007).*

4– *5 Design Updates to Make Sinks Safer, by Erica Mitchell, updated June 22 2022.*

5– *Surgical Gown Cuff Contamiation, Jonathan Miller, DVM, MS, DACVS, Vet Comp Orthop Traumatol. 2023;36(1):21-28.*

6– *Ancient Honey-and-Vinegar Combo Could Actually Treat Infected Wounds, Scientific American, Leo DeLuca, 10/01/2023.*

7– *Why Facts Don't Change Our Minds, New discoveries about the human mind show the limitations of reason, New Yorker, Elizabeth Kolbert, 02/19/2017.*

"The lesson is obvious. Your ultimate safety lies in never taking even the first enticing step in a direction you do not want to go."

Building off the author's prior volumes, Hoge's fourth offering traverses the spectrum of topics in a conversational manner, much like a friend would over a cup of coffee. The musings and observations, though, are carefully crafted and put together right from the beginning as the author juxtaposes Michelangelo's work and gender equality. While the author fearlessly analyzes his observations, he focuses more on creating a thought-provoking environment and a culture of conversation and discourse that can stimulate even more discussions and probing.

Early in his text, he dives into free will and presents vignettes that incorporate everything from murder trials and biblical narratives to physiology and cognition. Giving it a more nuanced dimension, Hoge even explores whether animals have free will, surveying concepts such as animal agency and animal nature. What's truly fascinating is that Hoge does not necessarily present new topics, but he examines known, relatable ideas from an extraordinary perspective. For instance, he uses evidence from the Bible to counter the argument from some theorists that only human beings have souls.

Although the topics meander randomly from section to section without any distinctive connection, the connection and relatability come from the notion that Hoge's work is truly a representation of how thoughts operate. Thousands of thoughts bounce around daily, pinballing throughout the brain, connected innately by their human experience. For example, in one bubble, there are Timothy McVeigh's last moments. In another, philosophy reigns supreme with the focus on starting with the end in mind. Yet another bubble comments on temptation, indulgence, and death through the frame of reference of a bee.

Whether the conversation revolves around the regeneration of 30,000-year plants derived from the "fruit tissue that had been frozen in Siberian permafrost" or the astounding fact that the often celebrated, even revered "sport" of bullfighting claims the lives of 250,000 bulls annually, the redeeming quality of this narrative lies in the undeniable evidence. Despite the tone being conversational, the content is impeccably researched and supported with insurmountable evidence that captures the spirit of the content. Hoge presents each of his topics with such clarity and force that he does not need to coax readers to believe him: the evidence more than suffices. In the case of bullfighting, it is particularly heartbreaking to learn about the mistreatment of the animals and humanity's penchant for turning the plight of animals into sport for nothing more than their own pleasure.

In the same vein, the author's veterinary background shines through when he examines the highly intelligent nature of pigs and, on a grander scale, their role in modern medicine in realms such as organ transplants. The history of pigs in medicine, such as how implants made of pig bladder were instrumental in regrowing leg muscles, is downright astounding. The author is the one choosing the topic he wants to discuss, so in that regard, this is no encyclopedia. However, the depth and uniqueness of the topics he has selected in this volume trend away from mainstream conversations and are genuinely enlightening, perhaps even providing more knowledge and context than any encyclopedia could. Overall, Hoge's thoughts encompass nearly six decades and an endless reservoir of highly intriguing and well-sourced topics that make this volume an undeniably meaningful read.

– Mihir Shah
USRB